Alone With Me

KITT, Eartha   B/KIT

Alone with me

7/12

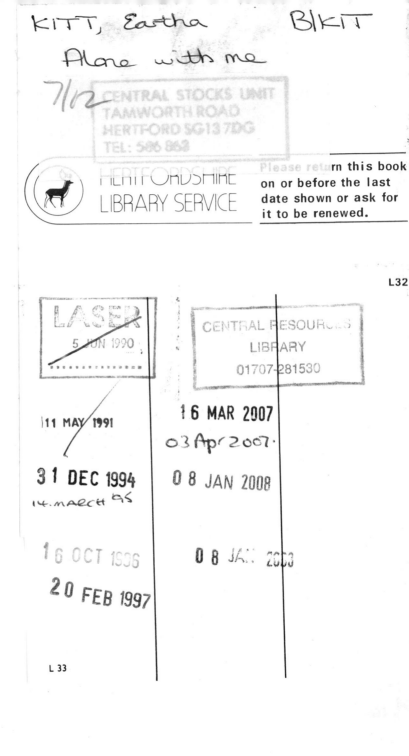

Alone With Me

a new autobiography by

eartha kitt

HENRY REGNERY COMPANY · CHICAGO

Library of Congress Cataloging in Publication Data

Kitt, Eartha.
   Alone with me.

    1. Kitt, Eartha.   2. Musicians—Correspondence,
reminiscences, etc.   I. Title.
ML420.K5A32   784′.092′4 [B]   75-13229
ISBN 0-8092-8351-4

Published by Henry Regnery Company
180 North Michigan Avenue, Chicago, Illinois 60601
Manufactured in the United States of America
Library of Congress Catalog Card Number: 75-13229
International Standard Book Number: 0-8092-8351-4

Published simultaneously in Canada by
Fitzhenry & Whiteside Limited
150 Lesmill Road
Don Mills, Ontario M3B 2T5
Canada

To my loving daughter, Kitt,
who has made me realize
what a human being really is all about:

the giving of love
and the taking of love
and never expecting more
than you're willing to give

and to the memory of my mother, Anna Mae Kitt,
and my aunt, Mamie Kitt,
and my mother-in-law, Nora McDonald

and, not least, to the public

Contents

Acknowledgments

There are people in my life who have been more than incidental to it, but whom I found impossible to weave into the fabric of this work without digression. So I couldn't quit the book without, at random, throwing a few brickbats at or bouquets to:

The CIA, who has established my reputation with men who want to believe that I'm a nymphomaniac but who should leave the writing of fiction to authors who don't write it at the taxpayers' expense.

Nancy and *Jordan Carlin*, who keep my head above water.

Aga Khan, who helped me with my shows.

Bellina Malach, who keeps the records straight.

Gerald Ford, who has made the world safe for mediocrity.

Jose Ferrer, who straightened the distortions in chapter 25 of my life.

Evelyn Lynch, who keeps the family ties.

Miss Beans, who showed kindness and understanding in my first school years.

Coretta King, who keeps the Martin Luther King philosophy alive and who is proof that woman is not of man's rib, but of his backbone.

Nmde Azikiwi, who almost made me First Lady of Nigeria.

Prime Minister Nehru, who served me chicken à la king instead of an Indian dinner.

King Farouk, who made me aware of what life should *not* be all about.

Prince Philip, who made me realize that, regardless of one's position in life, the development of children's minds is far more important.

Madame Golda Meir, whose strength seems everlasting.

Madame Indira Gandhi, who made me aware of the importance of women and strong decisions.

Sadrudin Khan, who gave me a garnet lion.

Rubirosa, who wooed me (platonically) and spoiled me with Dom Perignon and caviar.

Mrs. Banks, who taught at the New York School of the Performing Arts and who made me feel I was somebody.

Mrs. Bishop, who was my second school teacher and who encouraged me to study the performing arts.

Katherine Dunham, who gave me my start in show business.

Mr. and Mrs. Kabaz, in whose school my daughter is happily progressing.

Mr. and Mrs. Nesbitt, whose daughter (and telex) is very important to me.

Charles Revson, who was kind in time of need.

Doctors Charles Markman and *Joe Golenternek,* who helped me bring my daughter into the world.

Bill McDonald, who gave me a beautiful daughter and turned me off marriage.

Paul Lynde, whose sense of humor brings back wonderful memories of *New Faces.*

Marjorie Mead Bernhard, whose confidence and savvy I respect.

The Mothers of Watts, who keep me with my children.

Lady Bird Johnson, who made me remember that not all who ask questions seek truth.

Bobby Kennedy, who offered me an advisory position, but who died seeking truth.

Peter von Brochvitz, who made me realize again that a silver spoon in the mouth doesn't mean gold in the hands and that lack of money can kill you.

Don and *Barbara Shepherd,* with whom I can fight and who know my mind better than those who think they do.

Albert Popwell, who has remained my friend through the years.

Jimmy Komack, who proved to me the truth of Charles Schultz's epigram that happiness is a warm blanket.

Harry Harbour, who thinks like a father.

Natasha Reeves, who's like a sister to me.

Ann and *Roxie,* who never fail me as friends.

Food King, who allowed my Watts children to get food even when my bill was overdue.

Orson Welles, who made an actress of me and who stimulated my mind in spite of himself.

Richard Nixon, who showed the world that if you want to be dishonest and get away with it, take the White House.

Muhammad Ali, who shows that maybe the only way to make a decent living is to "knock 'em down."

Socrates, who set us all an example by dying for the truth.

James Jaeger (my pool man and gardener), who says, "It's okay, Eartha. I know you're good for it."

My neighbors (on La Collina), who believe in love thy neighbor as thyself, and show it.

Marvin Stern, whom I can challenge intellectually and have a good laugh with and who will probably never get back the five bucks I borrowed to get my car out of hock.

Hollywood, which made me realize that success begins at home.

Beverly Hills, which reinforced the adage that a house is not necessarily a home.

Captain, Deamon, and *July* (my dogs), who don't give a damn whether I'm Eartha Kitt or Eartha Mae; they still lick my face and make me laugh.

Arthur Lowe, who showed me that the strength of a man is in his mother.

All my lovers, who walked away when they couldn't handle it.

Duke, who taught me the tricks of his trade.

James Dean, whose spirit I always cherish and keep with me.

Judy Garland, a kindred spirit who allowed herself to be weakened by life.

Edith Piaf, a kindred spirit who allowed herself to be defeated by life.

Nora McDonald (my late mother-in-law), who proved to me that a daughter or son doesn't have to be born to you.

Mrs. McCoy, who can keep secrets no one else can.

People who didn't know what they were doing to me when they did it, but it worked.

Countries I've visited that made me understand that people are not all that politicians chop them up to be.

My country, which hasn't allowed me to work here but which takes a more than healthy chunk of my income because I refuse to be intimidated to leave it.

Congressman Roman Pucinski, who helped us in our effort to clean up the back streets of Washington, D.C.

Religion, which has become a big business because it doesn't practice what it preaches.

Me, who has learned that intelligence and sex are a difficult combination to handle.

And finally to all those whom I've momentarily forgotten to include—owing to deadline pressure—but whose names will spring immediately and embarrassingly to mind the very moment that it's too late for me to shout: Stop the presses!

Alone With Me

"This Is the Way She Is Now...."

Dear Miss Kitt:

You are cordially invited to create a scene, becoming ugly, unwanted, rejected, and hysterical in a corridor outside your dressing room at Carnegie Hall on Mother's Day, Sunday, May 12, 1974.

RSVP

That's an invitation I would have refused, had I known. I had given two concerts that day, one in the afternoon at Avery Fisher Hall and an evening performance at Carnegie Hall. Both were artistically successful, and they marked high points of my life. I hadn't worked in this country for a number of years—for reasons that I'll explain later—and I wanted desperately to be appreciated by American audiences again. I had never stopped working in those years, but I had appeared mostly in Europe, Asia, and South America, returning always to my home in California between engagements.

But this day marked the end of my professional exile, one not of my own choosing, and a return to my own country, a country I have always loved. It was Mother's Day. My daughter,

Kitt, then twelve, was with me at the Plaza Hotel in New York City, and I couldn't have been happier. Still, there was more to come that would send my spirit soaring—before the fall.

My concerts that day were a reunion of sorts, too. In attendance were fans and close friends and acquaintances I hadn't seen for years. They were overwhelmingly responsive to my performance; they reacted as though I was a worthwhile artist, and I suppose that's what we performers all live for. Their enthusiasm was wonderfully elating, making me even more vulnerable to the shock that was to come when I left Carnegie Hall that evening.

In my dressing room after the performance, it was one happy moment after another. Even the unfamiliar faces were appreciative, and I was glad that I had made everybody proud of me and proud that they knew me. No amount of money will buy an experience like that: the happiness one can give to others and the satisfaction a performer experiences in return. At that moment I was glowing, emotionally wealthy, spiritually soaring.

Because I was to do a benefit immediately afterward, a police escort waited outside my door. The hallway was still crowded, and as I started down the narrow corridor—Ann Grayson, a friend, on one side and a policeman on the other, helping to clear the way—there came from the crowd a woman's voice:

"Eartha Mae, do you remember me?"

I froze in shock.

"Eartha Mae," she said again, "do you remember me? I'm your step-sister. Your mother married my father."

When I heard those words, I stood there—not really looking at this woman even though I heard her—and I was afraid.

I remember gradually coming out of my shock and saying, "Who are you? What do you want from me?"

"I'm your *step*-sister," the woman said. "Your mother married my father. Don't you remember? We've been trying to find you."

And I heard myself saying, "After all these *years?* What do you want from me?" I looked at her and became hysterical. I was fighting against going back to the core of who I *really* was.

When Ann and the policeman saw my reaction, they started leading me down another corridor. The woman who called herself my step-sister had a young girl with her, and the girl kept saying to her, "Mama, Mama, leave her alone! You don't understand." And over the shouts of her daughter, the woman kept saying to me, "We don't want *anything* from you, Eartha Mae." And I heard the girl say, finally, "Leave her alone, Mama. This is the way she *is* now."

"No!" I shouted back at them. "*You* don't understand! Why, after all these years, are you trying to find me now? Where were you when I really *wanted* someone?"

I kept saying things like that over and over and, by then, crying uncontrollably. Ann and the policeman took me in one direction, and someone took the woman and little girl in another. I left the building still crying and screaming, "Where were they when I wanted and needed them? What do they want from me *now*?"

It's fortunate for me that there were no members of the press in the corridor at that moment, for I'm sure that some among them would have reported my actions as seemingly cruel and heartless. I would have understood that. I'm sure that my step-sister, her daughter, and the others who witnessed the hysterical scene must have felt the same way: This is the way she is now. Her long-lost step-sister is reunited with her at last, and Eartha Kitt screams, "What do you *want* from me?"

But it wasn't Eartha Kitt who was screaming. It was Eartha Mae. And none of them knew Eartha Mae—not the step-sister, or her daughter, or the people in the corridor that night. And none of them, not even the step-sister, knew that the words "Eartha Mae, do you remember me?" stabbed me to the core, just as surely as though she had used a knife.

Eartha Kitt didn't want to be Eartha Mae.

Eartha Mae is a yella gal. Eartha Mae is ugly. Eartha Mae is unwanted. Eartha Mae is rejected. Eartha Mae, at age three, was given away to strangers by her mother.

At that moment, I didn't want to be Eartha Mae, not in public—ugly, unwanted, rejected. I don't want to be given away again. I can live with the past as an intangible memory—as a nightmare that, even to this day, awakens me in the night, crying. That's in my mind. That's memory. I've had to learn to live with that. But that evening I met the embodiment of my memories, a flesh-and-blood woman who, in her childhood, had known me as that ugly, rejected yella gal and who was one of the reasons my mother had given me away. This was perhaps unknown to her, for she too had been a child then, just a few years older than I.

I went to pieces at the confrontation. I couldn't cope with that; to paraphrase the poet T. S. Eliot, one cannot stand too much reality. The appearance of my step-sister was reality personified, and my first feeling was fear, then mind-numbing shock—the purely emotional response of a rejected child, afraid and, once again, hurt.

It's a cliché to say that all of us are grown-up children, but it's true. From infancy to the toddler stage, we love and want to be loved. Perhaps from that point on we begin to emulate others to form what will be the adult. Hate, greed, prejudice—all of these things—have to be learned. They're not basic to our natures.

My child is Eartha Mae: ugly, unloved, unworthy, and therefore a loner. The adult I've molded is Eartha Kitt: self-reliant, afraid of nothing, even defiant. Ironically, I think of Eartha Kitt as practically nothing. True. She is so very far removed from the basic nature of Eartha Mae that I can—and do—think of her in the third person. She's *she*, not me. She's a name on a marquee. I'm curiously detached from her and yet suspended within her and totally dependent upon her for my survival. She has some of my better qualities, as a loving mother and as a friend to those who accept Eartha Mae, but I have none of hers. And until that evening at Carnegie Hall, no one ever got to Eartha Mae through Eartha Kitt. Never.

Eartha Mae psychs herself up to become Eartha Kitt for public appearances; she wears an impenetrable mental armor. And it was Eartha Kitt who appeared at Carnegie Hall and stepped from the dressing room that evening. But the woman who called herself my step-sister asked Eartha Kitt if she remembered Eartha Mae, and I was really torn. I was thrown into being both personalities at one time, and there was a tremendous conflict as to *who* I was.

I always knew that eventually I would come across these people; I thought it inevitable. There was, in fact, a prelude to our confrontation. It occurred the Sunday before my appearance at Carnegie Hall. I was in New York a week early to rehearse. That Sunday I went to church, and there a lady came to me and said, "You don't know me, but I know your stepsisters, and they've been trying to get in touch with you for years. But they've never been able to find you."

I didn't really take her seriously. I thought she might have been someone who had read my first autobiography, *Thursday's Child*, and had made up the story to get closer to me; similar incidents have happened over the years. I thought: That's very funny, because if my step-sisters—or anybody—really wanted to find me it would be very simple for them to do so. The whole story was mildly amusing to me, really.

But she went on to say, "I have their phone number, and I'll call them and tell them where you are." And I said, "Fine. I'm at the Plaza Hotel."

At that point, it crossed my mind that the woman might be sincere. Several days passed; I got very busy at rehearsals and simply put the incident out of mind. But one morning as I was preparing to leave for London, where I was performing at a crippled-children's benefit, I received a call from a woman who said she was my step-sister. And though I had not seen her since my childhood in the South, I knew in my heart that she *was*. The truth is, I didn't want her to be.

I should mention here that I have two half-sisters—each of us had a different father—and a number of step-sisters and brothers who belonged to the man my mother married after I was born. The woman who called me was one of my step-sisters, no blood relation. I never lived with them or really got to know them. I should also explain that I have a very personal prejudice—telephones. I hate them and consider them almost always an invasion of privacy. They're plastic and wire and a maze of metal that I consider totally impersonal, too mechanical for the transmission of genuine human emotion. I mention this to emphasize that this first encounter with my step-sister was insulated by plastic and wire and metal. It was my step-sister, yes, but our conversation had about as much emotional impact upon me as a recorded announcement.

It was restrained small talk, mostly. She said that we ought to get acquainted because we never had a chance to. I also got the impression that she was asking why I hadn't tried to contact them—as though it was obligatory on my part, because after I left the South I had never gone back to their family. The fact is, I was never invited *into* their family; far from it. When my mother and aunt died, that was the end of my family—except for my half-sisters, Pearl and Almita, who are blood relatives. I hired someone later to find them for me.

Anyway, there was no intimation that my step-sister would attend my performance at Carnegie Hall. By that time my trip to London and the concentrated rehearsals in New York had blunted the telephone encounter, and I thought I had forgotten about it. But subconsciously it must have been there—the feeling that this really was my step-sister—and I must have been fighting it even then.

The phone conversation still seemed unreal and strange to me. I had been an accessible public figure for twenty years. She could have found me far easier and quicker than it took me to find myself over the years. She could have found me on Broadway or in Hollywood or in nightclubs and theaters coast to coast. She could have found me by contacting news magazines or trade magazines. She could have found me in her daily newspaper.

My personal search for identity wasn't that simple. I had to search my memory, starting with a yella gal born in a small town called North, in South Carolina.

And then the question to Eartha Kitt: "Eartha Mae, do you remember me? Your mother married my father." Oh, yes. I remember. And her question forced me back into those painful years. From a corridor in Carnegie Hall, she sent Eartha Mae *and* Eartha Kitt back to the cotton fields.

2

Yella Gal

I have no idea how old I truly am. The ages given will be approximate. There are no records of my birth, which isn't at all surprising since I was born of mixed racial parentage on a plantation in South Carolina. I know only that I'm two or three years older than my half-sister, Pearl. And I know that my father was white and my mother was black, with Cherokee Indian blood.

In my memory there is nothing before the long, dark, dusty road. That's my earliest recollection—that road. It seemed to stretch endlessly before us. I remember holding tightly to my mother's hand. And I must have been very small, perhaps three at most for I had great difficulty walking, and Mama helped me keep my balance, half dragging me at times to keep pace and occasionally pausing to shift the weight of my baby sister, Pearl, in her arms. I couldn't figure out why the three of us were out in the wilderness so late. I wanted to ask Mama, but I feared that she'd be annoyed if I did.

As the sun sank into the ground ahead of us, I became more frightened. The evening breeze came up and the wheat began to sway in the fields near us. But the cotton stood still and glared out at me with a thousand bulging eyes. Mama must have sensed my fear. She began to hum, and once in a while she would look down on me with wet eyes and stroke my reddish-brown hair. Even so, something didn't rest right with me; I felt as though I had done something wrong and was going to get a whipping for it, but I couldn't remember what it was.

Perhaps it was guilt. Today, feeling back to that sensory impression in the light of what I have since learned of my past, I often wonder if someone's rejection of me had forced us out of whatever home or place we had come from. I'll never know, of course, but I remember no place, no home, before that road.

Before it was completely dark, we saw the silhouette of a house in the distance—a welcome sight, for houses in that area were miles and miles apart.

"Mama, are we home?" I asked.

"No, Baby, not yet," she said.

"Mama, I want some water," I said.

"Yes, Baby, I know."

She switched Pearl in her arms, grabbed me by my other hand, and quickened her pace until we reached the house. Then she paused and knocked softly.

A woman opened the door slightly and peered out at us. "Good evening," Mama said. "Would you mind if I came in for a while to rest and give my children some water?"

She was a kind-faced woman, and she opened the door wider, giving Mama a smile of complete welcome. "Come in, please," she said.

The first thing I saw was a fire burning in the fireplace, light and warm—inviting. I sat on the floor before it and looked into the flames in total comfort. And I began wondering if Mama was going to stay here for the night, or forever. I wanted to stay. I didn't want to go back into the night where spooks lurked to steal me away from Mama.

The woman soon brought me some bread and clabber milk (a thick, sour curdled milk) and a pan of hot soup. And I sat eating and dreaming before the fire, paying no attention to the mumbled conversation between Mama and the woman until, sometime later, I heard Mama thanking the woman for her kindness. She picked up my sister, who lay sleeping on the floor, wrapped in old blankets, and I knew that she was ready to leave again for wherever it was we were going. I bundled myself up and followed her out the door. And as Mama said goodbye to the woman, I peered into the darkness to see if there were any spirits around or if the bogeyman was watching us from behind some old tree.

Again we walked, this time by moonlight. It was a cloudless night and the moon was very bright, throwing what seemed to me ominous shadows of swaying trees in our path. We were now skirting the edge of a forest, and I knew that the bogeyman would be hiding in the forest if nowhere else. I imagined spirits behind every tree. And I clung closer to Mama.

How could I tell Mama that there was a spirit following us? I wanted to scream, but I couldn't. I wanted Mama to hold me in her arms, like Pearl. I wanted to say to her, "I'm too scared to walk down here by myself!"

It seemed years of walking with the spirits before Mama finally stopped. I remember looking up at her, and from my vantage point, she seemed nearly as tall and thin as the pine trees that surrounded us. I watched her, wondering why she was stopping in the cold, moonlit wilderness. She found a clump of small, overhanging bushes that would shelter us from the dew, and she laid Pearl down to arrange a bed of pine needles.

Why did she stop at a place like this? Where was a house for us? Where was our cow and horse? Where were our chickens and pigs?

After making Pearl's bed and comforting her until she was asleep, Mama made a bed for me and one for herself. She covered us with some old clothes we had carried with us and with pine needles; then she lay down to rest. I had no intention of going to sleep. I was determined to stay awake until sunup, when there would be no shadows to hide the bogeyman and spirits that might get us in the night.

I snuggled close to Mama, thinking of the ways I could escape a spirit if one came after us. I'll dig a hole and bury myself, I thought. No, that wouldn't be quick enough. Maybe

I'd hide behind a big tree. But no, spirits could see me. There was God, though. If I got on my knees and prayed for wings, God would give them to me and I could fly away. But God might not hear me.

The moon was full, and it occurred to me that perhaps only good spirits roamed on full-moon nights. Even so, if I prayed hard enough, maybe God would make me a spirit too, and the other spirits wouldn't bother me. Once that idea had settled—though uneasily—into my small mind, my thoughts roamed on to other fears. If I go to sleep, will Mama go off and leave me alone? Will she remember that I'm with her too?

I don't remember dozing off, but when I awakened it was daylight and Mama was standing above me, brushing the pine needles from her clothing. "You stay here and mind Pearl," she said. "I'll be back in a minute." Then as she walked away she called back, "Don't go off anywhere, now. Stay right there."

Pearl was awake too, and though I worried about why and where Mama had gone, I was occupied with the full-time job of trying to keep Pearl from putting handfuls of pine needles into her mouth. And I was beginning to get very hungry, wondering how far we were from people and plum and cherry trees and blackberry bushes. I didn't like the pine forest at all; one couldn't find hickory nut trees in a pine forest. And I thought: When I grow up, I won't be in any old pine-tree woods. I'm gonna sit in the shade and smoke my pipe all day and eat, just eat all the sideback, greens, cornbread, white bread, molasses and cream, sweet potatoes—all the eats I want. Pearl, I thought, could have all the string beans and okra. I didn't like string beans and okra.

I was wishing there was a spring nearby so I could get some water when Mama finally returned, her arms laden with fruit, including watermelon and cantaloupe. She must have stolen the fruit from somebody's field, for her skirt was dirty at the knees and her hands looked as though she had been digging.

After eating all of the fruit, we began walking again until we came at last to a strange kind of settlement, with lots of houses all close together and a road that was hard (paved, I learned later). We entered the yard of a house that seemed vaguely familiar to me, and a very pretty brown-skinned woman with long Indian hair greeted us.

Inside, the room was very pretty—like the woman—a nice chair, nice bed, nice fireplace. And it was cool. We stayed the night there, and I was hoping that this was our new home. But after breakfast the following morning, we were again on the road.

I don't recall the details of our journey this time, but I do recall the end of it. It was another house that seemed familiar to me, the house of my mother's uncle, but I didn't know that at the time. We crossed a small bridge connecting two fields owned by my mother's two brothers. A trickle of water flowed in the stream bed. There was an outhouse nearby, and ahead of us was a house. Chickens were running around the yard and dogs began to bark at us. Pigs stirred in their pen, mules raised their heads in the stalls, and children in the yard stared at us. I was scared.

Mama walked into the yard—reluctantly, it seemed to me—and climbed the steps to the porch. In the doorway stood a large, dark man I later learned was my uncle, and his expression was *not* one of welcome. It looked to me as though a battle were about to take place. From the looks of Mama, she was scared too. I clung to her dress, holding onto the hem for fear that she wouldn't win the battle. And Pearl began to cry without provocation. All our feelings were connected, it seemed.

The children—six or seven of them—were scattered about the yard, watching us to see what our next move would be.

"What do you *want?*" my uncle said in an unfriendly, booming voice.

"I have no place to stay," Mama said meekly. "Would you please let me stay here for a few days until I find somewhere to go?"

"I had this out with you before," my uncle said. "The answer's still the same. No!"

"Can't you see I've trudged from one place to another, trying and trying?" my mother said. "I won't be a burden on you. I'll work. I'll earn my board and keep." Mama began crying. "Just let me have some place to rest my children for a while."

My uncle stared hard at me, making me uncomfortable and even more scared. Mama looked at him, then at me. "She's no trouble; she's a good girl," Mama said.

"I don't care *what* she is! I . . ."

"Please don't hurt her now," Mama sobbed.

Suddenly, much to my relief, my uncle turned and stomped back into the house, mumbling to himself. Mama followed him, pleading. I didn't know what the quarrel was about and I wanted to follow Mama into the house, but I sensed that I should stay where I was, so I sat down on the porch and waited. None of the children came near me. They just went on with whatever it was they were doing, as though I didn't exist.

One of the dogs climbed up on the porch and approached me as though he might be willing to be friendly. I would have been delighted to have his attention, to take my mind off the faint, mumbling conversation going on inside the house. But the dog simply sniffed at my legs, warily, and went off. Then a cat jumped through the window onto the porch, mewing, and curled up on my lap as though she had known me forever. I was no longer alone.

Mama stayed in the house with Pearl for what seemed like hours while I played with the cat. I apparently fell asleep petting it. The next thing I knew, it was nearly dark. I was on the floor of the barn and Mama was pulling some raggedy covers over me and Pearl. The floor was strewn with hay, and there were bales of cotton stacked in one corner. I could hear the night wind wheezing through the cracks in the walls. I looked up at the spider-webbed ceiling and then drifted back to sleep, comforted that we had a roof over our heads at last.

I awoke at Mama's call the next morning. She gave Pearl and me each a piece of bread and a cup of clabber milk. Her face looked drawn. I thought she might have been crying, but she looked at me and smiled, running her hands over her disheveled black hair. She seemed distracted, and I wanted to ask her what was wrong, but I didn't want to disturb her thoughts. It seemed to me that she should have been happy now. I didn't realize why she wasn't until a couple of days later when, standing near a window, I overheard Mama and Uncle arguing again.

"You gotta leave here," my uncle said.

"But I haven't found any place to go."

"I don't care," my uncle said, "but you can't stay *here!*"

"I'm no trouble to you. . . ."

"I don't want that *yella gal* in my house. I told you that before!"

Yella gal, yella gal, yella gal. The sound of the words, the beat of them kept echoing in my brain like a chant, like a tune you can't get out of mind no matter how hard you try. Yella gal, yella gal . . .

"Don't bring your troubles to *me*. I have enough of my own, taking care of my children. . . ." Uncle went on and on, and Mama was crying now, her words exploding in sobs I couldn't understand.

Yella gal. Pearl was dark like Mama and my uncle. I knew that he was talking about me. And I ran into the woods and cried. There was something terribly wrong with me. I hadn't noticed that I looked different; I hadn't noticed until that moment that everyone was darker than me. I was a yella gal, ugly and terrible, judging from the reactions of my uncle to me. I wanted to run away, to hide from everyone forever. But there was nowhere to go, and I was too scared to leave Mama. At least Mama loved me.

When the sun sank behind the trees, I sneaked back to the house and hid beneath the porch until it was completely dark and no one could see me. I was to spend a good deal of my life beneath porches before I finally left the South.

A few days later, Mama said that we were moving to another house. I was both glad and afraid. I wanted more than anything to leave Uncle's house, but I didn't know whose house we were going to, or what the owner of the house would think of a yella gal.

The house was a full morning's walk from my uncle's place. It belonged to a pleasant, elderly woman who knew Mama and who was expecting us. She greeted us at the door and showed us through the house. It seemed like a palace to me. She showed us our bedroom, which had *two* beds—one for Mama and one for Pearl and me—and it had a window, and even a slop jar, so that one didn't have to go out to the outhouse on dark, cold nights. There was even a separate bedroom for the elderly woman, and a living room with a fireplace, and two windows, and a small kitchen, and a narrow hall that led to the backyard. Two bedrooms, and one bed just for me and Pearl alone!

Mama made us comfortable, then went off somewhere. The old woman sat in a chair knitting. I was afraid to go near her for fear that she'd notice that I was a yella gal—if she hadn't already. But Pearl was too young to know of such things, and, besides, she was dark like everyone else. She stayed at the old woman's feet during the hour or so that Mama was gone.

I learned later that the old woman was blind. To stay there with her, Mama had arranged to take care of the house and cook and tend to the fields and everything. The sightless old woman didn't know that I was a yella gal. Everything was going to work out fine.

3

Shock

Our new life was heaven. I joyously worked in the fields with Mama. But on days when the sun was too hot, Mama would leave Pearl and me at home. I'd take care of Pearl, feeding her, keeping her out of trouble, laughing and playing with her, rocking her to sleep. I made a playhouse at the edge of the woods, cleaning the ground of pine needles and roping the area into three sections: a living room, a bedroom, and a kitchen. It was a nice shady area, sheltered by overhanging trees and bushes. I gathered all kinds of old tin cans and battered pots and pans for my kitchen. And I made rag dolls to represent my children, though very often I used my sister as the child of the household. I'd play-cook for her, making mud pies and biscuits and other earthen delicacies.

But my playhouse was more than just that to me. It was my personal retreat, my Green Mansion. I'd often spend the entire day there alone in the peace and quiet, until Mama called me to eat. Afterward, I'd go right back to my Green Mansion. When it rained, I'd crawl beneath the bushes in a section of my playhouse where it was dry and watch the rain cleanse everything and listen to the staccato spattering of the raindrops on the leaves overhead.

It was a wonderful time, almost heavenly. Mama and Pearl and I were together in a nice home with a fireplace I could sit before and dream. And we had our own bedroom and our own beds and plenty to eat. The blind lady was kind and appreciative. There was no more aimless wandering or going without water or having to steal food or arguing with people who didn't want me. I would have been content to stay there the rest of my life with our little family.

Then one day an intruder appeared. It was a man, and he seemed to have come out of nowhere. Suddenly he was there. And just as suddenly—having courted Mama for a couple of months—he was gone. And Mama went with him.

He used to come to the house almost every evening. He'd lavish affection on Mama and play with my sister, coochie-cooing her and rocking her on his knee and talking baby talk to her. Mama would watch the two of them, smiling fondly, and I'd stare, ill at ease, into the fire, wondering why the man didn't coochie-coo with me.

I soon realized that as far as he was concerned I didn't even exist. He used to look through me as though I weren't there. And it gradually occurred to me that he didn't like me for some reason. After a while I became terribly jealous that he had stolen from me what little attention I had received. Mama seemed to notice me less and less, perhaps steeling herself for what she knew was inevitable.

Finally one morning Mama took Pearl and me and our few belongings to the house of a family called the Sterns. She didn't bother to explain why she was taking us there or why she was leaving us. But it was evident to me that this was to be our new home and that Mama wouldn't be living there with us. I remember a sudden feeling of loneliness, numbness, and then the terrible blow when I realized that even Mama didn't want me anymore. I can still visualize myself standing in the yard of the Stern woman's house and watching Mama leave us behind as she walked arm in arm across the fields with the man.

We didn't see Mama again for a long time.

The Stern house was occupied by Mr. and Mrs. Stern and their two grandchildren, Willie and Gracie, who were in their early teens. The talk that I heard in the Stern family was that the man Mama was going to marry had said he would accept Pearl, but not me. He had a lot of children of his own, and he didn't want to have a yella gal around to cause dissension among them. In order not to separate us, Mama gave both Pearl and me to the Stern woman. It was one of this man's daughters who approached me at Carnegie Hall—the eldest daughter, I believe—and asked me if I remembered her.

Well, of course, Mama's leaving was the ultimate rejection. I don't recall my exact reaction; perhaps I've suppressed it beyond recall. But certainly it must have been the shock of my life to hear the cruel fact. And I no doubt hoped that what they said wasn't true, that the man Mama was marrying would change his mind. He didn't, though.

My first impression of the Stern house was the bedroom. There were two double beds in it. Pearl, Willie, Gracie, and I shared one of the beds; the grandparents slept in the other. I never thought of the house or beds as being overcrowded because this was all very natural to me.

There was no time for me to lament, for I was alloted chores to earn my keep, and I plunged immediately into the work-a-day life of the Stern family. I awoke first at daybreak and went to the yard to fetch kindling for the stove. Then I'd cook breakfast, and when breakfast was over, I'd wash the dishes while the Stern family went into the fields to pick cotton. Most of the time my sister and I went with them. But when we didn't, I'd clean the whole house, feed the pigs, put the cow out to pasture, and let the chickens out of their coops and feed them.

All of this done, I'd sweep the yard. Then, while weeding the garden, I had to keep track of my sister and the cow, and try to keep the hawks from eating the watermelons. And in between I had to remember to give fodder to the mule at certain hours of the day.

The toughest part by far was keeping track of the cow, which was the Sterns' only source of milk and butter. It was my task to keep the cow away from the poisonous wild berry trees;

there were many of them near the swamp and one in the middle of the pasture. I could never understand why someone didn't chop them down if they were so poisonous to animals. But I guess it just never occurred to anyone to do so.

I must have been about four years old at the time. And if you think this a heavy workload for a four-year-old, you must remember that in those days—and perhaps it's true even today—it wasn't unusual for poor children of seven or eight to begin working full-time in the fields or mills or the mines to help support their families. Needless to say, I had little time to play. Sundays were the exception. But it was customary for nearby neighbors to make their weekly visits at the Stern house on the Sabbath, so I usually spent Sundays hiding under the porch, keeping out of sight so they couldn't make fun of me.

While my basic needs of food (leftovers) and shelter were provided for by the Sterns, I was never accepted as a member of the family. There was no love shown toward me, only indifference or, at best, criticism. It was simply a place for me to stay, and I was tolerated. I don't know what arrangement Mama had made with the Sterns, but I was obviously to pay for my board and keep by working.

I did everything I could think of to gain recognition and acceptance. I rarely spoke to anyone unless spoken to, and I worked very hard. I often worked in the fields picking cotton. At my young age, I thought that picking cotton quickly would win approval from the Stern woman. Unfortunately, in my haste, I wasn't very thorough, and the Stern woman would yell at me a lot and make me go back and repick the same stalk or row.

A couple of years later, though, when I was about six, the Stern woman sent the two grandchildren and me to work a certain piece of land. She told us to see how much we could pick in half a day. That was a challenge to me, and I decided that I wouldn't be outdone. At that time workers were being paid a penny a pound for picking cotton. By the end of the day when the white man came to weigh our work, the teenagers, Gracie and Willie, had picked 125 pounds between them. I had picked 100 pounds all by myself. I was very proud and happy to know that I had earned a whole dollar for the family, and I couldn't wait to get back to the house and tell the Stern woman about it.

As we walked back through the fields, one of the plantation owners threw me some pecan nuts and I felt as though everything was going for me that day. Upon learning of my feat, the Stern woman smiled at me and told me that I was a good child to have worked so hard. That was reward enough. I gave her the dollar I had earned.

I had all kinds of plans for earning more dollars and keeping them for myself. I figured I'd buy a new dress for myself, and I'd buy some bananas and something for Pearl, too. And I thought maybe I could work every Saturday and make lots of dollars and get rich and buy a house with a porch and sit in the sun, eating bananas all day.

Bananas were a passion at that time. They were an exotic fruit I had been introduced to one evening when the grandfather, Mr. Stern, returned from selling a good crop of cotton at the mills. God only knows how he had gotten home because he was falling-down drunk—no doubt his horse had found the way. And the timing was perfect. No sooner had his wagon pulled to a stop in the yard when Mr. Stern fell to the ground, passed out cold.

As the others rushed to his aid, I rushed for the package in the wagon, which was usually filled with goodies whenever he came back from the mills. There were usually cookies and candy and a loaf of white bread, but this time I found a strange kind of fruit; it was yellow and long and had little black spots on it. Not only did I not know what it was—nor did anyone else in the household—but I didn't know where to begin eating it. The smell was wonderful; it permeated the entire house, and I could even smell its aroma in the yard.

The next afternoon, when Mr. Stern finally recovered from his drinking spree, he told us that the strange fruit he'd brought home was called a banana and that, once peeled, the inside was good to eat. His instruction was a little too late. We had already eaten some of them—skin and all.

So I would buy bananas with the dollars I would earn. But as I said before, the Stern woman's smile and praise for me that day was reward enough. I can remember only one other occasion when she smiled at me and gave me some small measure of attention. It was on a night when the Stern woman had taken ill. She needed some kind of medicine, which meant that someone had to get it for her at the country store three miles away.

As usual, Mr. Stern was nursing a bottle and was in no condition to go anywhere. The Stern woman asked Gracie and Willie to go, but they began moaning about the darkness and about the young moon (a superstition about spirits roaming during periods of the new moon). They were too afraid to go. But when I saw how sick the Stern woman was, I said, "I'll go."

Everyone looked at me in complete surprise. I was told what kind of medicine was needed and given the money to purchase it, and I set out alone on my errand of mercy. Neither Gracie nor Willie offered to accompany me. I'm sure they thought I'd never reach the store alive. And I'm sure that they must have thought my actions stupid, rather than brave.

When I opened the door, the night seemed blacker than usual. And it became blacker still when I closed the door behind me. I followed the path leading through the fields and into the pine forest, my fists clenched tightly from fear. If anyone was afraid of the dark, I was, and I just knew that there were spirits lurking behind every tree just waiting for me.

Finally I came out of the forest, but there wasn't much solace in the fact, for directly in my path lay St. Peter's Church, with its school and its graveyard. There was a fork in the path that skirted a field and bypassed the church, but the graveyard path was the quickest and most direct route. The Stern woman needed her medicine quickly, I thought, and, besides, there was someone buried in the graveyard who I knew would protect me—but that's a story I'll get into later.

I stepped carefully through the graveyard, feeling for solid earth. Some of the graves were soft dirt, and I thought that if I stepped on one I might sink into the grave, never to return. I visualized spirits sitting on each grave, either cheering me on or trying to turn me back. My feet were covered with dew and held the dirt. My toes seemed to collect all the stones and my calves ached. My heart felt as though it would burst out of my rib cage before I finally passed through the graveyard and continued on the path leading across the fields to the country store. But I made it.

It was quite late and the store was closed. I had to hammer on the door a long time before a light went on inside. The white owner was surprised to see me. "My, my," he said, "what are you doing roaming around in all this darkness?"

I smiled, relieved that he had opened the door to a brightly lighted place of safety. I told him what medicine I needed and he went behind the counter and got it for me. I remember that my head barely reached the counter top as I pushed the money up to him.

I left the store running as fast as I could. I think I ran all the way back to the house, the entire three miles. I had more courage going back, for I had already conquered those dark pathways. And the exhilaration of having accomplished my mission gave me renewed strength. Now, I thought, the family will pay more attention to me. I've shown them that I'm not afraid of the dark. And I thought that maybe the Stern woman wouldn't beat me anymore.

When I gave her the medicine, the Stern woman smiled broadly at me, obviously pleased. I felt like a puppy being patted on the head by its master. This was all I really wanted. After giving her the medicine, I retreated to my corner by the fireplace and secretly watched the faces of Gracie and Willie. They were pouting. And it pleased me that, at my age, I had accomplished what teenagers had been afraid to attempt. I was in a state of near delirium to have been in that tiny limelight for a brief moment. The next morning the Stern woman was feeling much better, and I was the first to receive the breakfast she passed around the table.

I've made reference to the beatings I got from the Stern woman. She would occasionally give me whippings that only the devil could put in her mind, and sometimes I thought that the devil himself was wielding the whip because there'd be blisters on my backside for days afterward. She also had a penchant for slapping my face with resounding blows for the slightest of childish transgressions. For example, I had a habit of sucking my tongue, of doubling it backward and sucking on it, which gave me great pleasure. But to accomplish this I had to open my mouth slightly, and for this reason it was noticeable. No one paid much attention to me, so it was a long time before I got my first slap on the face for doing it. The slaps didn't break the habit, though. It was one of my few pleasures.

Another pleasurable habit I formed got me one of the Stern woman's devil beatings. I used to feel my breasts. I'd hide behind the house, run my hand inside my shirt, and feel the centers of my breasts. At my age there was nothing there, of course, but I wanted there to be. It seemed perfectly natural and harmless to me, but the Stern woman apparently thought it a sign of evil. I thought it no worse than eating sweet potatoes from the garden—for which I also got a sound beating. This was discovered because the tar from the sweet potatoes left a telltale ring around my mouth. After I was whipped, I switched to watermelon, which left no telltale ring and was never discovered.

My one vice deserving of punishment was smoking. I used to watch Mr. Stern smoke, and it fascinated me. He used to leave his tobacco and cigarette papers on the mantel, and one day my curiosity got the better of me. I wondered what it would be like to roll a cigarette, set it on fire, and eat the smoke. So one day when everyone had gone to the fields, I crawled under the house, rolled a cigarette as I had seen him do so many times, set it on fire, swallowed the smoke, and got sick. I figured that I was doing something wrong because Mr. Stern never got sick when he smoked, and I decided to watch him more closely to see how it was done.

After a couple of days I had it all figured out, and I began to make a habit of smoking. Every day, as soon as everyone had left for the fields, I'd crawl under the house where I had hidden the tobacco and paper and matches on a ledge, and roll my daily cigarette. I must have been five or six, I believe, and this went on for a long time. But one day I was having an afternoon cigarette when everyone returned from the fields earlier than I'd expected. And there I was, sitting under the house, sending up smoke signals for all the world to see. I got a beating, justly deserved for a change.

The whippings I got from the Stern woman were doubly traumatic to me. They were more often than not uncalled for and far more violent than the whippings she gave her own grandchildren. Then, too, the punishment was never counterbalanced by the slightest display of kindness, let alone love or affection. But for all their fury, the whippings were never equal to the maliciousness shown toward me by Gracie and Willie.

In the three years or so I spent at the Stern house, I was constantly provoked, ridiculed, and beaten by the Stern grandchildren. Children can be cruel and insensitive, but the teenaged Stern grandchildren could have given lessons in degradation and malevolence; they were masters at it.

At harvest time all of us usually worked in the fields, but when a field was nearly finished and not everyone was needed, we children would often be left at the house with set chores to be done by the time the Stern woman returned. These days were great sport for Gracie and Willie.

When the elders left the house, the grandchildren would begin their games. Willie would get a peach tree switch and begin whipping me on the legs to make me do his and Gracie's chores as well as my own. Gracie would sit in the shade and laugh while Willie brandished the whip and I worked. One of their favorite tortures was to put a croaker sack over my head and tie the opening of the sack around my waist. My hands were tied into the sack above my head. Then they'd strip me bare, tie me to a peach tree, and whip me with switches for what must have been hours. I'd try at first to keep from crying, but the pain usually became so unbearable that I'd cry for the earth to open and swallow me. Gracie and Willie would laugh and laugh at this, chanting "Yella gal, yella gal. . . ."

This went on for hours, until it was time for the rest of the family to come home. Then they'd untie me and dare me to tell on them. If I did, they swore to do the same thing again first chance they got.

I was in fear of everything and everyone. I didn't dare make a false move, so everything I did was carefully planned to please, to get a smile from someone—anyone. I never said anything unless it was absolutely important to do so. I didn't even talk to Pearl much anymore, for they had turned her against me too.

She wasn't old enough to understand the implications of what this meant to me. It was bad enough to have been abandoned by my mother, but to have Pearl side with the family against me hurt me very much.

It was Gracie and Willie who turned Pearl against me. They had her lying to the Stern woman about me—about little things, but it made my life miserable. They had Pearl telling the Stern woman that I was eating sand, for example. Every day for a period of about three weeks the Stern woman whipped me for eating sand. It didn't occur to her that the same story every day must have been a lie.

Having been beaten so many times for something I wasn't guilty of, I decided one day to see what there was in eating sand. Near the edge of the pine forest and across the road from the old well and the watermelon patch was a ditch of pure white sand. It was brilliant in the sun, and I sat in the warm sand, scooped up a handful, and licked at it like sugar. It became damp with the saliva in my mouth and seeped its way down my throat like honey. It tasted like the rain—that wonderful, pungent, earthy smell that is in the air before a rainstorm. I sat with my legs tucked beneath me in the softness of the warm sand and basked in the discovery of this new and different pleasure.

A few days later, I discovered an even newer pleasure: the taste of clay—red, yellow, purple, all the colors of the rainbow. It all had the same rainy taste. Pearl was playing with me in the ditch that day, so I kept the discovery to myself. But whenever I was alone, I would go to that ditch and combine my secret rain feasts. And, for dessert, I'd suck my tongue and feel the middles of my breasts.

4

Close to the Earth

North is a far-flung, backwoods plantation community in Lexington County slightly east of the center of South Carolina. I was born there and spent the early years of my life there, three or so of them at the Stern house. I have no idea what the area looks like today—I've been back there only once since I was seven—and have only a vague recollection of what it was like when I was there, in that era of black purgatory between the abolition of slavery and the beginning of the civil rights movement in the fifties.

It was in the thirties when I lived with the Sterns. The rural community of North was perhaps ten or fifteen miles in radius, and the wanderings with Mama in search of a home, which I described in Chapter 2, were probably circular. On foot, carrying a child and walking at the slow pace of a toddler like me, that must have taken days.

Life at the Stern house was close to the earth. Like most black people of that era, the Sterns were economically dependent upon white plantation owners. And the living was not easy. And for me, personally, the noun *purgatory* was most apropos, if one defines it as a place of punishment or remorse. I was a yella gal, accepted by neither white people nor black. To say that it was confusing would be the understatement of my life.

Still, I bear no malice and, on the contrary, I owe much to the Stern woman for taking me in at a time and place where yella gals weren't welcome anywhere. I earned my keep and took my beatings, yes. And though I was treated at best, with indifference and regarded as a servant, I wasn't kept in chains. I was sent occasionally to church and to school, and I was fed and clothed as well as the Sterns' limited means would allow. As for Gracie and Willie, well, they didn't know any better. They were still young enough to have a child's insensitive cruel streak and the backwoodsy prejudice of their culture. I was an interloping oddity to be toyed with, an interesting diversion. They had no way of knowing what wounds they were inflicting on my psyche. They were simply ignorant.

My abandonment and alienation made me a loner. I stayed away from everyone as much as possible. I was not the child of my mother or of the Sterns. Without thought, I became Nature's child. And I still am, as Eartha Mae.

I was happiest when alone. I lived in my thoughts, and when my thoughts and serenity were broken, I felt confused, unless Nature did it. She felt everything I felt and pitied me. I could talk to her without reproach. She accepted me without reservation. I belonged to Nature and Nature belonged to me.

When it was evident to me that I didn't exist in either Mama's or the Sterns' world, I spent as much time as possible in the pine woods gathering pine cones and lying in sunny places thinking of the Heavenly Father. I watched the birds build their nests and feed their young. I watched the squirrels and other animals gather food and run from danger. I ate hickory nuts, wild plums, and blackberries and sipped water from the running brook. I picked wild daisies and threw love-me-nots to the wind.

I loved the rain. When I wasn't in my Green Mansion, that roped-off playhouse beneath the bushes, I'd run in the rain, drenching my flour-sack dress, splashing barefoot in puddles, saturating my bushy hair, which would take forever to dry. And the thunder would shake me inside. I vibrated to its rumbling rhythm. The lightning would electrify my nervous system. Whenever it cracked across the sky, I would suddenly be charged with an energy that cried to be spent; I'd want to lift something and be destructive.

Nature had a curious effect upon me that was not fanciful, but very, very real. I was free in Nature, absolutely free. I was subordinate to no one, because I was a child of Nature, Who was God.

I didn't really give my freedom much thought, though, until one day when Pearl and I were playing in the yard and heard the chanting of a chain gang building a new road near the Stern house. We sat and listened to them, humming along whenever they sang a familiar song. We had seen chain gangs before; they were part of the scenery. But we had never paid much attention to them until that day when one of the prisoners, his feet chained, came riding a horse into the yard.

He was very dark and wore a torn sun hat. His shoulders were broad and strong, his chest and arms heavily muscled. He wore dirty, thread-bare trousers with faded stripes, and he carried a bucket. We sat and watched him as he asked the Stern man for water from our well. As he waited for it, he looked at us with eyes that envied us our freedom.

The Stern man returned with a bucketful of water, and the prisoner slumped down to take it from him, then turned his horse around and headed away. But as he reached the road that would take him back to the chain gang, he suddenly turned, dropped the bucket, and spurred his horse toward an opposite trail. He took off like a bat out of hell. Everyone at the house sprang to his feet and watched as he galloped off. We saw the guards go after him in swift pursuit, and we continued watching until they were all out of sight. Then we heard the sickening thud, thud, thud of their rifles and the deathly silence that followed. We all bowed our heads and went back to whatever it was we had been doing before. This, too, was all very natural.

In my first or second year at the Stern house, I saw my father for the first and last time. I was behind the house by myself, as usual, when I noticed a white man leave the nearby road and trudge across the field toward me. I don't remember what I thought at his approach. Not fear. Perhaps curiosity. I was sitting on the ground in the sun, my legs tucked beneath me, and I remember his pausing, towering above me for a second and blocking the sun, before he crouched slightly and gently cupped my face in his hand and turned my face up to him. He studied my face for what seemed like a full minute or two; then he turned, walked back across the field to the road, and was gone.

He had not spoken a word to me. And I had no idea who he was until I overheard the Stern people talking about him, after I told them of his visit. They later told me that he was my father. I don't remember thinking anything about it at the time, or connecting it with the fact that I was a yella gal. I was too young for that.

I said earlier that we lived close to the earth. This was taken for granted, for I had no basis for comparing lifestyles. But the condition was made frighteningly clear to me the year we damn near starved to death. To begin with, the lightning burned away the cotton. We relied on the forest more than ever to carry us through the winter. Never in my life had I eaten so much molasses and bread. For dessert, we'd have a piece of fried fatback.

Everything went wrong that strange and terrible year. Rabbits apparently didn't multiply fast enough. Possums were scarce. There were no fish to be found in the creeks. The trees didn't bear enough fruit to be preserved. Nearly all of the other crops failed. Sauerkraut, which we made from collard greens and cabbage, didn't turn sour. The sweet potatoes we banked in the ground rotted from the frost. We were very close to the earth, indeed. Nearly six feet under. I think we must have made it through that terrible winter with our prayers.

And prior to that year, I alone was responsible for a similar catastrophe—or at least I felt solely responsible. I have mentioned my daily chores of keeping the Stern cow away from the poisonous bushes and lima beans. One day the Stern woman had a group of women over for a quilting party. The Stern woman became thirsty and told me to fetch her a cup of water, which meant that I had to draw a fresh bucket from the well. When I left the well, the cow was ambling along, nowhere near the garden or the poisonous bushes. I took the bucket of water into the house, and most of the other ladies decided that they would have a cup of it too, as long as I had it handy. I kept looking out the window, keeping an eye on the cow while I served the ladies, when suddenly she was out of sight. I didn't dare say anything, but when I finally served the last woman, I dashed for the backyard.

The cow had edged her way toward the garden and was pulling away at the lima bean vines. My heart was in my mouth as I ran as fast as I could to get her away from the garden. But she had taken a real liking to the lima beans, and, try as I might, I didn't have the strength to pull her away from them.

I was too scared to cry for help; if the Stern woman knew that the cow was eating the beans, I'd get a whipping. Finally, in desperation, I managed to get the cow away from the garden, and I prayed, "Please, God, don't let anything be wrong with her. She's the only cow we've got." I was worried for the calf, too, because I knew that it couldn't live without its mother. And I kept saying, "Please, God, help me!"

As the cow took a few steps, she began to wobble and then foam at the mouth. Then her front legs began giving out on her, first one, then the other. I looked around quickly. There was no one in sight, and I thanked God for this, because I thought maybe I could pray hard enough to make her well again. But my heart sank as she went down on all fours, moaning, but not loud enough to be heard at the house.

I went down on all fours with her, begging her to get up again. The calf, which was locked in the barn, began to cry. The cow turned her head toward the sound of her calf and moaned again.

When I saw that there was no hope of getting her to her feet again, I called the Stern woman. She saw both of us lying on the ground and came screaming, asking what had happened. I tried to explain as well as I could, and she became suddenly calm, sending me to the house for baking soda. By this time, the rest of the women had come out of the house, and when I returned with the baking soda, they helped pry the cow's mouth open to allow the Stern woman to administer the soda. The calf, sensing something was wrong, was crying louder than ever.

The cow began to swell up. I knew that this was the end of her. And probably the end of me, too. The Stern woman sent me over the fields and through the forest to a neighbor's farm for help. I ran as fast as I could. The neighbor wasn't home. On my way back, I saw another neighbor hoeing a patch of land. I told him about the cow and asked if he could come over and help us. By the time we got there, the cow had swollen up three times its normal size. Everyone just stood around looking at it. The cow's head was resting on the ground and there was no hope. Minutes later, she began to gasp for breath and then choked to death.

I was numb. I couldn't move. I just stood there looking at the cow hypnotically and thinking: no more milk, no more butter, no more cream—and all because of me. I looked up at the Stern woman. She was staring at me with an expression of complete hate. I felt helpless. I could think of nothing to say, and I kept thinking: Why did God have to do this? Is the Stern woman going to whip me? If she is, why doesn't she do it and get it over with? But she did nothing. Just stood there staring at me as though to say, "There has been nothing but bad luck ever since I took you into my house!"

When the old man came home, all the men got together and dug a grave in the middle of the cotton field where no cotton had grown for a long time.

After the cow was buried, I sat on her grave until the sun went down. My sister played beside me, silently. The cow's death may well have been the final break in my hope to gain favor and acceptance in the Stern household. I don't know. But I do know that that poor cow has haunted me ever since. Even now I sometimes have nightmares about that poor cow and awaken sobbing uncontrollably, for I felt responsible for her death.

The only break in our daily routine came on the Sabbath, when I got to go to church, and during the winter, when I got to go to school. School was held when there was no field work to be done—which was only about two months out of the year.

For me the school days were cut even shorter because these months were winter ones, and I didn't have enough clothes to attend.

Our school—for blacks only, naturally—was a little one-room shack on the grounds of St. Peter's Church. I don't recall my first day there. I remember only that, when the time came, I was given some books and a writing pad. The school was very crowded; a lot of us had to sit on the floor. About the only thing I remember about those classes is that the teacher would pace around the room restlessly, threading his way among the children seated on the floor and mumbling things we never understood. I learned to read by listening to the other kids and to Gracie and Willie when they read their lessons aloud at home.

Though I don't recall much that happened in school, I do remember vividly an incident that occurred on my way to school. I had on high-button shoes and a croaker-sack dress, and as I neared the school, I saw a bunch of white kids running toward me with outstretched arms locked together. I didn't know what their intentions were until they reached me and began chanting, "Get in the ditch, you son-of-a-bitch!" And before I knew what hit me, they had caught me in their interlocked arms and hurled me headlong into the ditch. "You ain't got no business on the road going to school," one of them said. "You niggers got no business getting educated. You belong in the cotton fields!"

I scrambled to my feet and they went on down the road, laughing at the good job they had done. I looked down at my croaker-sack dress. It was filthy from the ditch. I was too hurt to cry, and too mad and frightened to fight back. I went on to school but was late. The teacher, ruler in hand, met me at the door. As I started to walk past him, he smacked both my hands with the ruler. I refused to cry. I just went in and sat down, hot all over. I was truly hurt.

But life wasn't always croaker-sack dresses. One day a big package came to the house addressed to Pearl and me. The package had been sent from someplace the grown-ups called "up-North." It contained clothes and shoes for both of us. I couldn't believe my eyes. The package was sent by my mother's sister, whom I learned was called an *aunt*. My aunt. The talk was that she had gotten angry with my mother for marrying a man my aunt didn't like. She had vowed that she wouldn't have anything to do with Mama or us anymore. But when she learned from someone that Mama had abandoned us, she decided to send us as much as she could, when she could.

One Easter Pearl and I received beautiful things. I got a dress of white chiffon with little ribbons on the sleeves and neck and with tiny flowers sewn all over it. And there was a white slip to match, and white slippers and socks. And a white bonnet. Pearl's outfit was exactly like mine, but in pink chiffon. We each got a parasol too, to shade us from the sun.

We went to church that Sunday, the envy of everyone who saw us. We were very proud of our Easter outfits, and so was the Stern woman, who had us get up before the congregation and sing a duet, just so we could be shown off properly. And as we sang, accompanied by a piano, the church seemed to rock with the people being moved by our wonderful spirit. That Easter Sunday was the most joyous of my young life. It was the first time anyone—everyone—paid so much attention to me. Our Easter dresses were the topic of the day in that small backwoods community, and my aunt became famous that Sunday.

Naturally, I absorbed every word mentioned about my aunt. I learned that she had run away from the South and had gone up-North. Mama hadn't seen her for years. She was living in a place called New York, they said, and she was very rich. The more I heard of her and that mysterious place called New York in up-North, the more fascinated I became with the thought of her. Whenever I could, I'd hide within hearing distance to learn more about this good woman in up-North.

5

Mama

Mama visited us twice in the three years I spent at the Stern house, and Pearl and I were taken to her house several times. She lived only a few miles away, but too far for youngsters to walk alone. We were always overjoyed to see her, but there was always deep despair when it came time to part with her again.

One day news came that Mama had had another baby, named Almita. I had a new half-sister, and I was extremely jealous. It had been a long time since Mama had come to see us, and I looked upon this new baby as someone else who would keep Mama away. When Pearl and I were taken over to see my new half-sister, I hated her on sight. She was dark in complexion, like Pearl, and I knew that she would hate me, too, when she grew old enough to see that I was a yella gal. And it made me even more jealous to see that the man Mama had married liked her and that she resembled Mama a little.

People thought Mama beautiful. And she was. She was part Indian and had the facial structure of an Indian, with inordinately large black eyes, jet black hair, and brown complexion. She was of medium height, thin, and curvaceous. Even her step-daughters were jealous of her beauty. It was the talk of the county, that jealousy.

About six months after the baby was born, Mama became deathly ill. I was sweeping the yard, with Pearl nearby, when a neighbor came to tell the Stern woman of Mama's illness. Everyone seemed gravely concerned, but told me nothing. It was all very mysterious.

It was getting to be evening, so the Stern woman put on a shawl, said that she'd return as soon as she could, and left for Mama's house with the neighbor. She returned late and sat for hours in front of the living room fireplace, telling her husband of Mama's sickness. I lay awake in bed, listening intently to the strange tale being told by the Stern woman and not understanding why Mama had taken so ill. She was young and vigorous. She was strong and lively and loved everyone. And I thought everyone loved her, even the envious ones. But the Stern woman talked as though Mama's illness was unnatural, that perhaps someone in the family had brought it about, owing to their jealousy of her. I began crying noiselessly, the tears flowing from my eyes and saturating my bumpy pillow. I wanted to wake Pearl, but I didn't want to make her unhappy.

According to the Stern woman, Mama became very sick after eating a plate of food that had been sprinkled with what looked like red pepper. Mama had asked about it and was told that it was a new kind of seasoning. After dinner, Mama made a fire in the living room fireplace and, hearing her husband coming home, went to the door to greet him. She collapsed in his arms. He put Mama to bed, then went to town to find the doctor. The doctor didn't come to the house until the next day. After he examined Mama, he said that there was nothing he could do for her.

She remained ill for quite a while. Whenever anyone came to the house, I'd find a hiding place to hear the latest news about Mama. I spent most of my time praying that she would get well. Each time I went to the woodpile, I'd pray as I knelt to pick up the kindling. No one had the faintest idea that I knew so much about Mama's illness. We were told about Mama the next day.

The Stern woman told us that we couldn't go to see Mama

for a couple of weeks. She was having fits and convulsions, the Stern woman said. I had overheard talk of the fits. They said that one night she'd wake up screaming, and another night she'd be up and walking around the house as though there was nothing at all wrong with her. There were times, too, when she'd ask someone to comb her hair—she wanted to look pretty for Saint Peter. At other times she wouldn't respond to anyone or anything; she would just lie dead still and stare at the ceiling.

One day a man came to get the Stern woman in his wagon. After she left, I learned that they had gone to my mother's house. Mr. Stern and the grandson sat by the fire in the living room and waited for the Stern woman to return. I tossed and turned in my bed, knowing that something was wrong. I tried to stay awake but dozed off.

I was awakened by excited voices. Everyone was talking about the back door, about how it had flown open when the Stern woman and several neighbors had walked in the front door moments earlier. Mr. Stern was swearing an oath that he had locked the back door, and his grandson was verifying the fact. It seemed strange to me that the back door should be a topic for excited conversation. That is, until I heard them theorize that Mama's spirit had entered the back door, that she had tried to reach us before the Stern woman and the neighbors to tell us that she was dead.

Mama was dead. When I heard the words, I felt Mama's presence in the room, hovering over the bed that held my sister and me. I could not cry until the thought of her death reached the center of my body and flowed through me from head to toe. I became damp and cold. I wanted to awaken Pearl, but I was afraid that they would hear me and know that I had been listening.

Soon we were called and told that we had no mother.

The next day we were taken over to see her laid out. They had placed her on a slab and covered her with a sheet. Her hair was neatly combed, her mouth curved into a smile. And it seemed to me that, even through closed eyelids, she was looking at me. My body was lead. I stood looking at her, unable to move, for a long time. I didn't want her to be dead, but she was.

Thinking back on it now, I don't know how, at that age, I accepted her death so matter-of-factly.

I was crushed at Mama's death, yes. Shocked, yes. But there was no period of the disbelief often brought about by a loved one's death. No shaking her and trying to awaken her. No screams of impotent rage. No crying that she can't be dead, I won't let her be dead. None of that. I accepted her death without question. Perhaps I did so because I lived so close to the earth, so close to Nature's cycle in which death is, in the true sense of the word, natural.

I don't know how long I stood looking at Mama, but finally one of the grown-ups guided me into the living room where people were talking in hushed tones. I didn't listen to their conversations, but I do remember them looking at me and saying, "Look at Eartha. She knows what's going on." I had known what was going on for a long time.

Mama was buried in the graveyard at Saint Peter's Church beside the graves of her mother and father. This was the same graveyard I had had to cross the night that I went after the Stern woman's medicine. That incident occurred not too long after Mama's death. And it was Mama's spirit I was referring to when I said that someone was buried there who would guide me through the night unharmed.

As her pine-box casket was lowered into the grave, I didn't cry at all. I just watched and wondered if my mother were going to heaven or hell. The sun was bright in the sky. That was a good omen. And I thought, God bless the child the sun shines on.

Perhaps owing to the shock, I don't remember dwelling on the Stern woman's dark declaration that Mama was murdered, poisoned by someone. But a ritual that took place after they lowered Mama's casket into the ground has haunted me ever since.

To understand its full significance, though, you should know that the community of North was superstition-ridden. There were incredible tales that people believed and lived by. I was no exception. Stories of the dead coming back to life were common. We lived by a code of don'ts: Don't sleep on your back when there's a young moon or a hag will ride you; don't step over anyone who is lying down or you'll catch all of his sicknesses; don't let a spider rise again if he descends from his web—this means death. Many of the superstitions have a pragmatic source. I'm sure the one about a hag riding you if you sleep on your back was perpetuated because of overcrowded sleeping conditions; everyone had to sleep on his side to make room for the others. And even though I figured that one out pretty early, the thought of sleeping on my back still unnerved me. I lived by many of these superstitions, and so did the others where I was brought up. That's why the ritual at my mother's burial has unnerved me ever since.

When the earth was shoveled back into Mama's grave, my baby half-sister was passed over her grave six times. This is a ritual practiced over the grave of one who is suspected of having been murdered; it is done to keep the murdered person from coming back from the grave to claim the youngest offspring. These people truly believed such things, and it was evident that someone thought there was cause to keep my mother from coming back from the grave to claim my baby half-sister.

Then there was the matter of her death bed. After the funeral, there was found in each corner of the mattress padding an object of voodoo: Knotted together were claws of animals, teeth of snakes, tails of weird things mixed with powders of swamp herbs. And tied neatly in the center of her bed between the springs and the mattress was a bundle of letters swearing death. This is done to keep the victim in agony until death comes. Voodoo objects and letters of death—if one method should fail, the other would succeed.

Someone wanted my mother dead. I don't know who. I knew little about the goings-on at the house in which she lived. I knew nothing about her adopted family or the people who visited them. It's an unsolved mystery that hurts me deeply.

After the funeral, everyone went home to continue life as it was. So did Pearl and I—without Mama. There seemed little hope for us now, little to live for, to look forward to—except maybe packages from that good woman up North. I thought about her often.

6

To New York in Up-North

Shortly after Mama died, my aunt sent for me. A box of clothing, with a letter and train ticket enclosed, arrived unexpectedly one afternoon. Everyone gathered around to see what the box contained. There were three pair of long underwear, three pair of long cotton stockings, three undershirts, three petticoats, a pair of gloves, a beret hat, a pair of shoes, a scarf, a woolen dress, and a winter jacket—along with some things for my sister.

The letter explained to the Sterns how to go about packing me up and putting me on the train. It said that my aunt would be at the station to meet me and described what she looked like. The letter also said that my aunt would send for Pearl as soon as she was able to and that Pearl should not worry about it.

My departure date was several days off, and never had time dragged so slowly. It occurred to me that my aunt was sending for me because she *wanted* me. It made me deliriously happy to be wanted. And for the next few days I did my chores automatically, thinking of nothing but my aunt and what up-North would be like.

As for the Sterns, I couldn't understand their reaction. I can only assume that they were jealous of my opportunity to go north, or that they were disgruntled at losing a combination field hand, housekeeper, and servant. This may seem a cruel observation, but I could think of no other reason or justification for their picking at me from the day I received the package and train tickets until the day I left.

"What do you want to go up-North for? It gets so cold up there that people freeze to death," they said. "People live on top of each other. You never have enough room to move around in. And the buildings are so tall they sometimes collapse and tumble down on you. The trains ride in the air and are always falling down to the ground. You don't know when you're well off! Why don't you tell her you don't want to come?"

I just let them talk, not bothering to answer them. I didn't care if what they said was true. My aunt wanted me, that's all I cared about. I'd take my chances with up-North!

The day of my departure, they put a wash tub in front of the fireplace and scrubbed me until I thought they were going to scrape my skin off. Then they combed my hair, put it up in three braids, and dressed me. My hair was so thick, even in braids, that the beret my aunt had sent me posed a real problem. They puzzled over it for quite a while, then in desperation, literally screwed it on my head. It was so tight that I knew it was probably cutting off the circulation in the whole top of my head. And though it hurt—until my head got numb—I suffered gladly: I was on my way to up-North, and I was never coming back!

For the long train ride, they had packed me a shoe box full of catfish sandwiches—on white bread—and a piece of sweet potato pie and some wild plums. It was the first time in my life that I had all the store-bought white bread that I wanted.

They even arranged for a car to take me to the train station at Orangeburg. I had never ridden in an automobile; in fact, I had seen few of them, and then only from a distance, on the main road. And I had never seen a train. I was so excited waiting for the car to pick us up that I could hardly contain myself. I was scared, too. But you can overcome a lot of fear when you've got all the store-bought white bread you can eat and you're going to up-North, where somebody wants you.

Pearl was very unhappy to know that I was leaving. She started to cry when the man with the car came to take us to Orangeburg. We all piled into the car, the Sterns, Gracie, Willie, and Pearl. And all the way there, everyone was telling me how miserable I'd be in up-North and how I'd soon be begging to come back. I just turned my ears off and enjoyed my first automobile ride, watching the scenery go by fast and listening to the motor. It sure beat the horse and wagon.

When we arrived at the station, the Stern woman spoke to the stationmaster about me, and he put a tag on my coat lapel that said who I was and where I was going and where I was coming from. Then we went out on the platform and waited. The tracks were there. I had heard about those tracks and how the train just stays right on them and goes wherever the tracks go. There were other people on the platform waiting, too. Some of them were looking up the tracks, so I figured that's the direction the train would be coming from. So I looked up the tracks, too—just stared at them hypnotically. I didn't say anything to anyone, not even Pearl; I didn't hear anything either. I just stared at the tracks until I heard the far-off chugging, and the train grew bigger and bigger as it approached.

It huffed and puffed, blew smoke out of its top and steam out of its sides, and it growled, and its wheels squealed and just generally made more noise than I had ever heard in my life. No one else on the platform ran away from it, so I figured that we must be safe where we were standing. But any fear I might have had disappeared when I saw the cars the engine was pulling. They were all shiny and the windows had real glass in every one of them, just like the windows in the automobile and the station. I had never seen so much glass. I had never seen glass in windows before; all the houses I knew about had shutters to close out the wind and cold, not glass.

No one got off the train, but all kinds of people got on. It seemed to me that everybody and his brother were all going where I was going, to up-North. A porter came out with a box that had steps in it, and the people started climbing the steps and getting into the car. When the porter saw me, he helped me up the steps. "Where are you going, little girl?" he asked.

I remembered what the stationmaster had written on my tag. "I'm going to New York!" I said boldly. I suddenly felt very grown up. I mean, wasn't I a full seven years old, and didn't I have catfish sandwiches with real store-bought white bread, and didn't I have all new clothes, and hadn't I come all the way to Orangeburg—and in an automobile? Now, that was fully grown, if you asked me! I was a seasoned traveler already. It seemed to me that I had seen just about everything—except New York in up-North, and I'd be seeing that, soon.

I went up the steps and into the car, followed by Pearl and the Stern family, who were chattering away. I didn't hear what they were saying to me. I was looking at the rows and rows of big easy chairs, all soft and covered with cloth. I took one by a glass window, and I heard the porter assuring the Stern woman that he'd look after me. Next thing I knew, Pearl and the Sterns were outside the window on the platform again. And the train began to move. I saw the receding figures of Pearl and the rest waving at the train, and I remembered that I had not said goodbye to them. I felt the smooth, tingly, vibrating sensation of the train on the track. I was off to up-North!

I didn't sleep the entire night. And except for the porter, I didn't look at or talk to anyone. I just kept looking out the window the entire night—except when I got hungry and ate my catfish sandwiches. But even then I kept my eyes to the window. I took in everything, as though I were memorizing it, every whistle stop, every town and light, every road and car and field—everybody and everything that came within my view.

The porter passed by once in a while to see if I was all right. He'd smile at me and go his way. And every now and then through the night I'd try to imagine what my aunt would look like, but I couldn't, and I'd stop trying until the urge to do so became irresistible again. Will she like me? The question recurred so often throughout the night that it was carried in rhythm of the train: *Will-she-like-me? Will-she-like-me? Will-she-like-me?* . . .

7

Discovering the Twentieth Century

My face was still pressed against the window, wide-eyed, when dawn broke. The blackness gave way to gray as the sun finally peeked its way over a nearby hilltop. Then it got brighter and lighter and colors crept back into things until it was full daylight. My eyes felt red and grainy from lack of sleep, and the new sunlight bothered them. But still I stared, afraid I'd miss something.

The porter came along, saying that we would be in New York shortly, and put the suitcase my aunt had sent me and my shoe box of food on the vacant seat beside me. As soon as this was done, my eyes were back to the window again.

Before long, the train began slowing down, as though deliberately teasing me. I wanted it to hurry. I kept thinking, if this thing was being pulled by a horse it would go faster than this! The station came into view ahead, and I began to worry. Will my aunt be waiting for me like she said? Maybe she forgot I was coming. Maybe the Stern people just sent me off to get rid of me. Maybe....

Then I saw all the people in the station. It was one of the

most astonishing sights of my life; I had never seen so many people. Hundreds of them. *Thousands* of them! They were skittering around like ants. They seemed to be pushing and shoving each other like cattle. How could my aunt possibly find me in a place like this? I was positive there were more people in that New York train station than there were in the entire South!

The porter had to literally pry me from the window. I was horror-struck to think that I was going to be thrust into that anonymous, unruly mob. I went down the train steps and just stood staring amid the giant grown-ups with intense faces who seemed to be going everywhere and nowhere at once. I'm sure that the porter must have stood by to see that my aunt found me all right, but I wasn't aware of him.

I searched the faces of the crowd until I saw a tall, pretty, brown-skinned woman walking toward me. She walked with an elegant, easy grace, and she had a smile on her face that made me smile. I had a feeling that she really wanted to laugh but was afraid that she'd hurt my feelings if she did. I must have been a sight, my beret screwed firmly in place and my eyes fearful and red from lack of sleep. I just knew that it was my aunt from the way she looked at me.

"Eartha Mae?"

"Yessum."

Being nearly three times my size, she had to bend down to look at my tag to see if I was really who I said I was.

"So *this* is what you look like!"

"Yessum."

She resembled Mama a little. Taller, and not quite as beautiful as Mama, but very pretty. She picked up my suitcase and grabbed me by the hand. I carried my shoe box as she threaded her way through the mass of people. Feeling the security of her firm grip, I was no longer afraid of the people; my fear turned to curiosity. And my aunt practically had to drag me along to keep me from stopping now and then to stare at the people and to figure out where all of them had come from and what they were all doing there. Everybody looked like they, too, had on new clothes—beautiful clothes.

We finally made it through the crowd and began climbing

the longest flight of stairs I had ever seen. They might have just kept going up and up into heaven, for all I knew. But when we finally reached the opening at the top, I knew I wasn't in heaven. I was stunned. I froze. I stopped breathing. In that one split-second, my senses were assaulted: New York City. The smell of it. The incredible *noise* of it. And the sight of it! Everywhere I looked there was snow—great piles of it, just lying there. I had seen snow once or twice in the South, where it melted as soon as it hit the ground, but nothing like this. And the people! There were more people up there than there had been downstairs; they were moving in masses—thousands of them! And the cars and trucks and buses, all shapes and colors and sizes, and they all looked as though they were trying to bump into one another. And when the shock from the motion of people and vehicles left me, I noticed the buildings. I kept looking up higher and higher until the back of my head was touching my back. I got nervous. I just knew that one of those buildings was going to collapse on me just like the Sterns had said.

My aunt was extremely patient with me and allowed me to absorb as much as I could in those first few minutes of complete bewilderment. She was eventually able to coax me to a bus stop beneath a steel road on which a train traveled in the air. Would one of those trains fall off on us—like they were always doing—before our bus arrived?

The bus came to save us, though, its doors whishing open, and we crammed inside, finally managing to find two seats way in the back. Once seated, my aunt—between chuckles—tried to adjust my beret, then finally gave up. I spent the whole bus trip silent, kneeling on the seat and looking out of the window at that wonderful, crazy New York.

When we finally got off the bus in Harlem, I noticed that there weren't as many people on the streets, and there weren't as many cars, and the buildings were not as tall. I grew less fearful and took great delight in the snow, which was falling heavily. I ran ahead of my aunt, trying to catch snowflakes and occasionally throwing myself headlong into snowbanks. I got so carried away that, before my aunt could caution me, I ran across a street toward a bigger, softer looking snowbank, disregarding the cars going up and down the street.

My aunt screamed at me, fearing for my safety, and the fact that she screamed at me hurt me deeply. I had come to expect her to be the opposite of everyone I had known in the South. I didn't think she'd ever yell at me. And I didn't understand that, for the first time that I could remember, someone was yelling at me for my *own* good, not for theirs. I didn't realize that I had frightened her half to death by running in front of cars that would have had great difficulty trying to stop in the snow.

We arrived at my aunt's apartment on 143rd and Eighth Avenue, which my aunt shared with a family of five called Wayde. The building is no longer standing; it was replaced in the early fifties by housing projects. It was a six-story building, run-down like every other building in that ghetto section, but inside it looked like a palace compared with the houses I had known in the South. The ghetto itself was heaven compared with the plantations.

We climbed two flights of stairs to the apartment, and several of the Waydes were there to greet us. The two youngest children, a boy and a girl, were still in school when I arrived. The girl, Joyce, was about my age, and we became good friends. She was to be a great help to me in that first year or so of adjustment to my new world. We've stayed in touch with each other over the years—she's now a pharmacist in New York City—and, in fact, Joyce and her husband and her brother and his wife came to visit me at the Plaza Hotel before the Carnegie Hall concert mentioned in Chapter 1. By being in school at that hour, Joyce missed the show, for my first couple of hours discovering the "new" technology of the up-North world were bizarre—mystifying and sometimes horrifying to me, hilariously funny to those watching me.

The show began in the living room. We sat for a while and got acquainted with the two older children and with Mrs. Wayde—whom everyone called Mama Wayde. Then someone flipped on the lights with a wall switch. I was astonished. I had never heard of electricity. Even the time or two that I had been to Orangeburg or Columbia, I could not recall having seen electric lights. But then our trips were always made during the day, so I hadn't had occasion to see electricity in use. Now, before my very eyes, someone flipped a switch and a light went on—there was no kerosene or wick or flame, and it was brighter than fire! I remember getting up and working the switch myself, the lights going on and off whenever I wanted them to. Everyone was amused for the first minute or so, but I was so fascinated that I just kept switching them on and off and on and off until I nearly drove everyone crazy and they made me stop.

Finally, it was time to get settled, so my aunt took me into another room to change me out of my traveling clothes; she got more hysterical with each piece of clothing that she removed: my coat, my beret, my dress, my three slips, three undershirts, three pair of long panties, three pair of stockings, and my shoes. Every stitch of clothing she had sent had been put on my back!

After my aunt had dressed me in something considerably more comfortable than the three outfits I had been wearing, I went through the apartment turning lights on and off and discovering things. I had led such an isolated, backwoods life that nearly everything New York people took for granted, I thought magic. Sometimes my discoveries were amusing to my aunt and the Waydes, as it had been when I discovered the radio. But sometimes I'd unnerve them—when I discovered the gas stove, for instance. Mama Wayde was preparing to fix dinner when I wandered into the kitchen. When she turned on the gas burner and blue flames appeared from nowhere, I let out a scream of such intensity that everyone in the apartment jumped about two feet off the floor.

I thought the gas stove was black magic and evil. And as far as I was concerned, there was ample evidence before me to support that opinion. Fire, after all, was always red or orange or yellow—never blue. One had to start a fire with matches— everyone knew that—and fire had to burn something like wood or paper. And here was Mama Wayde turning a knob, and blue fire appeared. She didn't use a match; there was nothing there to burn; and the flames were a bright blue. It was as though, by a flick of her wrist, she had summoned an evil spirit from the netherworld. It had to be the work of the devil himself, and I scared the hell out of everybody in the place screaming when the ol' devil jumped out of the stove.

Whenever my curiosity overcame my timidity, I'd ask

questions about my discoveries, not realizing that my seemingly simple questions don't have definitive answers even today. What is electricity? How does it get to the light bulbs? I figured that since they'd been using the stuff all along, they should have been able to give me simple, direct answers. They didn't know either, of course, but rather than telling me they didn't know, they'd usually have fun with me by making up some fantastic story a child might believe.

The radio is an example. When I discovered the little wooden box that music and singing and conversations came out of, I was told that there were little people in the box who sang or played music or talked whenever you wanted them to.

My discoveries were made over a period of weeks and months—the telephone, the elevator, clocks, the subway—marvelous things, but none more marvelous to me than modern plumbing: bathrooms right inside the houses and public buildings. I discovered the bathroom—the hard way—my first day at the apartment, too.

After my aunt had changed my clothes, I had to go to the bathroom. I was too embarrassed to tell anyone, so I decided to look for the outhouse myself. I looked from the second story glassed-in window to a yard of concrete below. No outhouse. Where did one go? I knew that it had to be on the first floor outside the building someplace, but how would I find it? In desperation, I finally gave up the idea of finding it myself and I asked my aunt. She took me to a tiny room, switched on the light, and closed the door behind me.

I looked at all the things in the room, weird looking bowl-like things made of what looked like white stone, and tried to figure them out. I managed to turn on water that ran into a bowl; I played with the knobs in the big tub; then I discovered what looked to me like a stone well with water in it. But if there was a place to go to the bathroom in there, I couldn't find it. I finally called to my aunt for help. She came in and showed me the proper bowl and how it flushed, then left the little room again, laughing and closing the door. It seemed to me awfully unsanitary to go to the bathroom right inside your house, but I eventually got used to the idea.

Later in the day, I went to the front window that looked onto the street and waited for the little girl who lived there to come home from school. I was told that she was about my age and that her name was Joyce. As the time for her to come home drew nearer, the street began filling with children, yelling and playing on their way home from school. Then I noticed one little girl walking all by herself. I thought it must be Joyce. And when the doorbell rang a few minutes later (another discovery), I knew that I was right. She came into the apartment, and we soon became friends.

After a few weeks, my aunt took me to be registered in school. It was a most terrifying experience. They put needles in my arm; my arm swelled up and I got sick. I had attended school in the South only a few times. And while the white kids had thrown me into a ditch once, and while the little school in Saint Peter's churchyard was tiny, overcrowded, dilapidated and didn't have an inside outhouse like this one did, at least the school in the South didn't swell my arm up and make me sick.

I was taken to a classroom of children much smaller than I. The teacher's name was Miss Beans, and after my aunt talked to her for a minute and then left, I was placed in a seat among snickering children. Miss Beans explained to the class that my name was Eartha Kitt and that I had just come up from the South and must, therefore, start my schooling from the beginning. My class was 1A.

None of the children took the initiative to make friends with me, and I didn't know how to go about getting to know anyone. For the first couple of weeks, my aunt took me to school each morning, came back at lunch hour to sit with me, and took me home at three. After I had gotten my bearings and a very small measure of confidence, she made arrangements for me to buy lunch in school and to come and go on my own.

I didn't have much trouble at first because I stayed to myself. Those who tried to pick fights with me soon gave up, because I wouldn't lift my arms to fight back, nor would I answer them back when they tried to start arguments. But fights were inevitable, and I was in school only a month or two before I got into my first one.

A girl pushed me down and hurt my knee. As I was bending down, tending to it, she kicked me in the behind—to the delight of everyone who was watching. I put my arms out to fight, but I couldn't get angry. I just got nervous and started to cry. I didn't want to hurt her, so I took all the blows. The more she hit me, the less I cried. The school bell broke the fight up, and we all went back to class. No one said anything to the teacher about the fight.

Unfortunately, word soon got around school that I was a coward, and everyone began picking on me. I wanted to tell my aunt, but I knew that it was a problem I'd have to figure out for myself. I was tense with anxiety every noon when school broke for lunch. But I wasn't angry with anyone, and I took the pushing, shoving, and derision from my classmates—until the big challenge came.

Shortly after my first fight, a bully girl started talking to me in the schoolyard as her followers surrounded us. They all began asking me questions, and I answered, and they began egging the bully girl on. I got the distinct impression that everyone in the gang was afraid of her. She told me she was going to beat me up after school if she caught me. Then everyone walked away, laughing. I sat frozen to my seat all afternoon waiting for the three o'clock bell to ring.

I didn't know whether to ask the teacher to let me leave school early or to stand and fight. I was too scared to ask the teacher, too scared to leave, and too scared to fight. But time flew that afternoon. I was still wracked with indecision when the hands of the clock zipped around to three and the bell made my decision for me.

My stomach felt as though it were being wrung through a wringer as I walked out of school. But to my joy, none of the gang was in sight. As I got around the first corner near a candy store, however, the bully girl came swaggering out of the store, with all of her little boosters right behind her.

"I told you, you'd better not let me catch you!" she said as her gang surrounded me again. "Why don't you run? Go ahead, run!"

I thought about running, but by then I knew from experience that if I did, this same scary scene would repeat itself. When this bully girl would get tired of it, some other bully girl would take her place.

"Ain't you gonna run?" she said.

I just stood there looking at her. I could see that she and the gang were getting nervous—so was I.

"Why don't you beat her up and get it over with?" one of the gang said.

"She's gotta hit first," another said.

"She ain't gonna move. Hit her!"

Suddenly, someone pushed her from behind, and she lurched toward me. By reflex, my hands went out, and she was knocked to the ground. This brought cheers from the crowd and infuriated the bully girl: "She knocked her down . . . she knocked her down . . . she knocked her down!"

This encouraged me. I doubled up my fists as tightly as I could and waited for a blow to anger me. The bully girl got to her feet in fury, and we went at each other like tigresses. I finally knocked her down, and she went off with a bloody nose and torn clothes. She didn't go to school the next day. And when word of our fight got around school, no one picked on me after that.

I gradually became very popular at school, not because of my reputation from having stood up to the school bully but because of my speaking ability. The teacher often called upon me to read before the class. And though I didn't notice it at first, I gradually began to realize that whenever I got up to read I had each class member's undivided attention, and the silence was frightening. I was embarrassed at first, but I soon learned to like the attention shown me when I read, and I loved to read.

I began participating in assemblies in recitations, speeches as representative of my class, and the like. The same strange reaction occurred then, too. Whenever I went before the assembly, it got so suddenly quiet that one could almost hear the students breathing. It was as though I had cast a spell over the room each time. I didn't at all understand it, but it seemed that I had some power that made people pay attention. And understand it or not, I loved the attention.

Though I had rarely spoken to anyone prior to my class

reading, I've always been a verbal person. Foreign languages are second nature to me, and I've always spoken clearly and distinctly. I don't remember ever having a Southern accent. I don't remember speaking any differently from the way I do today—which someone once described to me as Continental, a British accent with American and French influence. How I could possibly have learned this from South Carolina and Harlem is totally a mystery to me, as mysterious as that strange influence I had over my classroom and assembly audiences.

It was a wonderful feeling to be wanted by my aunt and to be noticed and liked by my peers and teachers.

8

Acceptance

As my first year in New York went by, I was getting along very well. My thirst for knowledge and insatiable appetite for reading enabled me to do two years' work in my first year of school, so I caught up with my age group and escaped the terrible feelings of inferiority caused by my being more mature and larger than my classmates. Later I would skip yet another grade, passing up my own age group.

At home things were going well with me. The Wayde family treated me very well, and I was being accepted as another member of the family. Joyce and I were great pals and spent a good deal of time together. Mama Wayde took a genuine interest in my welfare, making sure that I dressed warmly and ate the proper foods, and very nearly treated me as one of her own children. But there was friction between my aunt and Mama Wayde. A showdown was imminent.

Often I would hear them arguing. Mama Wayde complained bitterly that my aunt wasn't taking proper care of me, that she was leaving me alone too much and not seeing enough of me and, in general, neglecting me. It was true that my aunt would frequently go off to work in the morning and not come home until after I had gone to bed. When this happened, Mama Wayde or another member of the family would feed me dinner, put me to bed, get me up in the morning, and fix my breakfast before sending me off to school. My aunt, though, thought Mama Wayde's charges ill founded, and an argument would ensue.

I was seven or eight at the time, I guess, and didn't fully understand what was going on. No doubt, in light of what would happen later, my aunt was beginning to feel the tremendous pressure of her responsibility toward me. She was deeply religious and had a strict sense of ethics. And I'm sure that she sent for me when Mama died because she thought it her Christian duty to do so. But she was, after all, a single woman with a life of her own to lead, and I think that the cost in time and money and the responsibility of raising a growing child was beginning to wear on her. It's evident to me now that she was transferring more and more of her burden onto Mama Wayde, thinking that giving Mama Wayde money—which she always did—compensated somewhat for Mama Wayde's extra duties.

The break between them came during my second year of school. I was home sick with the whooping cough one night when my aunt came in late. Mama Wayde fired one of her verbal volleys about leaving a sick child alone, and my aunt blew up. Without thought of my condition—I was running a temperature and coughing my head off—my aunt scooped me up, yelled to Mama Wayde that she wouldn't have to put up with the two of us any longer, and stomped out of the building into a raging snowstorm. It couldn't have been a worse night for our departure, and there I was, dressed only in pajamas and covered with the thin blanket my aunt had scooped up with me, while my aunt, ankle-deep in snow, trudged up and down the street looking for a taxi.

Fortunately for me, a taxi finally came by, and she directed it to 136th Street and Seventh Avenue, where she awoke the building manager, who settled us into a furnished apartment. We never went back to Mama Wayde's place to live.

I liked the new place very much. It was run by a very nice

man who taught music, and the building contained not only a few apartments but a rehearsal hall as well. Ethel Waters and Bo Jangles used to rehearse there frequently. I didn't have the faintest idea who they were at the time, but I used to listen to them from the hallway outside the rehearsal room door.

My participation in both music and acting began about this time too. My aunt apparently made some arrangement with the music teacher in the building, and I began taking piano lessons—which I hated. My aunt's great desire was for me to be a concert pianist. I had no real interest in piano or music at that time, but I suffered through the ordeal to please her, thinking that perhaps I could gain her attention, maybe even praise. I took my lessons faithfully every Tuesday and Saturday. But my teacher went through absolute hell in getting me to practice. Finally, he forced me to practice in his presence before and after every class. Under his watchful eyes, I became fairly good, in spite of myself.

When my aunt was home, I would play the things I liked and knew well—usually the easy ones. I never risked playing the hard pieces when she was around for fear that I would play badly and displease her. The hard pieces I would put aside until I *had* to learn them, but once learned, I'd play them until I'm sure everyone was sick and tired of hearing them. To my surprise, I learned that I had almost a photographic mind when it came to music. I could glance at a composition once or twice and then play it almost note for note—provided, of course, that it was a relatively easy composition. Nevertheless, I still hated the piano.

Singing and acting came relatively easy to me, as easy as the speaking ability I mentioned earlier. And again, I had no youthful aspirations of becoming a singer or actress. It never occurred to me that one could be a professional singer or actress. I was simply drawn into it by circumstance.

My aunt had always been a great church woman, and she expected me to be a great churchgoer as well. I had joined the Methodist church and was a member for a long time. I was chosen for the children's choir, and for recitals and talks, and was always the star in church plays. I never competed for any of these activities. I was assigned them, like it or not, and accepted them without question.

There were about eight girls and six boys in the children's choir, and I was selected to lead the singing. When we were finished, the congregation would respond with amens and hallelujahs until the preacher would restore order to give his sermon. Sometimes the singing and preaching and hallelujahs went so well that everyone would begin shouting and jumping up and down with the excitement of a common spirit. I loved those moments; it seemed to me that the spirit of the love of God permeated the church during these magic moments, and I'd get warm all over. People would cry and hum, sing and pray with genuine love.

I starred in many plays both in church and in school. And the more I acted, the more word got to my aunt that I was a "great little actress."

"You must encourage her," people kept telling my aunt. And the more I overheard these remarks, the more I expected my aunt to praise me and encourage me. But I got no encouragement from her. Absolutely none. When she came to see me in a church play, I'd try to glance at her from the stage, but she usually sat way in the back where I couldn't see her. She'd come to take me home when the play was over, and people would tell her that they thought my performance wonderful. She would say, "Thank you." Nothing more.

We'd walk home in silence. I'd wait for her to make some comment about the play, perhaps tell me whether she thought me good or not. Nothing. Sometimes I would try to take her hand, to show her that I loved her and to get her to show that she loved me. But somehow she would always manage to avoid taking my hand.

At this new place, there was no one to awaken me, no wonderful breakfast aromas to look forward to. I would get up in the mornings and prepare myself for school. When there was something to eat for breakfast, I would eat; if there was nothing, I would go to school hungry. It puzzled me when I couldn't find food, because I knew my aunt was working—or at least I thought she was working. And my clothes became shabbier and shabbier. Those were troubled times, and as things grew steadily worse, I became aware of the word *relief*. That's what we were on: relief. I never really understood what it was all about, but after a while I realized that relief meant that someone, somewhere, was looking out for us. Relief meant food, a dress, and apples. How I remember those apples. It took me years to regain my taste for them.

One day my aunt sent me to collect what was due us from the relief station. She called me upstairs from my play and gave me the address. "Bring back as much as you can," she said.

The station was on the last avenue of the East Side and we lived on the last avenue of the West Side. When I finally got to the relief station, the smiling man looked at me and said, "You could have two ten-pound bags of apples, but you're too little to carry all that, so you better take one."

"I can do it," I said, remembering that my aunt had told me to bring back as much as I could. The bags seemed almost as large as me, and I took one in each arm and walked out. They were not heavy at first. But after walking two long city blocks, one of my arms began growing numb and its muscles wouldn't respond. No longer able to hold the bag up, I clutched it tightly to my body to keep it from falling. After another block my other arm gave out on me, and I had to put both bags on a step and rest a while. Then I continued my journey, my arms so numb they no longer ached, but my whole body ached and my legs were beginning to buckle beneath me. I began crying from the strain. But I was absolutely determined: I would not give up.

It was my mission. And I kept thinking to myself, the more apples I bring home, the more we'll have to eat. I concentrated on that idea, to take my mind off my physical discomfort: My aunt will make apple pie, applesauce, apple dumplings, stewed apples, apple cake, and apple salad, I thought. I kept thinking of these things over and over until I climbed the steps to our apartment and nearly collapsed. My aunt laughed until she could laugh no more. "I didn't tell you to bring home the *entire* relief station!" she said.

I just knew that my labors would be rewarded. My aunt would make all of the things I had thought about during my excruciatingly painful trek. But she never got beyond applesauce. I had just plain apples—morning, noon, and night for weeks and weeks. Still, I was thankful. As long as there was an apple in the house, I never got hungry.

Relief dresses bothered me. In my new environment it didn't occur to me that relief dresses were high fashion compared with the flour-sack dresses I had worn in the South. Everyone in school who wore a relief dress was known and snickered at. I was terribly self-conscious about them, but they were better than the ones I once had.

I began to wonder where we were getting the food and clothing. Who was so kind to give these things to us? I heard of something called WPA (Works Progress Administration). Everywhere I went I saw "WPA Project." Men were cleaning the streets and parks, or working on buildings—all for the WPA. I wondered what the WPA was, or *who* the WPA was.

We had begun to study government in school. We had to learn about the President of the United States, and after much avid reading of current governmental affairs, it seemed to me that relief, the WPA, and love were all embodied in the same person: President Franklin D. Roosevelt. He came to life in my mind, as God was alive, as my aunt was alive, as people were alive. He was my friend, a friend to all people who wanted to eat, to be warm, to work. For the rest of those troubled years, I thought of Mr. Roosevelt, and I was grateful because I didn't feel alone; I felt that he was aware of me.

With the help and encouragement of my junior high school teacher, Mrs. Bishop, I graduated into high school a year ahead of my time. Mrs. Bishop asked if I would be interested in attending a special school to study dramatics, the New York School of Performing Arts, known then as Metropolitan High School. I was very pleased at her suggestion, but when she told me what I would have to do in order to enter the school, I nearly gave up the idea. I would have to take an oral test before the students and faculty of the school, and to my mind, this sounded like the most frightening thing I would ever have to go through in my life. "Suppose I don't win?" I asked Mrs. Bishop. "Suppose they don't like me?"

"Well," said Mrs. Bishop, "I'll make an arrangement with the teacher of that school to have you go down and get acquainted with her. After you meet each other, if you don't want to go through with it, fine. It's up to you." She hadn't convinced me, but then she added, "No one has to know about it but us. If you don't pass, that's that. You'll continue here. No one will be the wiser."

That did it. That gave me the feeling of security I needed. If I didn't pass the test for the new school, I could continue in junior high for another year—I wouldn't have to skip a grade. I met with the teacher of the new school and we got along well. She told me what would be expected of me and asked that I prepare a speech to be recited aloud in front of a group of students and faculty members. I decided that I wanted to attend the school and that the fearsome ordeal would be worth it.

A few weeks later, I went back to the school. In those weeks, the butterflies that inhabited my stomach had been doing incredible gymnastic feats. They kept at it until I was finally called upon to recite. Then, standing before my anonymous judges, I became so paralyzed with fear that I would have preferred the butterflies.

As I began my speech, the room became still, and then even more still. At first I could not even hear my own voice. There was no sound, as though my mouth were only shaping the words. Then came the gradual realization that there was absolute stillness, except for my own voice. To my ear it sounded hollow; it reverberated as though I were talking in a vacuum, a glass cage in which the sound could be heard only by me. And the eyes of my judges became one huge eye, as though I were being studied through a microscope like an insect. Then the faces were no longer faces, but masks staring right through me.

I don't know how long it was before these impressions dissolved, almost melted in my mind, and I became conscious of that same electric feeling I had experienced when I first read before my classmates a few years earlier. I knew I had gained control of the room; I had won them. I just knew.

When I had given my speech and sat down, I noticed the teacher's pleased expression. Tears came to my own eyes, and an almost indescribable warmth passed through me because I knew that we would become great friends. Later she would encourage me more than anyone else to go into the theater.

The students were asked to explain what there was about me that they did not like. No one had anything to say. The class broke, and students left the room looking back at me. At that moment there were no thoughts of the school in my mind, only the wonderful feeling that Eartha Mae had gathered the courage, somehow, to face the possibility of rejection and had not been rejected. There were no thoughts of school until a couple of the students came over to me smiling, and one of them, a Jewish boy, said, "See you when the term begins." I'll never forget the look on his face, which said: Isn't it wonderful that you and I can be accepted here without prejudice?

I was in. Eartha Mae was in. . . .

9

"The Wild One"

By the time I entered high school, we were better off econom-ically—at least by ghetto standards. We were no longer on relief. I had a couple of decent dresses, a pair of good shoes, and some-thing to eat besides apples.

We had moved to a different neighborhood, which was rather unsettling to me for a couple of reasons. First, there was a man living with us now, or we were living with him—I never could figure out which was which. All I know is that he had a key to the apartment and that he came and went as he pleased. He was a very gentle man, though, and he treated me kindly. The apartment had one bedroom, a living room, kitchen, and bath. When I did not sleep with my aunt, I slept on a couch in the living room.

The second unsettling revelation was that I was an outsider again. The people in our new neighborhood spoke a language I didn't understand; most called it Cuban, though some called it Puerto Rican. At first, I would just stand by myself on the apartment stoop and watch the passersby, afraid to speak to them even if they tried to be friendly and talked to me. Everyone, it seemed, spoke this different tongue. And since I didn't attend the neighborhood school, having to take the subway cross town to my special school, I had little chance to learn their strange language except during the evenings and on weekends.

I listened to them carefully, picking out a word that was used more than once and memorizing it; then I would pick out another to add to my growing vocabulary. When I asked about the meanings of the words later, I was shocked to learn that some of them were not at all decent.

I began to make friends with the girls on the block and to join them as they wandered around the neighborhood. They would meet boys in the evenings and sit on neighborhood stoops and chatter away as though I could understand them. The girls spoke English to me, but when the gang would gather on a stoop or at the local candy store, they would speak this foreign tongue. I was ashamed to have them know that I hadn't the faintest idea of what they were saying, so I reacted accordingly: They would chatter and smile. I'd smile. They would chatter and laugh. I'd laugh along with them. They would chatter and frown. I'd shake my head in sympathy and frown fiercely. I became immensely popular with them; I'm sure they had never found a kindred spirit like me, one who shared their *every* view. Little did they know that I didn't know what the hell they were talking about!

Now and then I would hear an English phrase and, in context, I would get a notion of what they were saying. I became more curious, gained more friends, and was so determined, that I learned the language quickly. Without my aunt's knowledge, I began hanging around with the gang all of my spare moments. We would congregate about four blocks from my apartment building, where the boys would gather tin cans, garbage-can lids, boxes, and bells for instruments, and we would have Latin jam sessions. I fell in love with the sounds and rhythms and chants and words. They were a wonderful gang, and I loved every one of them. A couple would get up and dance in the middle of the street while I watched, my body moving in imitation of theirs. The rhythm would carry me away. It was wonderful.

Then there were the boys. And my aunt.

I would guess my age to have been about fourteen when I discovered boys and they discovered me. I liked them better than girls, for some reason. I didn't know why, didn't even wonder why. I suggested to my aunt that I bring some of the boys to the apartment to meet her. She struck at me like a cobra.

"You stay away from boys!" she said.

"Huh?"

"They're no good. They'll get you in trouble!"

My aunt knew that I had reached the age at which I was beginning to notice the opposite sex. But she didn't know how I was going about *noticing*. For a couple of years she had ranted and raved about men, and she didn't realize how much fear she had instilled in me about men and their ways with women. But I was interested in *boys*, not men. Friends. Still, her attack on boys scared me, too, and I didn't know what to think. I was not so naive that I didn't know of the relationship between man and woman, but the thought of it made me deathly afraid.

Soon the boys began inviting me to the Cuban dances that were given every Friday, Saturday, and Sunday night in some dance hall or other. They were good dances, and there was always a policeman there to keep order. The dances were wild, frenzied, and furious. I learned them quickly; I learned a lot in those dance halls. I learned that the boys thought me attractive and, when they saw that I had natural dancing ability, they were willing to teach me their dance steps as well as their language.

I had curfew to make every night: home by seven. On Saturday nights I was allowed to stay out until ten. I was good about keeping my curfew until I discovered that, owing to a new job, my aunt didn't get home until midnight on Saturdays. Sometimes I would stay at the dances on Saturdays until they were over—usually around midnight. If my aunt beat me home—which was frequently—I would get a beating for my transgression. But I loved to dance and gladly took the beating for the extra two hours of dancing. It was my one "vice."

Being very religious, my aunt looked upon dancing as sinful. And dancing with *boys!* She began calling me a "wild one" and berated me for my wanton ways. "You're going to come home pregnant!" she'd say.

Pregnant?

"You'll have a baby and bring shame on me. I'd have to take care of *both* of you! Then what would I do? How could I afford that?"

Baby? I had never even kissed a boy. I had never even held hands, except when dancing! If she had only known that it would have taken me weeks to work up enough courage to kiss a boy. She never knew how terribly shy I was with *everyone*, including boys—especially boys. I couldn't convince her, though. She firmly believed that I was a "wild one," and I couldn't prove otherwise. I couldn't make her understand that, to me, dancing set the spirit free, that it was a celebration of life and of the soul.

In all fairness to my aunt, I must admit that we lived in a tough neighborhood. There were gangs and street fights, but I was a maturing girl, and shy, and never entered into such things. My participation in gang activities was strictly limited to our street jam sessions and weekend dances. And, in truth, I spent more time studying my homework and reading and taking care of our apartment than I did with the kids in the gang. Still, I was human, and there was that first girlhood crush—but this was long after my aunt began calling me a wild one and yelling about boys.

His name was Alex. He was a soft-spoken, handsome, curly-haired, brown-skinned boy. And, as with my first crushes, I think I adored him mostly because every girl on the block wanted him for her boyfriend. Alex was the hero of our group, the one called upon to do the fighting and to lead the gang. But actually, Alex was an only son, spoiled beyond belief, lazy, a boy who hated school and stayed out all hours of the night. Who could resist such a "man of the world"? Much of his bravado was just that, however. Beneath the surface, Alex was very sweet— spoiled and lazy, yes, but sweet.

Before I got to know him, I used to sit on the stoop, watching for him. And I'd be thrilled to see him come around the corner, his shoulders hunched forward, head bent, smoking a cigarette. I'd hardly be able to contain myself in hope that he'd smile at me as he passed. Most of the time he would. The thrill, of course, was an electric feeling that I secretly knew was one that longed for satisfaction, that had something to do with physical contact. I had no idea how to deal with my attraction for him, though.

Alex was attracted to me, too, and we became friends. We spent the first couple of days getting acquainted, telling each other about our lives. We'd stand in the doorway of the candy store after it closed, or sit on a stoop somewhere on the block and just like being together. We were oblivious to the rest of the world; there was just the two of us. Sometimes we would hold hands or hug. Most of the time we were silent, enjoying each other, or he would teach me a new phrase in Spanish. When I tried to imitate his pronunciation, he would laugh until I got it right.

Soon I became Alex's girl. We used to take long walks. I remember one in particular; we were in Central Park, near the lake. The stars were out and the moon was bright. It seemed terribly romantic to me. We sat on a bench near the water and looked silently at the moon's reflection on the lake. Alex took my hand in his, and I suddenly became aware of my blossoming womanhood. A sensual urge shot through me like a bat out of hell. And so did fear. I could sense that Alex felt this urge too. I was young and so was he. Surely, I thought, he must have known that I wasn't experienced at the kind of intimacy the occasion seemed to call for. What would I do if he started to go further than I expected him to? The thought of how I would resist him came to my mind; the thought of offering no resistance came to my mind. Desire crept through me, part of me crying for satisfaction. If he tries to kiss me, will I let him? Why doesn't he make an attempt? Maybe it's best that he doesn't. Maybe if I hold his hand tighter, he'll try.

I held his hand tighter.

Alex took both my hands, faced me, and looked into my eyes. "How old are you?" he asked.

"Thirteen."

"You haven't been around much, have you?"

"What do you mean?"

"Well, I mean, well . . . you know."

"You don't like me because of that?"

"Sure, I like you. But . . . well . . ."

"Well what?"

"You know how the kids are on the block."

"You mean if the kids on the block are free with themselves, I must be too, in order to be your girl?"

"No. But . . . well, you know, everyone kids you when they know nothing is happening."

"Do you mean that all the kids get together and tell each other what they do with each other?"

"Yeah, well, you know how men are."

The desire of my blossoming womanhood left me as suddenly as it had appeared. I no longer wanted Alex to kiss me or hold my hand or even touch me. I pouted in silence, staring out at the reflection of the moon on the lake's surface.

Alex finally broke the silence in an obvious effort to comfort me. "I really don't care," he said.

"Alex, what do you think of me?"

"What do you mean?"

"Do you think I'm pretty?"

"Yes."

"Would you rather be with someone else?"

"No, I don't think so."

What kind of answer was that? He doesn't think *so!* One doesn't have a girl and go for long walks and hug her without being positive that he would not rather be with someone else. He didn't *think* so! What kind of game was this? I did an Academy Award pout on that one.

"Who were you going with before?" I said.

"Vickie."

"Do you still like her?"

"I like her, but not the way I like you."

"Does she still like you?"

"I don't know. She says she does."

"Why did you break up?"

"Oh, we just broke up, that's all."

I don't know what I expected, really. I suppose that, in a young girl's mind, it should have been like a scene in a Hollywood movie. There we were, sitting on a park bench, the moon dancing on the lake, the stars overhead. First love. Where were the thousand violins? Why didn't Alex throw himself in the lake and scream in anguish for all the world to hear: *"If you don't kiss me, I'll drown myself forever!"*

I became coolly, calculatingly feminine—or at least, I thought so. I got up and stretched, to make him think that I didn't care. And I decided to change the subject completely. I retreated into the world of my childhood. I walked to a nearby tree, sprang to catch an overhanging limb, and swung back and forth.

Alex watched me with a smile on his face. In a showoff manner, I climbed like a squirrel from one limb to another until I reached a resting place, then looked down on him from my "heavenly" perch. I had planned to look down on him with a good measure of disdain, but his bemused expression made me laugh. He stood in silence, and I wondered what his thoughts were at the moment. Maybe he doesn't like me anymore, I thought. I will not let him know that I like him as much as I do. But if he likes me, why doesn't he say so? Why must we play cat and mouse? I decided I hated that kind of game.

"You better come down from there."

"Why?"

"It's pretty late."

"I'm going to stay up here forever. You won't ever be able to bring me to the park anymore. Won't you be sorry?"

He laughed. "I'll go back to Vickie if you stay up there."

"I *hate* you!" I screamed.

"Come on down and prove it."

In my pretense of fury I began scrambling out of the tree. At the last limb, I jumped, but lost my footing in doing so and landed flat on my dignity—which hurt my pride and one of my fingers, not to mention my derriere.

Alex laughed as he helped me to my feet. I had bent the finger backward in the fall, and it was throbbing. I looked at it, then held it up for him to see. "It's broken," I said.

He took my hand and examined the finger. "No it isn't."

"How do you know?"

"Well, it doesn't feel like it's broken."

"You don't care if it is or not!"

"I do care."

"Then why do you say it isn't?"

I wanted to hurt him. I wanted him to feel sorry for me. I wanted him to give me attention, attention, and more attention. He looked at me, laughed, and said, "Oh, you poor baby." Then he kissed me on the cheek and walked me home.

The following day I put a splint on the finger and wrapped it in about six feet of bandage to make it look worse than the simple sprain it was. But this awkward attempt at gaining attention and sympathy didn't work very well. Alex took little note of my injury, as I recall, and my aunt simply said, "Playing rough again, huh?"

The heat of my first Great Romance gradually dwindled, and Alex and I went our separate ways. It had something to do with his getting mad at me and hitting me in the stomach with his fist. Those were the highlights of my first love: the moon on the lake, falling from a tree and landing on my fanny, a sprained finger with about three pounds of bandage on it, and a punch in the stomach. This was the girl my aunt described as a "wild one"!

* * *

If I wasn't accepted and loved as a daughter or niece, at least I was getting more attention and admiration from the boys. It gave me a measure of self-confidence to know that they thought me attractive. But there were times when I wished they didn't.

One morning my teacher kept me after class in the main building to talk for a few minutes. My classmates had already left for academic classes in the Monroe Building two blocks away, and as I walked alone along a brick wall that separated a group of apartments from the street, I noticed several boys from school huddled together ahead of me. I tried to skirt quickly around them, but they closed in on me.

"Where you going?" one asked.

"I'm going to class."

One of them, big and muscular and more than a little menacing, obviously was the leader. He regarded me for a moment, then said, "You wanna be my girl?"

I tried to giggle my way out of the situation. "I'm not interested in being anybody's girl," I said.

"Well, you're gonna be mine."

"If you want to be my friend, okay," I said.

"Either you be my girl, or you'll be sorry."

There was a tone of finality to his voice that frightened me. They all looked tough, and the leader was a typical bully. They began pressing in closer. I felt a hand grasp my arm; the grip tightened. I wanted to scream for help but was afraid that I might frighten them and then they'd really get rough with me out of revenge. I was really scared.

"If you don't like me," the bully said, "you'll learn to."

I tried stalling for time. "Why aren't you boys in school?" I asked.

"Don't worry about us."

"I'm going to be late for my class."

"Well, why don't you answer our questions?"

"I told you, I don't want to be anybody's girl."

"Well, you better make up your mind, if you wanna go."

Pinned against the wall, I tried to figure a way out of the horror. Then my prayers were answered. A teacher came along and the boys scattered, leaving me to explain why I was late for class. I said nothing about the threats. I was too scared.

After that, every time I had to go between buildings in the mornings or at noon, I made sure I was surrounded by friends. I had become more popular because of my singing and acting in assembly, and this worried me because it brought even more attention from the boys in the gang. One of them would always catch up with me and ask if I was ready to be the leader's girl. My silence was always met with a pulling of my hair or nasty words, or both. Fortunately most of these boys, including the leader, apparently lived in Brooklyn, so I wasn't worried about running into them on the subway.

But one day, as I left the main building to go home alone, one of the gang caught up with me. I talked to him as calmly as I could on the way to the subway, and when we reached the station I breathed a sigh of relief and started toward the uptown subway. But the boy put a tight grip on my arm and said firmly, "You're going with me."

"But I have to get home."

"I don't care about that. Come on!"

What is he going to do with me? Every frightening thought under the sun came into my mind. How am I going to talk my way out of this? Besides, I only have one nickel; how am I going to get back home? The boy pulled me along, ignoring my fears.

On the subway to Brooklyn he seemed very sure of himself. I listened in agony as he told me how I'd better give in to his leader or it would be too bad for me. He said that his leader had never had his mind on girls before I came along. He looked at me in expectation, as though I should show some sign of gratitude at being the "chosen one."

"Why don't you wanna be his girl?" he asked.

I didn't answer.

"You're not a bad lookin' chick," he said. "You'd make somebody a good partner. I'd go for you myself if he hadn't put his bid in first."

I studied him. His clothes were shabby, a little dirty, and he handled his books as though he didn't care about them. His face was hard. He looked as though he had always had to fight for *everything*, even his existence, and was resigned to the fact; that's the way things were, and the way they would always be. You grabbed what you wanted and fought to keep it.

I tried to bring out a little kindness in him. I thought that if I could weaken him, make him give me a sincere smile instead of one of bitterness, perhaps I could persuade him to let me go. But he didn't react at all to my friendly words. When we finally came to his stop, he made me get off with him, gripping my arm tightly as we walked down the stairs of the station. I wanted to pull away and run, but I knew that he would only get even with me in school or drag me off to Brooklyn again. It seemed hopeless.

I was never more astonished in my life than I was when we got to the street and he said, "You can go now." And I stood there stunned as he walked away. I never learned why; I can only assume that it was a cruel joke that the gang had devised to teach me a lesson. But none of the other gang members were there to witness the "fun."

I stood wondering what my next move should be. I had no money, and I walked back up the stairs trying to think up a nickel. I stood near the cashier's window for what must have been fifteen minutes before I had nerve enough to tell the man that I had gotten on the wrong train and didn't have another nickel. He looked at me and, without a smile, pointed to the spoked gate, motioning me to go through. I didn't report the boy at school. If I had, he would have paid me back. And I was beginning to believe that perhaps he had let me go out of kindness.

A few weeks later, I was off guard again thinking the gang had simply forgotten me. I was hurrying to the subway to catch up with my girl friends, who usually waited for me if I was detained at school. This time the gang followed me, heckling and yelling, and I ran down the stairs to the train with them close behind.

My friends were waiting at the other end of the platform, and we saw each other at about the same time. We began running toward each other so that we could enter the same car. The noise from the approaching train was deafening, so I have no idea whether they cried out to warn me or not, but just as it came blasting full speed into the station, someone shoved me violently toward the tracks. Before I could realize what had happened, one of the girls grabbed my clothing and yanked me back from the train.

I saw the boys running down the platform, laughing, as my friends tried to calm me—and each other. This time it had been no joke; the gang was deadly serious. We talked very little on the way home, but all the kids got off at my stop and escorted me to my door and the next morning they went with me to school.

I said nothing to my teacher; the problem seemed insoluble. If I reported the gang, they might simply redouble their efforts;

if I didn't, they might still try to kill me. I couldn't spend the rest of my school days in fear, always looking over my shoulder. But the boys were ruthless. Would I have to quit school to be rid of them?

Fortunately, my friends and teacher weren't as indecisive as I was. They took the problem to the principal without my knowledge, and my friends continued to escort me everywhere. Within a few weeks, none of the boys were in school. It was then that I learned that they had been conveniently drafted into the army. My life at school was peaceful again, but life at home got worse.

10

"Tramp"

The relationship between my aunt and me, which had never been very close, had grown more strained as I got older. Now, when she came home from work or wherever, I'd go from one room to another in our small apartment trying to avoid a confrontation with her. She was always yelling at me, frequently slapping me, and occasionally beating me. There was no pleasing her.

"Don't talk to boys!"

"Clean this house!"

"What are you reading for? Why can't you find something to do?"

"You've been in my things!"

And so it went, constantly. Being in her things was an obsession with her, and purely imaginary. She was so fastidious that if an object was moved half an inch on her dressing table, I would get a tongue lashing. I was even afraid to dust for fear of touching anything. So I dusted around every object that was hers.

Apparently there were economic troubles again, too. She

began leaving me less and less money for school and never bothered to tell me why. I had to have a dime for subway fare and at least fifty cents for lunch—that is, if I were to eat. She used to leave the money on the table for me each morning. One morning I found a dime for carfare and twenty-five cents for lunch. Then I found a dime and fifteen cents. I figured that she was temporarily broke, and I figured I could manage. Then I found two dimes, and wondered whether she cared if I ate or not. She seemed to have money, and it puzzled me.

Half the time I found nothing but bread and milk when I came home from school. I began to worry, making up all kinds of excuses for her. My clothes were beginning to get shabby again, too, so I had to think of ways to make them look decent. I would wash my good blouse every night and iron it in the morning, until my aunt began complaining about the waste of electricity. Finally she hid the iron from me, so I began pressing my blouse by pulling it as hard as I could to and fro across the steam pipe in the bathroom. I had to get up a half hour earlier to do the job well.

Once I found a box in the top of the closet containing some of my aunt's old, out-of-style clothes. I selected a blouse and skirt that I thought salvageable and decided to alter them. Afraid to ask my aunt for them, I decided she wouldn't care, since they hadn't been worn for years. Besides, it would save her the cost of a new outfit for me. But when she discovered my newly altered things, she gave me a terrible whipping. She said they belonged to her and I had no business touching them. I suppose she was right.

One day I found only a dime for carfare. I went to school and sulked through lunch hour. I finally decided that things could be much worse, but when I got home there was no food in the house. My aunt was apparently eating in restaurants and bringing no food home at all. How *could* she? What possible motive could she have for not providing for me at all? I knew she wasn't *that* broke. Anger overcame me. I slammed the cupboard doors; I slammed the door of the smelly icebox that contained no ice; and I laid my head down on the kitchen table and cried.

It was dark when my aunt finally came home. Without a

word to me, she put her bundles down on the table, changed clothes, and left. I searched through the bundles for food. Nothing. Something must be wrong, I thought. Surely my aunt wouldn't do this to me deliberately. She knows I have no way of eating except through her.

I was hurt. I could take the slapping and beating and yelling, even if I thought the cause unjust. But for the life of me I couldn't understand or forgive the silence and failure to provide food.

I began visiting friends at dinner time in order to eat. Or sometimes I'd sit in their apartments for hours in hopes that someone would get hungry and bring out some kind of food. I didn't want anyone to know how starved I was, so at first I would refuse their offers of food, hoping they would insist. But often they didn't make a second offer, and I soon lost my pride, grabbing anything that was offered to me. In school I even began playing up to the boys to get them to take me to lunch.

My teacher noticed that something was wrong. Sometimes she would keep me after school and ask questions about my home life. I wanted to tell her about my troubles, but I couldn't. Occasionally she would treat me to lunch or take me for an ice cream sundae. It gave me great joy to know that someone cared, but still I began to pity myself and to build a hate inside me that was to bring me more pain as I grew older. I began thinking of myself as a tortured child; then I began to think that I really was a good-for-nothing. I withdrew more and more into myself.

Passing a store on my way from school one day, I found a solution. In the window was a sign for part-time help. It was a job of packing writing paper and envelopes into boxes, and it paid seven dollars a week. I took the job because it made me independent of my aunt—that is, until she noticed that I was no longer taking the carfare she left me and inquired about it.

She said that she had no objection to my working but that seven dollars a week was too much money for a young girl to have. She began taking my weekly pay, giving me enough money to get to school again—including a quarter for lunch. The job didn't last long. For one thing, the late hours made it difficult for me to keep up with my studies. And since my aunt was keeping most of my salary, I still had no decent clothes. That was one of the reasons I had taken the job, so I eventually quit.

Before long, I got a job as a salesgirl in a shoe store near our apartment. The store also carried a small inventory of dresses. I was making ten dollars a week, and after a couple of weeks I bought a new dress and a pair of shoes the owner let me have for half price. As soon as my aunt saw the dress, she wanted to know where I got it. I told her about the new job.

"Why didn't you bring the money home before you went off and spent it?"

"I wanted to work and buy nice things for school."

"Don't you know it costs money to take care of you?"

"I thought it would be all right to buy something I needed and to show you I wasn't throwing the money away," I said.

"If you want to work, bring the money home and help me pay the rent and buy food!"

Other than her questions about my working, she rarely paid any attention to me. I seldom saw her, and when I did she either totally ignored me—as though I weren't there—or she yelled. It was my impression that she simply didn't care whether I was there or not; she just lost all interest in me. I kept up my regular routine. My only recreation was the Friday and Saturday dances. I loved the Cuban dances so much that I started coming home at one on Friday and Saturday nights.

For a while my aunt ignored the late weekend hours, but one night after a dance she met me at the door. "Give me my key," she said.

I was puzzled. I thought maybe she was going to confiscate my key on the weekends to keep me from coming in late, and her sudden interest surprised me. I gave her my key and was shocked when she said: "Get out of this house and don't come back! You're a *tramp*, a no-good. You stay out all hours of the night. Nobody knows where you are. One day you'll turn up pregnant, and then who'll take care of you? *Me!* I don't want anything like that in *my* house! Go on back to the street where you belong!"

And she slammed the door in my face.

I stood staring numbly at the door for a moment, and then

my anger rose. Teenage defiance. I wouldn't beg to get back in. Pregnant? I had yet to kiss a boy; how could she think such a thing? I didn't smoke. I didn't drink as the other kids did. And my self-respect—being a "good girl" among some pretty wild kids—was my pride and joy. A tramp? I was so shy it was painful. My aunt had no idea what I was really like.

Where does a teenager go after being thrown out of the house at one in the morning? I headed for the subway, paid my nickel, and made the train my hotel for the night. It would be the *last* place in the world I would think of going today. Fortunately the night passed without incident. When day broke, I went to a friend's house and stayed until evening. And then, too proud to ask for shelter, I went back to the subway for the night. I still had my part-time job in the shoe store, but what little money I made was spent buying ice cream, candy, and sodas for my friends. I rode the subways at night until my money ran out. I didn't go back to school because my clothes were locked in my aunt's apartment and, anyway, I needed to think things through. My days were usually spent in Central Park, where I slept for the most part. I couldn't sleep on the subways because I was always dodging the conductor. At the end of the line, I would always get off with everyone else, then get back on when the conductor wasn't looking and ride to the other end of the line. This went on for several days and nights.

The night that I ran out of nickels I spent near my aunt's apartment, on the roof of a tenement house in which a girl friend of mine lived. No blanket, just the clothes I was wearing when my aunt kicked me out. And I learned what a bum must feel like; it was a terrible, lonely feeling. For some reason—perhaps the fear of embarrassment at being discovered—I moved around the next few nights. I slept in doorways and on other roofs. During these days I stayed in my neighborhood, hoping that my aunt would come looking for me and find me. But she didn't. In the afternoons and evenings I visited girlfriends at their homes, helping with chores and usually being invited to dinner. This also gave me an opportunity to take a bath occasionally. I must have been a sight by then.

Finally, perhaps a week or so after my aunt had slammed the door on me, I was offered shelter. I had been playing stick ball in the street with a bunch of friends. When the game was over, a boy who liked me insisted upon walking me home. I told him that I couldn't go home, and he insisted on taking me home to his mother. I stayed with them a couple of days, then went to stay with a girl friend named Carmella, who had apparently learned of my problem from the boy.

I decided to quit school and to work to earn my keep. Carmella helped me get a job as a seamstress in a factory where army clothes were sewed and mended. With the help of her parents, I got a fake certificate showing that I was sixteen. After a few days' work and a few good meals, I was my old self again.

I loved working in the factory. I began to laugh all the time, to tell jokes, and to sing at my machine. I sang Cuban songs, black spirituals, all kinds of songs. The other workers encouraged me to sing all the time. We were working the five to midnight shift, and I became the featured entertainer who helped them pass the long, dark hours.

One night as I sat at my machine, the floor manager said that I was wanted in the main office. Those around me looked up in curiosity. No one was ever called to the front office unless something drastic had happened.

"What do they want to see me for?" I asked.

"I don't know," the woman said.

I walked to the main office, thinking that they must have found out about my fake birth certificate. As I entered, a man with papers in his hand asked, "Your name Eartha Kitt?"

"Yessir."

"Your aunt claims you've run away from home. Why?"

I couldn't tell him that I had not run away, that my aunt had put me out. I said nothing.

"Don't you like your aunt?"

"Yessir."

"What does the trouble seem to be?"

I remained silent, not wanting to get my aunt in trouble.

"She's very worried about you," he said.

I wondered how she could claim to be worried about me when she was the one who ordered me to leave.

"You know, children who run away from home are put into a special home for kids if they persist in this kind of action," the man said sternly.

"Yessir."

"Do you want to talk to us about it?"

"No, sir."

"I'll give you until midnight tonight to get home," the man said.

I walked back to my machine, thinking that they must have known that I was under sixteen. I finished work, wondering how I was going to greet my aunt or how she was going to receive me. I figured that she must be sorry about what had happened and that perhaps we could be friends again. That was my hope.

After work, I walked the snow covered streets to my aunt's apartment and knocked on the door. I wished she would greet me with a warm smile and tell me she was sorry, so that I could say I was sorry too, and then we could forgive and forget and live happily ever after.

I knocked again and the door finally opened. My aunt peered into the hallway and said, "Oh, it's you." No smile. No greeting. She simply opened the door wider for me to enter and, without another word, went back to bed. I wondered why she had bothered to find me if she was going to treat me with such indifference. I finally decided that she was motivated not by love or deep concern for my welfare, but by her Christian duty. Kicking me out had been un-Christianlike; had something happened to me, she would have felt responsible. In her mind, I'm sure that she felt she could atone for her actions by simply reversing the process. She had kicked me out; now she would bring me back. But nothing else would change—that was obvious.

It was evident to me that she really didn't want me back but wished only to clear her conscience; if I left of my own volition, she could not be held accountable. When she went back to her bedroom, I went into the bathroom, took a bath and washed my hair, put on clean clothes and a warm coat, and walked out. My hair was still wet, my body damp from the bath, and it was freezing outside. I should have known better than to go out in such weather so soon after bathing, but I was acting emotionally.

Resigned now to working at the factory, I rented a room from a man and his wife in an apartment house closer to the job. But after a few days' work, I became very ill from that night of overexposure. I didn't tell the couple with whom I was staying that I was sick, fearing that it might make them uncomfortable. I locked myself in my room and came out for soup or something only when they left the apartment. Then I'd walk around the house in agony, trying to stay on my feet but having to lie down every few minutes.

My illness lasted about two weeks, and by the time I was fully recovered I had lost my job. Rather than look for a new one, I decided to finish my education. When I told my teacher that I had been ill and had not been living with my aunt, she said that I had a lot of grades to make up but that I could do it if I got busy. I had enough money saved from the factory to support myself for a while, but I knew I'd have to find work soon. This worried me, because it was difficult to hold a job and do my school work too—particularly since I had fallen so far behind.

I budgeted my money and concentrated on my studies—having decided to catch up as quickly as possible before looking for work—when one day my aunt walked into my classroom. As unpredictable as she was, I was still astonished. She told the teacher that I had run away and that she wanted me home. My teacher talked with me after class and convinced me that my place was with my aunt.

We were at peace with one another for a whole month. She came home smiling, kept food in the house, and gave me money for school. But as the days grew warmer she began reverting to her old ways, dropping broad hints that I was really too big for her to be taking care of and complaining about me being home all the time again. The nagging became more frequent and bitter.

Occasionally my aunt's boyfriend would come home from

the army on furlough or weekend passes. I was glad when he was around because the apartment was more peaceful. He liked me and would give me fifty cents now and then, or sometimes a whole dollar for running errands. He was Cuban, and he'd talk to me for hours in Spanish while my aunt sat and listened, not understanding a word. He would tell me Cuban jokes to make me laugh, and I had to repeat them to him to be sure I could remember them. Quite often he sided with me, too, which didn't make my aunt too happy.

"You're not treating that child right!" he'd say.

"It's none of your business how I treat her."

"I know. That's why I don't interfere more often than I do, but you have no gentleness with her. She wants to be loved, like any other child does."

"And what makes you think that I don't?"

That was a curious way of putting it: What makes you think that I don't? The word *love* was not in my aunt's vocabulary. She would talk all around it but I never heard her say it. I listened closely to their discussions about me, but there was never a reasonable conclusion to them. My aunt would never admit that she was not treating me as a child should be treated. It was nice of her boyfriend to take up for me. It was a waste of his time, but it still gave me hope that perhaps something he told her might sink in eventually. It didn't.

The final break was a violent one. I had gotten my aunt very angry one night—I don't even remember why. But I do remember my sitting in a corner of the bedroom on a stool while she beat me with an ironing cord. I covered my head and tightened every muscle to keep from crying. I wouldn't cry. I refused to cry. She whipped me on the back and shoulders and arms and hands and legs until either her anger subsided or she was exhausted.

When she stopped I looked her straight in the eye, defiantly. This angered her more and she brought the cord down on me again and again, saying: "You miserable little wretch! All I do is work and slave for you. You're no good. You hear me? No good!"

She stopped again and was about to walk away when I

looked up to show her that I was stronger than the ironing cord and all her muscles. Something must have really snapped in her. Her face turned red with rage, and with incredible strength she jerked the stool from under me. I went to the floor on my knees, and she raised the stool high above her head and was about to come down on me with it when her boyfriend came running into the room, grabbed the stool from her hands, and stomped out of the apartment, slamming the door behind him.

I, too, left my aunt's home that night—for good.

11

A Person of the Theater

I never returned to school. By the time of that final break with my aunt, I had determined to be—as I often told friends and fellow workers in those days—a person of the theater. I didn't have the faintest idea how to go about doing so, but I was determined.

My teacher had encouraged me; once she had even arranged for me to audition. The play was *Carmen Jones*. She gave me a pass to see the show and carfare to get there, telling me to put on my best dress and to take along the semi-classical music I had learned. I sat in the balcony all by myself and marveled at the dancing and singing and scenery. It was very exciting.

When the play was over, I was to go backstage and ask for a certain man. He wasn't easy to find in the labyrinth of sets on the huge unlighted stage. And when, after walking in darkness through countless doors and passageways that led nowhere, I suddenly found myself on the front stage where they had set up to audition, I didn't know what to do. There was a man sitting at a piano, another standing onstage holding a book, and a man and woman sitting restlessly in the front row.

I stood in the wings waiting for someone to notice me. The man who finally did was gentle and kind; he took my music, gave it to the pianist, and announced to the man in the front row that all was ready. The piano began to play. My throat closed up on me and I swallowed, choked, thought about things I would rather have been doing, and prayed. When it came time for me to sing, I opened my mouth but nothing came out. We started again. The faces looking up at me from the front row seemed inhuman; the theater was dark and cold; the seats were empty and ugly. I wondered why they didn't turn on some lights. No one could see a thing.

The song started again and this time my voice responded: "Because you come to me. . . ." But it was as thin and fragile as the whisper of a bamboo reed, and it was dissipated in the immense theater like a wisp of smoke in a windstorm. My voice got stronger toward the end of the song, and I was in very good and strong voice on the last four measures.

As I was going out the stage door one of the cast said, "Why didn't you sing the whole song the way you did the last four bars?" I couldn't give him an answer. I just smiled and was grateful that I hadn't been accepted and that I was getting out of that theater. I just wasn't ready, and certainly not determined.

On another occasion, my teacher had sent me to see Jose Ferrer in *Cyrano de Bergerac*. I was fascinated with Cyrano's nose. I adored him. I loved the way he spoke his lovely lines; I loved the way he moved around stage; I loved the love he loved, and cried the cries he cried. And when he was left broken-hearted at the end of the play, I too was broken-hearted. I left the theater in a daze. I had never been so moved. I felt more alive and suddenly saw the world in a different light. People on the street seemed more alive to me, and I felt more akin to them. Even the buildings and streets and skies seemed suddenly more wonderful to me. I was happy to be alive in a world in which such beautiful thoughts and sentiments could be transmitted from one human being to another.

If only I could do what Jose Ferrer had done. If only I could give the feeling of happiness to people—or to any one person, for that matter—that he had given to me. . . . If only I knew how. If only I had the opportunity. The wonderment of the idea began to haunt me. I could do it, I kept telling myself. I could do that.

This view of what the world *could* be helped me to crystalize ideas that had been passing through my mind. The crystals didn't fall into an orderly pattern, rather they were just lumped together awkwardly in my head. I hated the idea of going back to school, of having knowledge stuffed into me whether I liked it or not. I hated the idea of having to go back to the factory. I wanted to change the world to my way of thinking. I wanted a law passed forbidding people to work more than four hours a day. I thought that people should be free of restrictions and that they should never be made to do things that they did not like.

It seemed to me terribly important that people should eat because they were hungry, not because it was breakfast or dinner time. It seemed to me that people should love because they loved and hate because they hated, not because someone told them when or how or where. As for me, I wanted to think of myself as a human being, not as a person belonging to any one nationality or people. I didn't want to be conscious of the fact that my skin was black or brown or white or gray. I felt that there was one race: the human race. I wanted a place in life to call my own. When I wanted to share it, I would share it. If I wanted it alone, I would be alone.

What I did not know was that I was becoming suspicious of everyone who tried to enter my world. I was beginning to analyze people. But I forgot to analyze myself. I felt that people should accept me as I was or not at all. The only thing that mattered to me was how people affected me, not how I affected them. Years later I learned that life is both give and take, not just take. I also learned that I should give freely, without expectations.

More than anything in the world, I wanted to know how to think, to make decisions independently. I wanted a clear, bright mind, one that knew where it was going and why. I was not looking for anything definite, but I wanted to see beyond yesterday, to have a feeling for tomorrow. I was not looking for the sun, just a spark to give me hope. And I knew that I couldn't get that spark from my aunt or from anyone else I knew, so I set out to find it away from home. I became an adventurer. That is to say, I no longer felt afraid of anything. I no longer felt afraid of being hurt by anything (Eartha Kitt) except people (Eartha Mae). I became immune to hunger and to physical discomfort.

So when I left my aunt's, I went back to the Cuban family in the Bronx and found a job in Brooklyn. My job was hunting for empty bobbins on a machine that seemed a mile long. The machines made Swiss-like embroidery and emblems for soldiers' uniforms. If a bobbin was empty, I had to tell the foreman to have it threaded again. It was to be a temporary job, but it lasted through the spring. I made quite a bit of money by working overtime, usually working about ten hours a day.

When summer came I joined the Farmerettes, a group of about a thousand girls who went to camp in upstate Connecticut to help out on the farms. The obligation was to earn not less than ten dollars a week to pay for room and board. I had joined to get away from New York and to think things out. It was light farm work, picking onions and cherries and currants and hoeing the land. I enjoyed that very much—and still do, for even today I spend as much time as I possibly can working in my own large organic garden. Because I was a good worker, I was soon in demand. I won a contest picking currants at five cents a quart, and my earnings ran up to fifty or sixty dollars a week. I spent it all on goodies or clothes or taking Saturday bus trips to New York—which I had joined the Farmerettes to get away from!

In September I returned to live with the Cuban family. One day a girl friend and I decided to take in a movie and stage show downtown. But it was standing room only, and we decided to stay just for the stage show, which was about to begin. The featured star was Carmen Miranda, and I was glad I had waited. I had wondered what there was about her that all those people around us would stand up so long to see. I soon found out. She twitched around the stage and went sheeboom, sheeboom. And before I knew it I was twitching right along with her. I had forgotten how wonderful it was to see live entertainment. All I could think of as we left the theater was her twitching and sheeboom, sheeboom.

Outside the theater on Broadway, we were wondering what to do (should we spend a dime for candy?) when we noticed a girl pacing up and down as though she were lost. She reminded me of myself, when I had first come up North. Finally she noticed us and asked, "Can you tell me where Max Factor's makeup shop is?"

"Do you have an address?" I said.

"Yes, but I still can't find the place."

Curious about such a young girl looking for the makeup shop, we went with her to find it. Inside, she began buying all kinds of theatrical makeup. I asked her what she could possibly do with it all. She said that she was a Katherine Dunham dancer and that the makeup was for Miss Dunham.

"I'd love to meet Miss Dunham," I said.

"Well, why don't you come down to the school with me now, and I'll introduce you. As a matter of fact, she's looking for dancers. Can you dance?"

"Oh, yes, I can dance very well," I said. After all, hadn't I just gotten through twitching with Carmen Miranda?

"She's having auditions now," the girl said. "Why don't you come along?"

Miss Katherine Dunham, according to an article I had read about her a few days earlier, was a noted choreographer, anthropologist, and expert on primitive dance, and I wasn't about to pass up a chance to meet her.

The school was filled with dancers—a group doing a routine and individual dancers prancing up and down the studio. We watched a while, and finally my girl friend said, "Go on."

"No, she won't like me."

"How do you know?"

"Well . . . you know I can't dance like that!"

"These kids don't look so hot, either," she said. "Besides, you're always dancing around the house, doing acrobatic things and whatnot. Just do the same things you do at the house."

"Noooo," I said.

"I dare you!"

I was never one to refuse a dare, but I was scared. "I don't have any dancing clothes," I said. Just then a tall woman came up and asked if we were going to audition.

"I'm not, but she is," my friend said, pointing to me.

"The dressing room is upstairs," the woman said, indicating a flight of stairs.

"Go on," my friend said. "Maybe someone will give you something to wear. If not, audition in what you have on."

Maybe I wanted to be coaxed, I don't know. But I do know that my friend had a lot more confidence in me than I had in myself. I climbed the stairs and found an older girl there. When I explained my problem, she found a garment for me to wear. I changed clothes and began to practice what I thought I might do on the dance floor. "I really don't know how to do anything," I kept saying to her, while doing a split and then a head stand, kicking my feet in the air and contorting my body. "What should I do?"

"Just go down and follow the leader," the girl said.

Finally, I was called to join the others. I looked them over apprehensively; all of them were aspiring young dancers. I realized that this was an important test. We would either prove our potential within the next few minutes or be told to go back where we came from. What was I doing here? I had just come downtown to see a movie, and suddenly I was to be judged to see if I should continue my career in dancing! Continue? It was crazy. All I knew about dancing was what I had learned in the Cuban dance halls, but it was too late to back out.

I stood with the rest of the group and watched the leader. Whatever he did, we were to imitate. I watched him hypnotically, with the most intense concentration I could focus. I watched every body and head movement, every arm, hand, and foot movement until I thought I had it.

The whole group tried out at once. I went down on the floor, imitating what I had seen as though my mind were programmed like a computer. I was terribly disappointed whenever any part of my body didn't respond exactly as I expected it to. I worked wildly, freely, managing unintentionally to get into everyone's way; I was nearly oblivious of everything around me. When my movements didn't satisfy me, I wanted to quit but I wouldn't. I jerked my pelvis, worked my feet furiously, wiggled, twitched, bounced, writhed, twisted, and nearly turned myself inside out until I was exhausted. Then it was over. I slumped into a chair against the wall beside my friend, too breathless to talk.

Moments later the tall woman came over to me. I didn't know what to expect, and I didn't have energy enough to care. "Can you be here Monday morning at ten?" she asked.

"Yes, I guess so," I answered in surprise. "Why?"

"You've won a scholarship," she said.

12

Early Dunham Days

Those of us who had scholarships at the Katherine Dunham school received ten dollars a week. We couldn't take outside jobs because our hours were too long and the training too rigorous. It was a constant battle to make ends meet—both financially and physically.

I thought I was in good shape, until our training started. Our day began at 10:00 A.M. with ballet class, which I didn't like because I had no conception of what ballet was. We'd start each day at the warm-up bar before dancing. This wasn't very strenuous for me for I had always been active and had kept my body limber. But I soon discovered that ballet required great strength, constant practice, and incredible self-discipline. I found that my thighs were particularly weak, so I worked hard the first month. Then I began getting lazy, as I'm naturally lazy unless I really have to prove myself. I soon learned, though, that being good is not enough; one has to be better than good.

After an hour and a half of ballet, we got to do what I liked best—the Dunham technique, a more free-form, interpretive dancing that is not limited by classical restrictions. I liked it not because it was easy—it wasn't—but because it represented the more free-souled spirited kind of dancing in which I expressed myself naturally and found the most satisfaction.

We would train from morning until dark until we wanted only sleep. We lived to dance. But we practiced and practiced and practiced until it began to seem that practice was the end itself and pointless. When we became exhausted physically, mentally, spiritually, and emotionally, we'd ask ourselves why we were foolish enough to subject ourselves to such torture. We were all well aware that being in the Katherine Dunham school didn't ensure appearance in her productions—far from it. She chose only the best and most promising. The others—the majority—would be left behind with Miss Dunham's assistants, practicing, practicing, practicing, and trying somehow to get along on ten dollars a week.

I ran into financial trouble quickly. I had saved a little money before I entered the school, but I began lending it out to the other kids in the class even though I knew they couldn't pay it back—and they didn't. The borrowing never ceased. Even after I ran out of savings and was trying to get along on ten dollars just as they were, I continued to lend them money— sometimes half of my weekly income from the scholarship. I don't know why I was so foolishly generous; I had always been that way. Maybe it was because I wanted to feel needed.

I thought little about my financial situation until the people from whom I rented a room began demanding payment. I tried to figure a way to set aside at least five dollars a week for the rent and have enough left over for food and carfare. That wasn't possible, of course, especially since I was lending my rent money to my friends so they could eat. I finally had to give up my room.

For a while some of us sneaked back into the school at night to sleep because we had no place to stay. Miss Dunham didn't know this, of course. We'd spread the Haitian straw mats on the studio floor and cover ourselves with whatever clothing we had. Then we'd be up and out of the place before the school opened in the morning. But we soon gave up that impractical and risky practice.

Soon several of us got the idea that if we pooled our money we could rent a halfway decent place to live—which is what we did for most of the time we remained in New York. The idea worked, but not well. Sometimes one of the girls would leave the school and, unable to find a replacement for her, we'd have to find something cheaper. Usually those places were in pretty rough neighborhoods, and we'd be forced to move when the neighborhood toughs learned that three or four girls were living alone and began to make advances. I had more than one close call.

I remember a two-room apartment in particular; it was typical of the one- or two-room apartments we shared. Madeline, Othella, and I found the "apartment" (dungeon would be more appropriate) on Forty-fifth Street near the school; the price was right—very cheap—and with a little cleaning, we thought, it would be suitable for condemning. But on the positive side, it had two beds—if we took turns, every three nights each of us could have the luxury of a whole bed to herself! And besides, it had a stove to cook the food we couldn't afford to buy. All it needed was a little elbow grease; we could imagine it sparkling clean.

We pooled our money and bought soap. And we scrubbed. Then we pooled our money and bought more soap, and scrubbed some more. Then we pooled some of our food money for more soap. Finally, after scrubbing for days, we found the surfaces of walls and a ceiling in each room—we even unearthed a couple of windows! All of this was done in the wee hours of each night after eight to ten solid hours of exhausting dancing. But it was worth it. The apartment looked like hell, but it smelled clean.

The floors were something else; they were layered with at least a half-century of dirt. We scrubbed them for days with soap and tears of frustration. And no matter how much we scrubbed, the dirt remained. Nothing short of dynamite or a blow torch could have removed what seemed to us a solid inch of impenetrable filth. Needless to say, we never invited anyone to our rooms; we were too ashamed of them.

Food. For a couple of years—between Dunham productions—we lived on hot dogs and Cokes. We jumped at every party invitation; our sole aim was food. Sometimes, to get a meal, we accepted dates with boys we didn't care for. In my naivete, I could never understand why the boys I got stuck with *always* offered me drinks quicker than food. We'd pool our dimes for a coffee breakfast. Sometimes we'd pass up the coffee breakfast to save up for the one luxury we occasionally allowed ourselves—a movie. But then, we *had* to keep up with show business; we knew it was out there somewhere!

Katherine Dunham was an enigma to us. She spent much of her time traveling, arranging for her various stage productions or trying to find backers for them. She was tall and erect, carrying herself with a noble grace that commanded attention in any setting. Whenever she came into the studio I would stop whatever I was doing and look at her in hope that she would say "Hello, Kitty"—everyone called me Kitty. Sometimes she did and sometimes she didn't, but we all lived in hope that she would stop and joke with us; we'd be in our glory to be able to laugh at something she did or said.

But there was fear of her, too. She held a power over our lives that we didn't understand and that we resented. Sometimes we would talk about her unmercifully—anything to downgrade her in our eyes. Yet at the same time we idolized her for the courage and strength to accomplish what she had, for her leadership and protection. We were afraid to leave the company and afraid to stay. Occasionally she would lecture us on not getting discouraged, telling us that the outside world was cruel and hard and that we didn't know how well off we were in getting such training and experience.

We would find fault with this kind of talk: She was holding us back. Once we even decided to leave the company; we would prove ourselves in no time. Why was she so unfair at times? Why didn't she give us a better chance at showing off our talents? It wasn't until years later that I learned for myself how right Miss Dunham was about the outside world being difficult, about the obstacle-strewn road to success, and about what the word *success* really meant.

Miss Dunham did indeed create a better world for many of us, making the path easier for those of us who had the determination to follow. I wanted to get closer to her, to talk to her and ask questions, but I was afraid. She wasn't the kind of person one walks up to and buttonholes. I could never really reach her, but I got sensitivity from her, a spiritual, inspirational feeling, like a thought wave being received—however imperfectly. Our verbal communication was always rough; it was rare that I ever got a warm word from her. Every day she would come down hard on someone. When my turn came she would watch me dancing and just laugh coyly. I could never tell whether I was doing something wrong or whether my whole body was all wrong for dancing, my rear end too big, or what. Then one day, after I had been with the company for a whole year, she let me have it. "You'll never be a good dancer," she said. "You have too much excess baggage." She was staring at my breasts as she said it. The company snickered and I began to cry.

"Why did you take me for a dancer then?" I retorted. "You knew what I looked like before I joined the company." I don't remember her reply. I left the room to pout while the class continued.

The Dunham company was very active. About a month after I had joined the school, Miss Dunham returned from a tour of California to cast for a new show, *Blue Holiday*, which she was preparing for Broadway. We knew that not all of us could be in it. When the day arrived, she came into the studio with her secretary and other members of her entourage and sat quietly while the audition went on.

I wanted more than anything to be in the show, but I tried not to let my hopes build up. Disappointments always hurt, and I didn't want to be hurt. After all, I had been in the company only a few weeks and had no right to expect that I would be chosen. But I was. So was Roxie Foster, my best friend in the Dunham company. At that time I had just given up my room, unable to pay the rent; Roxie and her mother invited me to stay with them until I could make other arrangements. They had an apartment on Convent Avenue. I was very comfortable there and stayed on probably longer than I should have, but we pooled our money and got along very well.

Blue Holiday featured many well-known entertainers

including Ethel Waters, Willie Bryant—and Josh White. Josh is a man I shall never forget. I remember vividly the first day I saw him. He walked into the rehearsal studio with his guitar, went straight to the piano, stuck a cigarette in the side of his mouth, and began playing.

The sound of his guitar stirred me sensually. It was irresistible and enchanting and seductive. It tantalized my senses and wined my bitter blood. I watched his hands as they caressed the guitar, telling of love and hatred, of faithless women. His mouth moved as though he was making love to the words he spoke; his eyes had a come hither look that said, "There's no woman I cannot have and any woman can have me."

"Who's that?" I asked Roxie.

"Don't you know who that is? That's *Josh White!*"

I said nothing, still not knowing who Josh White was. I moved nearer so that I could sense him better and to make him sense me. When our eyes finally met, our senses touched, and he finished his song to me.

After rehearsals we went our separate ways, but not for long. A few days later he gave Roxie and me a lift to our apartment. Soon after that he asked me if I'd like to have dinner at the place where he was working, and I gladly accepted; it was my first opportunity to see a nightclub. When we arrived I trailed along behind him, not knowing how to act. Josh was greeted by everyone—the owners, the musicians, the waiters, the patrons. Everyone seemed to like him, and I was proud to be with him.

Josh sat me at a table with some of his friends and told the waiter to pay special attention to me. I felt very important; I had never been treated so royally. Since I didn't drink, I asked the waiter for something to eat: a steak. I had heard talk about steaks but I think this was the first one I had ever eaten.

Finally the house lights dimmed and drums began to roll. I expected to see Josh, but instead Imogene Coca stepped into the spotlight, a microphone before her. As soon as she appeared, people began smiling and chuckling; I thought they were terribly rude. It wasn't until she went into her act that I learned that she was a comedienne and that the audience had begun laughing in expectation. She was the funniest woman I had ever seen and the funniest I have seen to date, besides Bea Lillie and Carol Burnett. In truth, I don't remember Josh's act that night, but Imogene Coca stayed in my mind.

Blue Holiday closed after a five-day run in New York and we were almost back where we started. Rehearsal pay had been a little more than our customary scholarship money, so we had eaten better for a while. My only regret was that I was so busy making costume changes that I never got to see much of the show. But I had my first New York credit, and I was proud of that.

13

Sweet Misery

Miss Dunham returned to New York a day or two before *Blue Holiday* closed to select members for her new production, *Carib Song*, and again I was chosen. I knew little about the new show except that Miss Dunham herself was going to act and dance in it. So it was back to rehearsals.

During the run of *Blue Holiday*, the Dunham school had moved from Fifty-ninth Street to Forty-third Street, which was nearer to that terrible-looking, clean-smelling apartment on Forty-fifth I shared with Madeline and Othella. That saved carfare and, more important, time, for it was back to the old 11:00 A.M. to 11:00 P.M. routine: classes during the day and rehearsals at night. We rehearsed for about six months, then opened in New Haven to fair reviews before going to Broadway. Miss Dunham sang, danced, and acted; she was marvelous opposite her leading man, Avon Long. *Carib Song* also featured the wonderful singing of Harriet Jackson, but the show closed after about an eight-week run.

What followed was a year or so of the twelve-hours-a-day, ten-dollars-a-week routine I was growing to loathe. I was young and impatient and couldn't see where my training was leading me. In two years of nearly constant rehearsal, I had been in two shows with a combined running time of about two months. Would that be the pattern of my professional life? Twenty-two months of rehearsal and two months on stage? It was demoralizing. Still we were ambitious and determined. By this time, I was about seventeen and rehearsing for another Dunham review, *Bal Negré*, which turned out to be not only spectacular but also very successful.

Bal Negré opened in Philadelphia, moved to Broadway, then went on the road for six months. I don't remember much of Philadelphia or Broadway or cross-country. I was too preoccupied. I had fallen deeply in love, and for the first time in my life my love wasn't unrequited.

It happened while we were still playing Philadelphia. I was standing in the wings one night, waiting to go on, when I noticed a husky, brown-haired man crossing the stage, checking lights. I couldn't recall having seen him before, and I was immediately attracted to him. He came off on my side of the stage. Miss Dunham's secretary was standing beside me and I whispered, "Who's that?" But before she could answer, I heard my cue and was on stage. By the time I had finished my number I had forgotten about the man—that is, until I saw him again a few days before we left for New York.

One of the musicians asked one of the dancers for a date and told her to bring me along. When we arrived at our meeting place, the man I had seen on stage was with the musician. He was introduced to me as Charlie. It was a pleasant surprise, and although it all began very casually we liked one another immensely. We began having sandwiches and coffee together. Then lunch. Then dinner. From sandwiches and coffee in Philadelphia, we went to champagne and caviar in New York. I have since learned that I don't fall in love easily, but when I do it takes the kick of a mule to put me straight again.

I knew nothing about him, really, just that he was an expert electrician. And I marvelled that he was so good in his field at age twenty. From New York the show traveled cross-country. We were inseparable. And by the time the show returned to New York—six months later—we were deep in caviar.

There was great excitement within the company upon our return. The show had been booked for Mexico, and later in the year we were to go to Hollywood to appear in a movie. The Mexican engagement was particularly attractive to me because it meant that Charlie would be traveling with the troupe; I'd worry about Hollywood when the time came—I didn't want even to think of being separated from him.

After eight weeks of rehearsal we boarded a train for Mexico. The trip took four days, as I recall; Charlie woke me each morning and gave me little signals all day long that I was on his mind. We were so attuned to one another that it was astonishing. A touch, a glance, a moment of silence told all we felt. I was delirious with this wonderful thing that had happened to me, but I couldn't put my feelings into words. I tried once to tell him how I felt about him. He put his fingers to my mouth to quiet me, saying, "I know." I loved him more for that.

The company may have had ideas about our feelings for one another, but they didn't really know. We were discreet. It was our business and no one else's, our world, and we didn't want intruders; our secret, which belonged only to the two of us. In the evenings we would sit at the rear of the train watching the desert unfold at our feet until the sky turned to pastel shades and then cloaked itself with night. Each moment grew into a more beautiful one. I smiled at everything and angered at nothing—except night. Sleep separated us, so I loathed the night; it was made bearable only by the thought that each night foreshadowed a new day with Charlie.

It was summer in Mexico, so once the show had settled into an established routine we did a lot of sightseeing. And we became so accustomed to being with each other that if I went somewhere without him he became lonely, and if he was away from me any length of time I grew apprehensive. I remember one night when we went to a party with the rest of the company. As usual everyone in the show performed individually to entertain the others. When my turn came I didn't want to leave Charlie's side, but I couldn't refuse. There were a number of Mexicans present, and the crowd began yelling, "Sing 'Babalu,'" which was fortunate because it was one of the few numbers I could sing in Spanish at the time. When I finished the song the Mexicans surrounded me, congratulating me on my interpretation of the Cuban song, patting me on the back, and asking if I were Cuban. I tried to catch the eye of my lover, but it was fifteen minutes or so before I could free myself. Charlie was no longer in the room.

I looked for him in the bar but found only Dunham dancers. He was not in the garden either. Something was wrong; I could sense it. Finally I spotted a figure coming up the path towards me. Hoping it was Charlie, I sat down and waited. I heard him say, "So you finally got away!"

"Where have you been?" I asked.

"Walking."

"Why?"

"Lonely."

"Lonely?"

"Yes."

"Well, I'm here."

"No, you weren't."

"I've been here all the time."

"Not with all those people around you."

"Well, I won't do it anymore."

He sat on the bench beside me. "I don't mean that," he said. "I mean I hate people to touch you. I don't want any hands on you." He took my hands, holding them tightly, and added, "I love you so much it scares me."

He took me in his arms and we sat in silence, in the warmth of the darkness, in the pleasantly flower-scented garden, and I wondered if heaven could be so lovely.

And we were kids. Some nights Charlie and I would take a taxi into the nearby woods, discharge it, and then run through the woods and grass, throwing our laughter to the wind as though it could sweep up our joy and spread it like the seeds of wild flowers. We'd lie in the sand and count the stars: He loves me, he loves me not, he loves me.... Finally we'd lie in silence until dawn, then shake the sand and dew from our clothing and return to the hotel for breakfast before other members of the company awakened.

We had breakfast every morning on the roof of our hotel. Lunch we would have at "our" restaurant, away from people we knew, and we usually had dinner with the gang. Often we were content just to stroll the city streets in silence—just being together. I would have been content to live my life out in that fashion—changing nothing—but it couldn't be. All good things come to a close.

Two months went by, and our engagement in Mexico was ending. A company meeting was called to find out what we wanted to do. We had a choice of staying in Mexico and rehearsing until our picture commitment in Hollywood, or returning to the States to wait. For those in the company who wanted to stay, Miss Dunham had arranged for the girls to have a house and for the boys to stay at their hotels, with expenses paid. With few exceptions the company decided to stay in Mexico, where the living was far cheaper than in New York.

It would be fun to stay in Mexico, I thought, as I looked at Charlie's reaction to the news. But Charlie's job would be finished when the review closed. He wasn't a member of the Dunham company, and he'd have to stay at his own expense. I feared he wouldn't want to stay, doing nothing. I waited patiently for the meeting to end so that I could make my decision with him. His expression wasn't a happy one; I could sense that he was thinking desperately. As the others discussed the alternatives, I wondered if I could persuade him to get a job in Mexico. I began inventing possibilities for our remaining there together, knowing none of them would work.

The meeting finally broke, and we had a couple of days to make our decisions. I knew by Charlie's expression that he wouldn't stay. But maybe.... We all walked home from the theater together, each of us thinking secret thoughts, and at the hotel I left my door open and sat down on the bed, thinking that if Charlie didn't stay I'd return to New York with him. I looked up, startled to see him leaning against my doorjamb, hands thrust into his pockets, gazing intently at me. "Are you going to stay?" he asked finally.

"Are you?"

"For *three months?* Doing nothing?"

"That isn't very long," I said hopefully.

He came into my room and paced the floor. "I have to do *something!* I can't just sit around and waste three months just like that." Very upset, he stopped and looked me straight in the eyes. "Are you going to stay?" he repeated. There was fear in his words.

"I don't know. I'm waiting for you to decide for me, I suppose. Of course I don't want to stay unless you do. But if I go to New York, I'll have to work, too. I have a little money. If I stay here with the company I won't need it, and we can get along on what I've saved. There's no point in both of us starving to death in New York."

"Then you mean you want to stay?"

"I don't care what we do, stay or not. Whatever you say, Charlie . . . but I want us both to stay."

"I can't."

"Why not?"

"I just can't. I must work. Three months. . ."

"Why are you so concerned about working? Three months isn't long. We could have a vacation before going to Hollywood. It won't cost us much to live. We can have lots of fun without lots of money."

He sat down beside me on the bed, and I held his head to my breasts. "We don't need lots of money," I said again, trying to convince him that as long as we were together we were one, and that it didn't matter whose money we were using; it was *ours* and it would keep us together.

Suddenly his arms tightened around my waist and his body quivered. He was crying. I held on to him, ashamed to look at his face. I didn't want to see him cry. I didn't know how to react; he had never done this before. What does a woman do when a man cries? I felt helpless and stupid. I wanted to pull away from him, to pretend it wasn't happening. But I could only hold him tighter, touched by the love strong enough to bring tears. My heart swelled with the joy and sadness of love.

"I don't ever want to lose you, Kitten," he whispered. I kissed his hair. He held tight. Suddenly I began to laugh and so did he. What crazy emotions love brings. Our eyes met. And I cried. When love beckons, follow it. I followed. We went to sleep with our problem undecided, but the following morning at breakfast we talked about it again.

"Are you going to meet the company in Hollywood, Charlie, if you return to New York?"

"I'd like to, but I can't get work at the studios. I've already asked."

"We'll know people after we get there. I'll introduce you to everyone I meet, and you can take it from there."

"Yeah, I could. I've always wanted to live in California." He thought about it for a while, then said, "But how will I get there? I can't ask my dad for the fare. He's done too much for me now. I don't have any money at all."

"If I stay here for three months, then go to Hollywood and do the picture, I could send you the fare," I said.

"No, that isn't right. You can't do that."

"Why can't I?"

"Because it isn't. . . ." He paused, looked into my eyes, and finished with, "I love you."

"I love you too."

Charlie left for New York a few days after the show closed. We didn't say a word to each other in the cab to the airport. I looked out one window while he looked out the other, too sensitive to touch, too lost in our misery to search for comforting words. At the airport he paced nervously waiting for the plane, occasionally glancing at me. I watched him pace, remembering all the wonderful times we had had and wondering if, when I saw him again, we could resume exactly where we left off. I worried about whether his love would diminish for me or whether someone else would claim him. I longed for a last minute reprieve, longed for him to turn quickly to me and say, "I can't leave you." But I knew that was impossible.

I was startled by the call to board the plane. For a final moment we stood face to face, reaffirming our love for one another with our eyes as passengers pushed their way past us. He kissed me lightly on the cheek, without a word—no goodbyes. Then he turned and quickened his pace almost to a run, passing through the ticket gate without looking back, until he was lost in the crowd. I felt empty, hollow inside, as I watched his plane become a tiny dot in the sky and then disappear.

Our little hotel was not the same. It was the first time I had walked through the doors alone. The lobby was cold; the furniture was shabby; the walls were ugly; and the curious little elevator now seemed ancient and exasperating. My room, which I had adored, I now hated. The old telephone that had been so quaint was now useless and impractical. I loathed everything I touched.

I took a shower, trying to wash away my misery—I thought. But I didn't want to be rid of the misery, really; it was all I had at that moment to make me realize that I was young and alive and loved. It was a sweet misery.

14

Triangle

We girls moved into the little house Miss Dunham had rented for us in Villa Obregón, about a half-hour from Mexico City. It was a nice place, with three bedrooms, a living room, kitchen, and bath. Othella and Dolores took the bedroom that opened onto the brick-walled yard; Jackie and I shared one with a window facing the dirt road; and Lucille and Richie had the upstairs room.

We especially liked the kitchen and the fact that we could cook our own meals. Lucille had become the self-appointed head of the household. She did the cooking and made sure we each did our chores, which included cleaning house and taking turns doing the day's shopping. We had a budget of twenty-five dollars a week for food. This was a lot of money by Mexican standards, but we couldn't afford to be extravagant—we were growing girls, expending incredible amounts of energy at all-day rehearsals six days a week. We had big appetites.

But we soon grew tired of our everyday fare—the vegetables and tough beef that were plentiful and cheap. We longed for something different. One Sunday afternoon I was in the yard with a little black pointer dog someone had given me, which we had named Babalu. We were just sitting together in the sun when out of the drainpipe—which ran beneath the brick wall—came a young pullet. Babalu sat up straight, looking in wonder at the chicken. My first thought was to shoo it out of the yard, but hunger brought back the remembrance of fried chicken. And as Flip Wilson would say, the devil made me do it.

"Get him, Babalu," I said. The dog leaped joyously at the opportunity. He caught the chicken without hurting it, and just as I took it from him another chicken peeked from the drainpipe. He was within easy reach, and I grabbed him.

The kids screamed with excitement when I walked into the house with our dinner. "Kitty, where did you get those? Did someone give them to you?"

"No," I said.

"Oh, you little devil," they yelled, laughing. Then Lucille said, "Who's going to take the job of killing them?"

The laughter died. Everyone was silent as the horrible thought came to our minds that chickens didn't just take their feathers off and jump into the frying pan. I looked from girl to girl, but none of them could meet my gaze. Then, with great bravado, I said, "I will. I know how!"

I went out the back door carrying one of the chickens, while Dolores followed with the other. I'd never killed a chicken, but I'd seen it done in the South: Just grab the old head, give the chicken a twirl to break its neck, and *snap*, that's all there was to it. Just like that. I grabbed the chicken's head and twirled it. Nothing happened. I began feeling sorry for the chicken. How could I be so cruel as to even think of killing the helpless creature?

"Maybe we should only have one and let the other go," I said to Dolores. Her head was turned away so that she wouldn't have to witness the cold-blooded murder. I felt like hitting her in the head with the chicken! If I had to do the dirty work, the least she could do was suffer with me, I thought.

"One won't be enough, silly," Dolores said, still looking away. "They're too small. Go on, you caught them. Finish the job."

I twirled the chicken again. This time I only half broke its neck. I got sick. Tears came to my eyes. "I can't!" I said. Then, to console myself, I started talking to the chicken as though the whole disgusting thing had been its fault and not mine. "You walked right into my lap!" I said. "If it hadn't been meant to be this way, you wouldn't have found your way through that drainpipe. Who ever heard of a stupid chicken walking through a drainpipe? One of you is as stupid as the other. I have no choice but to do my duty as a hungry human being. Off with your heads!"

I twisted and pulled and twirled the chicken's neck, getting sicker by the minute and hoping that each twist would be the last. But the devil himself was in that doggone chicken, keeping it alive to torture me. Finally the skin of its neck broke, and I *really* got sick. I wanted to forget the whole thing. I wanted to put the chicken's neck back in place—all nice and neat—and shove it back through the drainpipe and forget that it ever happened at all. But I had to go through with it.

The neck was broken, and the chicken was flopping all over the place as I got a knife from the kitchen to sever the head so that it would bleed freely. I remembered that this had to be done so that the blood didn't spoil the meat or something. The knife was dull, though, and I ended up sawing the head off and thinking of the men in history whose job it was to bring the ax down on the heads of queens—either they must have been without souls, or they must have died a thousand deaths along with their victims.

Dolores handed me the second chicken. My body shivered uncontrollably as I laid its head on a rock. No neck wringing this time; I was going to end it quickly and mercifully with one swift chop of the knife. Whack! Nothing happened. That knife was really dull. And in my horror and sickness I cried, "I can't go through with this one!"

Dolores finished the job as I went into the kitchen to regain my composure and to put water on to boil; somebody else could pull the feathers. By dinner time, I was myself again as I bit into the tender meat of a young stray chicken.

On Saturday nights we gave parties at the house. All of our

friends would drive out from the city, loaded down with food and drink. Faithful to my soulmate, I would sometimes sit in front of the fireplace moping and panting from loneliness and generally feeling sorry for myself. But mostly I'd remain in my room, where I could hear the music from the phonograph in the living room. The rhythmic tunes stirred my loneliness. The slow tunes melted me to tears. A few times I joined the fun and would have a swallow or two of tequila, but this only depressed me more so I stopped that.

Charlie and I wrote to each other every day. I lived for his letters. Each night I'd go to bed thinking of what the next day's letter might say. One day I was delirous with joy when I read that he was on his way back.

The evening of his arrival, I spent hours grooming myself and patching up an old dress as well as I could. Then I borrowed cab fare and went to the airport to meet him. He didn't arrive on the flight he was supposed to have taken. I walked the airport grounds for an hour before deciding to go back home. I thought maybe he wasn't coming after all. I was furious by the time I reached the house, wondering why he would disappoint me so.

The usual Saturday night party had begun, but because I was too hurt to make excuses for him, or to consider the possibility that he might have taken a later flight, I went directly to my room and sulked. An hour or so later I heard someone yell, "Charlie!" I was too amazed to move. Then someone yelled from the living room, "Kitty, Charlie is here!" I sat resolutely on my bed, thinking: If he wants me, let him come and get me.

The door opened, and he stood there for a moment or two looking at me before plunging in to take me in his arms. "Oh, Kitten, how I've missed you!" In his powerful arms I felt like a doll being squeezed. When he finally let me go, the air rushed back into my lungs and precious joy replaced the anger I had felt.

Charlie got a room in town and we met every day after my rehearsals. We used to walk for hours in Obregón Park, mostly in silence, until the hour for sleep arrived. Then he'd return to the city. There was a monument to General Obregón in the park. The monument contained the General's hand—preserved for posterity. The general had been one of the great leaders of the Mexican Revolution. It was said that he had a powerful left hand that could shoot a peanut off the head of an elephant from a distance of five miles. His left hand was the envy of his enemies and the pride of his people. It was the strength of Mexico. No one dared challenge Obregón's left hand.

Although the idea was horrifying to me, out of curiosity I decided to go see Obregón's left hand, this hand of strength and beauty. It was preserved in a large jar of alcohol or formaldehyde. And it was horrifying to see. But even more horrifying was my discovery that someone had made a mistake and preserved the right hand instead of the left! I stayed inside the tomb for a long time comparing hands—left against right, right against left—until I was convinced that I had made no mistake. The mistake was in the jar. I didn't tell any of the villagers of my discovery. I didn't want to start another revolution. One doesn't tamper with the artifacts of history— even if right is wrong.

Charlie had been promised a job with a utility company, but when he arrived the position wasn't open. I didn't care whether he worked or not so long as we were together. But he worried and hunted work for a week, finding nothing. One evening he came out to the village two hours earlier than usual. I saw him walking down the road and ran to greet him, jumping into his arms and nearly knocking him down, expecting him to be overjoyed at my reception. But his arms were weak when he caught me—no enthusiasm, no joy. I pretended not to notice, thinking he was depressed because he couldn't find work. "Hi, Charlie! You're early."

"I know."

"What's up? Get lonesome for me?"

"Yeah," he replied without conviction. He was tense and uncomfortable. "How much time do you have?"

"Oh, I don't know. We just broke. Maybe half an hour."

"I have to tell you something. Let's walk." He didn't take my hand but instead strolled along with his hands in his pockets, kicking at the dirt. "I can't meet you tonight."

"Why not?"

"I have to go to the airport."

"The airport? What for?"

"I have to meet someone."

I didn't like the sound of this someone. It was a feeling. The strangeness of this someone didn't settle lightly with me. This someone had a special kind of meaning and I didn't want to know what it was, but I couldn't keep from asking.

Charlie had his back turned to me, his head bent. I could barely hear his mumbled words: "My fiancée."

I was stunned by the word. My brain didn't want to register or acknowledge the word. But it had to, and I began trying to think of other meanings for the word *fiancée*. Surely it didn't mean what I thought it meant. There had to be at least two meanings for the same sound. Truly weak-kneed, I held onto his arm and said, "What? What did you say?"

"I wanted to tell you before but I couldn't," Charlie said in anguish. "I thought I'd wait until I made up my mind to break off my engagement."

I felt a terrible hatred for myself. I had given all there was to give. Flesh for flesh, yet separate hearts. I knew then why he felt such concern for work in New York. There was a fiancée between us. She was coming here. No doubt she had become suspicious of Charlie. He had phoned his parents that morning and learned that she was on her way to Mexico City. It was a complete surprise to him.

"When did you first think of breaking it off, Charlie, before or after me?"

"Before," he said.

I didn't believe him. I couldn't look at him anymore. I couldn't stand next to him or talk or breathe the same air with him anymore. I walked slowly toward the house; halfway there, I broke into a run. I would have felt better had I been able to cry but I couldn't. I went back to rehearsal as though I were the happiest person alive; no one knew that only half of me was dancing. That night in bed I looked up at the ceiling and prayed for strength.

Charlie didn't come to see me for a couple of days after his fiancée arrived. I felt very inadequate as a woman, unattractive, unwanted. After three or four more days of absolute loneliness, I decided to go to the city for dinner. It was really an excuse to catch a glimpse of him, if I was lucky. I knew he would eat in "our" restaurant because it was the only place where one could get good American food.

My roommate, Jackie, went with me. I looked for Charlie as we waited for a table, but he wasn't there. Jackie suspected nothing until she heard me ask the headwaiter if Charlie had come in yet.

"Is he still here?" Jackie asked.

I pretended not to hear her, as the waiter led us to our table. I had decided to sit there until Charlie showed up. If he didn't, I decided I'd come back every night if necessary. I wanted to see the other woman; I was curious to know whether she was small, pretty, ugly, or what. And I wanted to see Charlie's face when he saw me in the restaurant. I wanted to see his reaction. If he was a coward, I thought, he would pretend not to see me. If he acknowledged me, I wondered what his fiancée would do—probably pretend to know nothing.

We had eaten a full dinner and had spent more than an hour in the restaurant when I decided to give up for the evening. We paid the bill and were heading for the door when Charlie walked in, his fiancée just ahead of him. He did what I feared he might do—looked directly at me and cringed, passing me by without a word. She was pretty, and that made me feel ugly. I watched him for a moment, not letting on to Jackie that anything was wrong. But in the cab on the way back to the villa, I broke down. Jackie tried to comfort me, understanding at last what was happening.

I didn't see Charlie again until he came to the house one evening to tell me he was returning to New York. Feeling awkward and tense, we said very little to each other. He swore again that he was going to break his engagement. I told him I didn't want to be responsible for that. He swore again, asking me to bear with him and telling me the decision had been made before he met me. He said that he'd become engaged out of loneliness and with the encouragement of his family and hers. He had become engaged without really questioning whether he loved the woman.

I didn't know if Charlie was telling the truth or not. But I wanted to believe him, so I did. I began making plans to help him get to California.

A few weeks after Charlie left, the company was offered an engagement at Ciro's in Mexico City. It lasted two months —until we had to leave for Hollywood. During that time I moved to a small hotel in the city, which cost me ten dollars a week, and I saved what I could of my thirty-five or forty-dollar salary from Ciro's to help Charlie get to Hollywood. I was very emotionally unsettled; I wanted to get Charlie out of my system, wanted to be rid of him and the anguish he was causing me. I wanted no part in being one of the corners in a triangle. But at the same time I wanted us to live happily ever after. Hollywood was certainly the place for happy-ever-after endings, wasn't it?

15

Hollywood

I expected Hollywood to be movie stars on every street corner.
My expectations had been formed in the dark, popcorn-smelling,
thickly carpeted cloisters of the silver screen in Manhattan.
Breakfasts on an open veranda, accompanied by a thousand
unseen violins—and no flies. Life with precise beginnings,
middles, and endings—always happy. Shirley Temple. That was
my lasting image: Shirley Temple in a mansion with dolls in
every room, a swimming pool, a chauffeur-driven car, a dog,
and lawn, lawn, and more lawn. Shirley must have had a new
dress for every hour and ice cream whenever she wanted it.
I pictured her ordering her chauffeur to the nearest ice cream
parlor. So much for childhood impressions.

We arrived, very tired after three days of travel, with no
place to live. We were told that we couldn't stay at hotels like
other people, so we made arrangements to stay with families
who rented rooms in their homes. Two of the girls, Richie and
Dolores, got a place with a woman they knew who catered to
entertainers. They tried to get me a room there too. I spent the
first three nights sleeping on a couch in the living room, ap-

parently waiting for a vacancy. But when the woman who owned the boarding house finally saw me, she said, "Out," making it clear that I was unwelcome not because there was no vacancy but because my skin was too light for her taste. I found a place down the street and settled in.

A few days after our arrival, Miss Dunham took Jessie Hawkins and me to see the man who was to direct the picture. She parked the car on the Universal-International lot. When we started toward the director's office, I realized that I was carrying my coat and that the day was too hot for it, so I ran back and threw it into what I thought was her car.

The director's office was in a little cabin. He wasn't in when we arrived, so we waited. Soon a curly-haired dog came bounding in, followed by his master, who was also curly-haired and handsome. He was introduced to us as John, and the moment our eyes met something happened; no one had ever looked at me quite like that before. He didn't take his eyes off me throughout the business transaction. Feigning nonchalance, I played with the dog, paying little attention either to the business at hand or to John. The meeting didn't go too well for Miss Dunham, and the idea of Jessie and me doing something special in the production was ruled out.

At home that evening I discovered that I had forgotten my coat. But the following day I learned from Miss Dunham that, in my haste, I had obviously thrown my coat into the wrong car. After the first day's work at the studio, I went looking for the other car and discovered that it belonged to none other than the director; he had thrown it into the back seat, figuring someone would eventually claim it. When I did, John invited me to dinner at a restaurant across the street from the studio. As time passed, we became close friends and frequently had lunch or dinner together.

I had a strong fear of Hollywood but was fascinated by it. Like most youngsters, I had dreamed of becoming a part of that glamorous world, but now that I was in its midst it didn't seem real. I felt as though I, too, were some sort of prop, something between fantasy and reality. I loved the illusion created by the men who made the sets. It was exciting to discover a seventeenth-century French drawing room or an 1860s vintage Western town, to turn a corner and find a city block of New York City tenements and candy stores. And exciting, too, to see all the cameras and the dozens and dozens of people who worked on a single film, and to see the takes and retakes and to hear yells of "Quiet" or "Cut" or "Take" or "Wrap it up!"

It was a quiet, controlled fascination that I just stored up. I was too busy absorbing everything to give vent to my excitement; my eyes and ears missed nothing. When I finally saw Tony Martin and Peter Lorre and Yvonne De Carlo, the stars of our picture, I wasn't moved as I thought I might have been. I took it all quite naturally; it was just another phase of my dream coming true.

When we weren't needed on our set, we visited others. We saw Deanna Durbin and Vincent Price on the set of *Up in Central Park*, Louis Jourdan and Joan Fontaine on the set of *The Letter*, Edward G. Robinson and Burt Lancaster on the set of *All My Sons*. We went from lot to lot, getting acquainted with everyone and being invited into people's cabins for drinks and lunch.

There were the legendary Hollywood parties too, but I never participated—probably because I didn't drink and because, having to get up early in the morning, I didn't like night life. I was always home at a decent hour.

The picture we worked on was fun and rather strange. It was, of course, shot out of sequence so that I never really knew quite what was going on. We were supposed to be Arabs, and in the scene in which I made my film debut we wore fezzes and bolero jackets and flare skirts. And I had a line of dialogue. During the dance I snapped my fingers in Tony Martin's face and said, "Come on, Pepe." In another scene we had a frenzied dance in which everyone, including Miss Dunham, fainted into delirium for some reason. I was the second girl from the left, the last to twirl into unconsciousness, falling on top of everyone who had already twirled into unconsciousness.

The picture made me feel more important because everyone—except the stars—got the same salary: $150 a week. With this, I opened a bank account and started saving.

A few days after we started the film Charlie arrived,

checking into the hotel where I had made a reservation for him. I was very happy to see him, but when he moved a few days later to a private home nearer my apartment I had mixed feelings about our relationship. He was still engaged to marry the family choice. I didn't want to be in love with him anymore, but being around him again made it difficult for me to put him out of my life. The satisfaction of knowing that someone really cared for me was too great to let go without a substitute. It was very selfish of me, but women will be women. And then there was still hope that he would make a decision that would allow us to have our life together.

Even more disconcerting was that "triangular" feeling; it hung between us like black crepe. It gave me the sensation I had when I was a kid and had done something wrong, knowing that I was going to get a whipping when my aunt came home. And it angered me because I was feeling the guilt that rightly should have been Charlie's. I kept saying to myself, why should *I* feel guilty? It's Charlie who should feel guilty for not being honest with his fiancée. Still, my guilt persisted.

Charlie became very casual with me in public, as though I were just a good friend. At first I thought that perhaps this lack of affection was simply my imagination, but after about six weeks he began seeing me less frequently. One night at my place I cooked dinner for the two of us. He ate heartily, drank gluttonously, kissed me coolly on the cheek, complimented me on my cooking, and said, "Let's talk."

I knew from his actions and tone of voice that I had to brace myself emotionally. He sat me down at the kitchen table next to him and said, "I don't think we should see too much of each other."

"What do you mean?"

"Well, you know how people are—especially out here. I'm trying to get somewhere and so are you, so I think we should be discreet about ourselves."

"You mean we shouldn't be seen in public together?"

"Well. . .yes."

I was deeply hurt but determined not to show it. "How do you intend to manage that?" I said.

"I'll come and see you here, whenever I can. We can meet

(Left) Eartha at eleven—New York City grade school days. (Above) Taken when she was thirteen, this photograph won first prize at Metropolitan High School: "I was just beginning to recognize who I was." (Below) Metropolitan High singing group, a year or two later. Eartha remembers Barbara, Lucille, and Yvonne as good friends. The school is now known as New York School of Performing Arts.

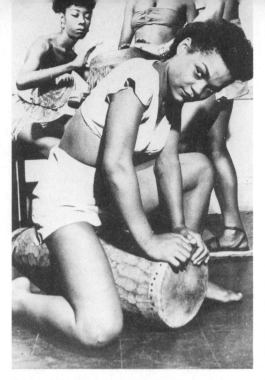

(Above left) First week with the Dunham dancers, September, 1946. (Below) Touring Mexico with the Dunham Troupe, 1948. (Above right) "Lean days" in Paris, 1949. This photograph led to her first appearance at La Vie en Rose in New York City.

(Above left) Istanbul, 1951: It took a court fine to stay, and an appeal to the consulate to get out. (Below) At Bricktop's in Paris, 1951, with Duke Ellington (behind Eartha) and Orson Welles (right), with whom she was starring in *Faust*. The French called her voice "the most haunting in the world." (Above right) Opening night, *New Faces*, May 16, 1952, with Ronnie Graham and a backstage visitor, Franchot Tone.

(Associated Press photo.)

(Above left) Return to La Vie en Rose, a 1954 engagement. (Above right) Break during 1953 RCA recording session with Henri Renée. (Right) Acclaimed for "Salome" on TV's "Omnibus" in 1954, she gave all credit to Patricia Neal and Leo Genn, who "made me come alive every time they spoke a line of dialogue with me."

(Herman Leonard Photo.)

(Irv Haberman photo.)

(Above left) Philippe Halsman's famous study and cover photograph. (Below) With Cab Calloway and a visitor, Cary Grant, on the set of St. Louis Blues, a 1957 picture with a black, all-star cast. "I felt I was standing in two different worlds," says Eartha. (Above right) 1958: with Sammy Davis, Jr., in Anna Lucasta.

(Above left) Eartha appeared on the Ed Sullivan TV show at least four times a year, and at his request, always sang at least one Hebrew song, 1960. (Above right) Eartha's dance workshop in Harlem, 1963. She started another in Watts when she moved to California. (Below left) Starring in the stage play *The Owl and the Pussycat*, 1966. (Below right) As the Cat Woman in a 1967 "Batman" episode on TV, with Cesar Romero (left) and Pierre Salinger.

Eartha and her daughter, Kitt, 1971: "Here we are, working together, playing together, and . . . just together."

(Indoor photo by Par-Ola Folcker; others courtesy of Kristianstadsbladet.)

(Above) Her 1973 visit to Swaziland in southern Africa. (Right) Onstage at the Mandarin Hotel in Hong Kong, 1974.

as usual in our eating place, but you know how people talk. I don't want to ruin my chances of getting a job before I get started."

Now I looked at him in dismay. After all the joy from the self-giving, wonderful love we had shared, after all the promises he had made, he wanted me to be a back-street wife. He was afraid, afraid of loving a black woman in a white man's world.

I haven't mentioned Charlie's color before this point in the narrative, and it occurs to me that you might think the exclusion of fact was deliberate, like that of a bad mystery writer who springs a surprise he should have told his readers about much earlier. But I couldn't say Charlie was "white" because, to me, he wasn't. He wasn't any color. He was Charlie, handsome and strong, and we loved each other. I wanted you to see how it was with us: two young people who found each other in a world where color didn't exist—not for them, not yet. But now Charlie had become conscious of color for the first time in our relationship, and it hurt deeply.

If white men were put against walls and shot for loving black women, I could have understood his fears. But I truly felt that he was afraid for all the wrong reasons. He was afraid of the men who would dictate what and how and whom to love. He was afraid to rebel against a conformity that was wrong. He was afraid to fight for what would make him happy.

I knew and sympathized with what he must have felt to bring himself to this confrontation, and I was terribly frustrated because I didn't know how to show him that his thinking was wrong. If he wanted to let me go completely, that was all right. But he was asking me to love him in dark corners and to walk alone in the white world of glaring neon, where blacks huddled in darkness trying to make neon light of their own.

Finally I said, "I'm sorry, Charlie, but if this is what you want of me, I can't accept. I can only see you in a light that we *both* hold the string to, to turn on, to stand in the circle of that light, to see each other as we are—people. I must be free to love; I won't be bound to hate."

We discussed the point to its exhaustion and until I finally said good night to him, never conceding a point. At the door he said, "I don't want to lose you, Kitt. Can't you understand?"

"I understand," I said, "but I can't accept your terms."

He left, head down, probably thinking that I would call him later asking forgiveness—as I usually did when I found I had been a fool about something. But there would be no call to him. Hiding in dark corners is beneath human dignity.

I continued with my studio work and continued having dinner with John. I tried to put Charlie out of my mind. I hadn't spoken of him to others and hadn't seen him for a week when John drove me home from dinner one night and saw me to the door. I had a strange feeling that we were being watched, and I thought immediately of Charlie. John held me in his arms, and I tried to chat with him as I peered into the darkness, looking for lurking shadows, but I saw nothing. "You go right to bed now. Don't stay up," John said.

My instinct told me not to let him go but my head told me that I was being silly. Charlie wouldn't spy on me. "All right, John. Good night."

I went into the house and to my room, a little worried that there was no one in the house but me. But when I had finally dismissed the thought of being watched, I heard a knock on the front door. I knew who it was, knew he was mad, and knew he had been watching every move I'd made. I opened the door, and there stood Charlie. "Is this what you've been doing, not to be home when I've called? This must have been going on for some time!"

Before I could tell him that was none of his business, he grabbed me by the collar and threw me to the floor. "How dare you make a fool out of me," he said, glaring down at me. "Who do you think you are? Who is that man who brought you home? Get up off the floor!"

I didn't move. Charlie had never roughed me up that way before, would never have dreamed of doing so. I was scared. He towered over me angrily, hating me for being a woman, I thought. I didn't know whether to cry so that he wouldn't be rough with me again or to stand up and take it. I settled for something in between: I whimpered a little. Then I wished I hadn't. If he began to feel sorry for me, he might want to make me feel secure again—which might shake my firm resolve to be rid of him, might awaken again the love for him that I knew was there, might weaken me as a woman and get me to do his bidding. I wondered if a better course might not be to kick him in the groin and make him crawl out my door on his belly.

Before I could make a decision, he dragged me roughly to my feet. That angered me so much that I did exactly what I had done in my grade school days when cornered by the gang at the candy store. I doubled my fist and socked him right in the jaw. He was so startled that I got a good shot at his abdomen and was aiming a beauty at his left cheek when he grabbed both my wrists, dragged me into my room, and threw me on the bed, pinning me immobile with his body. Then I felt his lips on mine, and our battle ended in love.

The next morning at the studio I made up my mind that Charlie and I had to part. Miss Dunham had mentioned a possible tour of Europe and I hoped that it would come about. There would be an ocean between Charlie and me, no phone to pick up when I was miserable. Charlie had heard of the possibility but had laughed it off. "You won't go, anyway," he said. I said nothing to Charlie about my plan to leave him.

There was another motive for my wanting to go to Europe. The few parties and studio functions I had attended had made me acutely aware of my ignorance. Everyone seemed to be stirred up about something called the world situation. I knew nothing of politics and very little of what was going on in the world. People were talking about what Russia believed or what we believed, and I was horrified to realize that my thoughts were restricted to the last dance we had learned or the audience's reaction. I couldn't discuss world events. Since school, I hadn't read a book cover to cover, and my newspaper reading was confined to the comic strips. I had concentrated so thoroughly upon my career that the world had gone right by me.

I wanted to know what those people knew who sat around at parties discussing politics and world leaders and economics. When I heard people talking on subjects that were foreign to me, I was awed. One night, while visiting some friends who talked world events the whole evening, I was very embarrassed because the woman of the house tried to bring me into the conversation by saying, "Don't you think so?" And I was unable to answer her. Others looked at me and smiled politely, but I was sick with shame. When I got home that night, I cried.

I knew the solution was to teach myself to think, absorb, retain. Somehow I had neglected all this. I began inquiring about books to read and had them explained to me when I didn't understand them. My principal advantage was that I wasn't afraid to admit that I didn't know—which is an art. I have always found that honesty is the best course, regardless of the consequences.

Charlie used to sit with me for hours explaining the hows and whys and whats of many things. With him, I could be as ignorant as I really was without shame. And he enjoyed the role of tutor; it gave him someone to mold and a way to command respect and admiration. I was going to miss those tutoring sessions when there was no more Charlie.

16

Crossroads

When the film was finished, we went to Ciro's in Hollywood for a two-week engagement. There the Dunham troupe was made very proud by the presence of Hollywood's elite. With the club filled to capacity every night, we regarded ourselves as the hottest act in show business. Our pride in being what we were—a black group—was diminished only by our position in society. I felt that we were on the edge of being accepted, that there was an opening somewhere, and that all we had to do was find it. I felt that the white world was not afraid of us but that we were afraid of it, and that if we presented ourselves on equal terms we might not even be noticed—which would mean understanding, not tolerance. To be tolerated would be worse than not being accepted.

I wanted the world to understand me so that it would accept me. I believed that one day I might come back to Hollywood to meet people face to face and hold my own with them. I wanted to be able to distinguish truth from opinion, to have my own values and be able to express them. I had no real grasp of what I was aiming for, but the drive and desire were there. Very often I could feel that deep inside me. It was a question of direction.

Charlie wasn't the right direction; I knew that. But, for a while, he was love. I had a feeling that the other direction held great fulfillment but that there would be no genuine love. The question I pondered was: Which was more important? Charlie's indecision settled the question for me. Whatever direction I took, the search for love would always exist.

When our two weeks at Ciro's came to an end that winter, the Dunham show toured the coldest and most horrifying cities imaginable. Particularly Chicago. What an impression it made on me! I was ready to leave the moment I arrived. Being a person who hates cold weather, I was prepared to dislike Chicago from the start. The snow seemed at least seven feet deep, the icy fingers of Lake Michigan chilled me to the bone, and I immediately dubbed the city "the old icebox."

As in every city we played, except those in Mexico, we had to live in segregated parts of town a long way from the theater. The company manager made reservations for us at a hotel on the South Side, about five or ten miles from the Loop. A large part of our small salary was spent on trolley and bus fare.

After being in Chicago a few days, we began meeting people and having an enjoyable time. Soon I began to get fond of the old icebox. The people were friendly, and I came to the realization that it's one of the few cities in the country with real character.

Dale Wasserman, who had been stage manager with the company off and on for many years and who was Miss Dunham's personal manager, took over as stage manager again while we were in Chicago. By this time we were talking seriously about Europe, and Dale was giving everyone his third degree: "Are you going? If not, why not? Don't you want to see Europe? Don't you realize what an opportunity this is?"

I had been doing a lot of thinking about Charlie who was still on the coast, and I was sure that I could get him to change if I went back to him. I told Dale: "I don't want to go to England."

"Why not?"

"I want to go back to Hollywood."

"Kitty, be sensible! Come to Europe—you won't regret it."

We debated, but Dale was persuasive. Every day he talked of Europe and the advantages of the tour, finally convincing me that if I was ever to see Europe it was now. We returned to New York to prepare for the tour.

During our time in Mexico and Hollywood, I had corresponded with my aunt. I wanted her to know what I was doing so that she wouldn't worry about what happened to me and think that I had gone off to become a "bad girl." Our relationship by mail was a good one; she had come to realize that I was very serious about my profession and had no doubt read or heard about the fine reviews the Dunham troupe was receiving across country. And while her fundamentalist religion caused her to see dancing as sinful, once she had accepted the fact that I had made my career decision she said nothing more about it.

While I was in Mexico, my aunt had invited me to come back home when I returned to the United States. I stayed with her for the ten days we were preparing for the European tour, and we were close for the first time in our lives. I had learned a good deal and matured considerably, and my aunt's attitude toward me had changed as well. I realized that she was a warm and sensitive woman. She wasn't afraid of life and the payment for it. She looked to no one on earth for anything; she looked to God for strength—particularly for strength to keep going. For although I didn't know it at the time, death was close by.

I continued to call her "Mother," as I had since my first weeks in New York. She was indeed my surrogate mother, and I think she began to consider me her daughter at this time. Before, her relationship with me had evolved from a sense of duty. Now it was love.

The house was warm—a home. I felt as though I belonged there at last. There was love and comfort and the scents of home-cooked food, and when I had to leave the house for rehearsals or something, I could hardly wait to get back home to my aunt. I had mentioned to her that I wanted to do some shopping. I had saved a little money and was going to buy suitcases and clothes for my voyage. I think I even suggested that we might go shopping together. But one day when I returned from rehearsal she was waiting for me with everything I needed, including new suitcases.

She showed me all of it, piece by piece, saying, "If there's anything you don't like, I can take it back." It was, in my eyes, an act of love. In my excitement, I wanted to talk to her more and more, to tell her how I had longed for her to show such interest in me, to show me love. But instead I said, "Mother, I started a bank account in Los Angeles. I can have Miss Dunham send the money to you."

"Never mind," my aunt said, "I know how you are with money."

"But I *am* saving." I didn't have my bankbook with me to prove it, so I couldn't make her believe me. She got her handbag and brought out two bankbooks, opening one and showing it to me. My name was at the top of the first page. A few lines down it gave dates and sums, the total being $1,300. The book in her name totaled $2,300.

I felt ill. My thoughts went back to the empty iceboxes and no shoes and the shabby clothes she used to wear, to the hand-me-downs we both wore from the white world. All that time she must have been putting money aside for me to have when I grew up. "Of course, if anything happened to me, all this, along with the insurance I've taken out, will be yours," she said.

I had a mother—one who cared. She wanted me home. She was proud that I had not turned out a no-good. I wished that the troupe were not going away, or that I hadn't committed myself to the tour. I wanted to cherish those days, to prolong them. But I found some solace in the fact that I would return and that we could begin again where we left off.

The day before we left I called Charlie to tell him I'd see him in six months, after our engagement in England. He begged me not to go but I was committed. I told him that my absence would give him a chance to decide which woman he was going to choose. He couldn't have both, and he was on his own. I was upset after the call, but I knew that time would make it work out for the best.

The next day at eleven, my aunt took me to the S. S. *George Washington* to join the company. She talked and joked with members of the troupe and their mothers. I was proud to stroll among the others saying, "This is my mother." Like them, I had family.

The ship's whistle blew and there was a call for "All ashore." My aunt looked at me and said, "I feel I shall never see you again." That brought tears to my eyes; I was very moved that she was sad over me for the first time since I could remember.

At sea we went about choosing beds and unpacking. Then everyone but me went around the ship getting acquainted. I lay in my bunk with no intention of getting up until we reached England—unless, of course, I was on the verge of starving. That bunk would be my home for the eight to eleven days we would be at sea.

Staring at the emptiness of my cabin I was suddenly overwhelmed by the realization that I was really going abroad. It wasn't leaving Charlie that bothered me. I wouldn't get over him for a long while, but I was resigned to the fact that he had, in effect, rejected me because he thought I might harm his chances of making it in Hollywood (he never did make it, by the way). And it wasn't the fact that I was leaving everything I knew for a strange and foreign world. It was my aunt.

Now the memory of those last few minutes on deck with her hit me like a swift and stunning blow to the solar plexus: She had remained *close* by my side, she had evidenced *pride* in me when talking to the others; and the expression in her eyes when she spoke her parting words—an expression I had never seen there before and hadn't recognized—was one of *love*. But it had happened so quickly; her fear that she wouldn't see me again, the look in her eyes, the call to go ashore. And then I had been caught up in the Dunham troupe's enthusiasm at getting under weigh.

What a terrible revelation of loss: I was leaving the one thing I wanted most from life. Feeling the tingling vibration of the ship's engines beneath me, I realized that the love I had been longing for since childhood had been expressed and then instantaneously smothered in the confusion and excitement of the moment. And now I was being carried away from my aunt, the one person in the world who truly cared for me. It was as though the devil himself was at the helm, and he had fiendishly allowed me a momentary glimpse of heaven before transporting me across the Styx to purgatory.

I lay in my lower bunk for four days of deep, soul-searching depression. To avoid conversation, I pretended to be asleep all the while. And I thought and slept, and thought and slept some more. Only the expectation that I would be reunited with my aunt at the end of our six months' tour brought me out of my lethargy, determined to work even harder so that she'd be even more proud of me.

When I finally decided to get up, I couldn't; I was terribly seasick. I lay in bed for the remainder of the voyage, no longer emotionally upset but too ill to care about living or dying. There were times when the sea was so rough I was sure we were goners. My bunk would tilt so far that I thought the ship had turned on its side in mortal agony. But when we docked at Southampton, I suddenly felt like Alice in Wonderland. I was glad I had decided against returning to Hollywood.

17

England

The year was 1948 and Europe was suffering economically from the war. London still grieved from that horror; I could see and feel her wounds, as I was to witness the vestiges of war in other parts of Europe in the ensuing months. I was glad to have been born in America and to have been so well protected, but I felt guilt, too, for having been totally safe while so many suffered and so much of the world was destroyed. The experience made me appreciate my birthright even more.

Food was still scarce in England. Meat, milk, sugar, coffee, cheese, and the like were being rationed. Knowing this, Miss Dunham had shipped crates and crates of food with us. When we reached customs, we learned that we were allowed to import only a few pounds of food per person. Miss Dunham solved the problem by giving away canned food at the dock; the expressions on the recipients' faces was worth the trip.

In London, we were taken by bus to the private homes we were to stay in, hotels being too expensive. Most of the girls were put in one house—three in one room, four in another, with a bath on a level between the second and third floors. Since none of us liked the barracks arrangement, we began looking for vacant apartments the next day.

A girl named Julie Robinson (now Mrs. Harry Belafonte) and I pooled our money and found a nice apartment at 10 Manchester Square in a beautiful neighborhood. There were two bedrooms, a living room with fireplace, a large bath, a kitchen, and a telephone. It was expensive, but by now I was making ninety-five dollars a week. Julie and I enjoyed dividing the cooking and cleaning. We had our ration books for foods like meat and eggs and milk. And as we became known to our neighbors, they helped by showing us the best stores. Julie's mother occasionally sent food, as did my aunt, and we'd invite our English friends to dinner whenever we received boxes from home. Most of the other members of the company eventually found apartments, so we rotated our dinners on Sundays when we didn't work.

We were playing the Prince of Wales, which was considered *the* theater in London at the time, just as our show was considered the biggest stage event to have hit London since the war. The house was packed for our entire six-month engagement. It was exciting introducing Londoners to primitive dancing and singing—exciting, too, to play for royalty. Every theater in London had a royal box. When the curtain went up each performance, we'd look to the royal box to see if it was occupied, which it often was, and we'd be disappointed if we found it empty.

A few months before our London engagement ended, I was introduced to a young man who had taken a fancy to me. I don't recall his name, but I remember exactly what he looked like; all of the girls in the show thought he was an extremely handsome son of a gun. But going out with him made me realize that I had yet to get Charlie out of my system; in fact, it took me a year and a half to get over Charlie. Consequently, I wasn't the warmest person in the world to my English beau. If he tried to touch me, I'd turn against him immediately. I didn't like myself for it, but I suppose it was my mind's way of protecting me from being hurt again.

Fortunately, he was the perfect gentleman. He didn't try to

get fresh with me, and my coolness toward him didn't affect our friendship. He lived on the outskirts of town, but whenever he was in London proper he would pick me up at the stage door and drive me home in his little Jaguar. And he spent Sundays with Julie and me, eating dinner and sitting at the fireplace telling stories. Sometimes he'd bring a friend; sometimes members of the company would spend the day with us. In the evenings, we would go to the movies, or for a ride in his car, or just for a walk. I felt that I could have grown to like him even more had there been time, but memories of Charlie stood in the way.

The Londoners' response to us was wonderful and gratifying. There's one incident I'll never forget. I was walking alone one afternoon just a few blocks from Piccadilly Circus when an elderly man wearing a raincoat and derby hat pointed his umbrella at me and asked, "I say, aren't you Eartha Kitt?" It was startling enough and enormously pleasing to have someone recognize me by sight, but to know my *name* as well! All I could do for a few moments was stand there grinning at him. When I finally gathered my wits and answered, "Yes," he took the carnation from his raincoat lapel and handed it to me.

"I must pay you a tribute," he said. "I love your singing." He smiled, looking me up and down, seeming more surprised to find that I was me than I was to be recognized. "The way you move around on stage is fantastic. But you are smaller than I thought you were."

I don't remember what I said, but as I began to walk away he took my arm gently and said: "You must come and have lunch with me. I assure you I'm harmless, and this is a great privilege for me."

I must have looked apprehensive—I certainly felt so—for he added hastily: "You needn't worry, my dear. Here is my card of business. Everyone in London knows me around here, so you're certainly safe. We can go to a restaurant where they know me."

It was astonishing for me to realize that he was actually jittery with pleasure at the idea of escorting me to lunch—as though I were a celebrity. And since it was to be one of the finer restaurants, one I would not otherwise have been able to visit, I accepted. Besides, I was really hungry.

The restaurant was indeed fine, and everyone did know him—or at least it seemed that way to me. I had an expensive meal for the first time in ages, and he was a pleasant conversationalist. After dinner, I was a little afraid; after all, he was a stranger. But I told myself that he would probably walk me to the theater, leave me at the door, and that would be the last I'd see of him. But to my surprise—and growing delight—that wasn't the last of him at all.

Every night when I left the theater he would be waiting outside the stage door, carrying the same umbrella and wearing the same raincoat and derby hat, but with a fresh carnation in his lapel which he always presented to me faithfully. Then he'd bow and disappear into the shadows of the London streets. This went on until we left the city. Neither rain nor fog nor whatever kept him from being at that stage door every night for weeks with his carnation. What a kind, sweet gesture that was.

When our London engagement finally ended, we were booked to tour the provinces. My young English beau came to see me on the day we left to ask that I write to him often, which I did once a week, despite our busy schedule. He wrote to me twice a week.

Liverpool was our first stop on tour, and what an impression it made on me! This was the town of the old slave markets, of flesh for gold. I don't remember whether we were there one week or two; I remember only the waterfront. I was drawn to it, despite my loathing of it. This is where the slave boats docked, where it all began, with Africa directly across the sea. I used to stand on the pier and stare out at the ocean. The dark aura of the place—the eclipse of human dignity—was almost palpable. I could sense that horrendous era as though it were taking place at that very moment. I felt great sorrow, not sure whether it was for those who were no more, or for myself, a descendant of them. In today's vernacular, Liverpool gave off bad vibrations I couldn't shake, despite the friendliness of its inhabitants. And I wasn't unhappy to leave the place.

I liked Birmingham, but as in Chicago, I could well have dubbed it the old icebox. I mean, *cold!* Throughout our stay, I wore fleeced boots and pajamas made of fleece wool. For two weeks I wore those pajamas, taking them off only when I had to go on stage. I also wore several long-sleeved sweaters at a time. I was corresponding frequently with my aunt, keeping her abreast of our adventures, but I don't recall telling her about the pajama episode. She would have enjoyed it, I'm sure, for it would have reminded her of my first arrival in New York, when I was wearing every stitch of clothing that she had sent me.

I was chilled to the bone when we arrived in Birmingham. Julie and I could hardly wait to get into the warmth of the house. What optimists! It was nearly as cold inside as it was out. The lady of the house had the tiniest fire in the fireplace I had ever seen. We discovered that coal was scarce and very expensive; one seldom found more than one lump of coal burning in a stove or fireplace. But the English are resourceful; they warmed themselves from the inside out, as we were to learn when that kind and gracious woman sat us down and filled us up with steaming hot tea.

Manchester was the most pleasant city of our tour. We all stayed in a lovely small hotel, which was surrounded by trees and had a garden. I was happily at home there. My room was large and beautiful—and private. It had an old-fashioned, high-post bed with quilted bedspread. And there was a fireplace too. All I needed to start a fire was a shilling, which of course I never had.

At most of the places on our tour, we had been given large and noisy send-offs. But since we didn't stay in Manchester long enough to make friends, all was orderly and quiet as we boarded our train for London, on our way to Paris.

We had half a day in London, so I called my English beau. "Come out and spend the day with us," he said. "I want you to meet my mother and dad."

When I arrived at the station on the outskirts of London, he and his parents were there to meet me. I wondered nervously what his mother thought of me: a toy for her son—one he would soon tire of? The day was pleasant, under the circumstances. She accepted me cordially, but I suppose I was looking for more. My English beau was another matter; his manner toward me was unchanged, but I saw something in his eyes when he looked at me. He was so gentlemanly and understanding, but I had the distinct impression that he was on the verge of becoming not so gentlemanly.

My intuition eventually proved correct. The place to tell people's truths is Paris. We were settled in, playing the Théâtre de Paris, when my so-far-angelic Englishman came to see me. I had just gotten the five-minute curtain call and was putting the finishing touches to my makeup when I heard his voice bellowing my name backstage with sufficient volume to be heard not only in the audience, but probably in the lobby and out on the street as well. Mortified by the disruption, I hurriedly opened the door to my dressing room to hush him. When he saw me he came into my room, the gleam in his eye like that of a child bent upon irresistible mischief. The quiet one (on English soil) took me in his arms, squeezed me, and said, "Baby, are we going to have fun *tonight!*"

I talked him out of my dressing room and into the idea of going out front to see the show. Waiting to go on stage, I tried to rationalize his behavior: Paris is too drastic a change for him; maybe he's been drinking. I had heard of those Air France flights from London that served champagne, with no limit to those little bottles of whiskey. But when cue time came, I decided I'd figure him out later; I went out and danced and sang my extra best.

When the curtain came down, Jackie and I went to the dressing room we shared and began changing. There was a knock at the door.

"Who is it?" I asked.

"Me!" came the familiar voice. "Let me in."

"Just a moment. We're not dressed."

"That's why I want to come in. Ha, ha, ha!"

I was so disappointed I could have cried. I wouldn't have minded the joviality, but there was more than a hint of seriousness in his suggestion. He had always been so chivalrous in London; now it was like turning over a card and finding a joker.

He waited outside until I emerged, then gave me a long look and said, "Darling, I thought you'd never come out." Laughing, he took me by the arm and started walking me through the streets of Paris. After the show I usually went with Jackie and the

others for food before going back to my hotel. And that was my
intention until he asked, "Where are we going?"

"Aren't you hungry?" I asked. "I thought we'd go with the
others for supper. There's a wonderful restaurant up the street.
We always go there. Would you like to?"

"No, I'm not interested in food. I just want to go home."

Home, I thought. We walked toward my hotel. "I couldn't
get you a room here," I said. "There are no vacancies."

He stopped and eyed me. "Why don't I stay with you?" I
looked at him in dismay, but not surprise. "Come on," he said,
"I hope everyone in the hotel is a sound sleeper, because we're
going to have the time of our lives. Ha, ha, ha, ha!"

I loathed him and all men at that moment, as I fought for
restraint and calmness. "You can't stay with me," I said.
Apparently my expression had more finality than my words, for
when I walked briskly away he neither protested nor followed.
He just stood there in the middle of the narrow Paris street, his
overnight bag in one hand, a cigarette in the other, looking after
me as though I should be as unvirtuous as Lady Paris.

18

Paris and Beyond

Paris was fascinating. And, at first, frustrating. Julie's mother had told us about an attractive hotel, so we went there by cab to look the place over. It was far from swanky, but the price was right—seven hundred francs a day, which in those days amounted to two dollars. We had separate rooms, each fifteen feet by ten, with a wash basin in the corner and an iron bed that reminded me of my childhood days.

We registered in late afternoon, writing in the large space provided for personal information—which we guessed at, since neither of us spoke a word of French. And after putting our things in our rooms, we set out to explore the city and to find a good restaurant. We told Othella and Jackie about our quaint lodgings, and they took rooms next to ours.

To our delight, we found that the Théâtre de Paris was only ten blocks from the hotel. This was another convenience, for we could walk and save money. But it soon became apparent that Julie's parents were unaquainted with the Paris night shift; if they had known what they were getting us into, they would have had about two hemorrhages apiece—as Holden Caulfield would say.

We met the night shift while walking back and forth between our hotel and the theater. After the first few nights, we found that we'd have company once in a while. If the four of us walked together we had little to worry about, but with two of us—or one—it wasn't so good. At first we had trouble shaking our followers. And a couple of times Julie and I were trailed into the lobby of our hotel, where we called the manager. Our not knowing the language made it worse; I had never seen such tenacious fans. Then we learned that our hotel was in the middle of the streetwalkers' section—that also explained the hard stares we were getting from some of the women on the street. The professionals apparently thought we were moving in on their territory!

We thought of moving, but since we were to be in Paris only eight weeks, and since the hotel was clean and inexpensive and convenient to the theater, we decided that we'd walk to and fro in fours and not be intimidated. It was a little embarrassing, though. The ladies swarmed around our hotel like flies to chicken gravy, and our hours were the same as theirs! But we got used to it, until the morning we were awakened by heavy fists on our doors.

My room, nearest the elevator, was first. The pounding wrenched me from sleep: *Boom! Boom! Boom!*

"Who is it?" I asked.

"Open the door!"

My first thought was: What have I done? Then, maybe the hotel's on fire. But I couldn't smell smoke and I was groggy from sleep, so I said to hell with it, they must have the wrong door, and I lay back down.

Boom, boom, boom again.

"What do you want? Go away!"

Then I heard banging on other doors and voices in the hallway, and thinking that something was definitely wrong I opened my door. All the other doors on our floor were open too, and there were officious-acting men in the hallway. One of them pushed into my room with exaggerated authority, and his eyes darted around suspiciously. "Your passport!" he said. He spoke French, but I understood the word.

"My passport? What for?"

He spoke no English and he was adamant. If I had known French in those days, I would have told him a thing or two for waking me up at such a ridiculous hour. I tried to ask him who he was and what right he had to barge in. But it was impossible, so I looked for my passport. It was missing. Could I have lost it? Could someone have stolen it? American passports were at a premium in those days.

I ran to Julie's room—the knobby-knuckled door boomer close at my heels—thinking in my half-awake state that perhaps Julie had my passport. But she couldn't find hers, either, and it was then we remembered. The company manager had taken all passports to get visas or work permits or something. Now, somehow, it was made clear to us that if we couldn't produce our passports, we would be thrown into jail. Someone got on the phone to our manager, and he came to our aid within the hour. We all went back to bed, and the next day we learned that police had been rounding up prostitutes in the area. No doubt the hotel manager had told them that we were with the Dunham troupe, but they had needed the passports to verify that.

Fortunately, the police had waited for our manager to arrive with our passports. The newsmen evidently hadn't—or, if they had they ignored the facts. One newspaper carried a small but prominent item:

FOUR DUNHAM DANCERS SEIZED IN RAID

The four of us thought it enormously funny. But although the subject was never mentioned by the Dunham hierarchy, I doubt that they were amused.

Our show was a hit in Paris, and what was supposed to have been an eight-week engagement stretched for months and months. We were soon involved in a social whirl, relentlessly probing the city's fascinating night life. For one three-month stretch we didn't return to our hotel until dawn, and I became so exhausted that I came to hate Paris and everything she stood for. I'm not a night person—and wasn't then—but I didn't want to miss anything. It was an exciting time, shortly after the war and the occupation. Paris was, indeed, young and gay again.

My first plane trip was from Paris, and it was as awesome to me as my first train ride from the South. We were scheduled for one performance at a festival in Cannes, and the trip turned out to be an almost somnambulistic blur. Our evening performance in Paris ended at eleven, so it was nearly one o'clock in the morning when I got to bed. Then it was up early to be at the airport by seven. Six o'clock in Paris is like six o'clock anywhere—only more so. My eyes smarting and my nerves raw from lack of sleep, I took a window seat on the plane, just behind the propellers, and fastened my seat belt.

At first I could hardly keep my eyes open. But if there was any doubt that I would be able to stay awake during the flight, it was dispelled when the engines began revving up. The sound and vibration nearly shocked me out of my skin, and I knew that if it didn't stop, I'd simply run out of nerves. But once the plane lifted from the runway, I calmed down. And when we rose through the clouds, I had never before felt such serenity.

I pressed my head against the window so that I could see everything passing below us. I watched every object, every cloud, and secretly looked for angels too. After a while everything seemed quite natural—though it felt strange to be eating a meal in the sky.

Cannes was romantic. The palms, the architecture, the blue waters of the Mediterranean were beautiful. But we didn't get to see much. We walked around until rehearsal time, did the show, got back on the plane, and returned to Paris.

I had had a few dates in Paris and enjoyed an increasingly large circle of friends, but doing the same show night after night in the same theater for so long was terribly boring. Until Philippe. He was a handsome young man, a free-lance journalist who suddenly appeared one day—I don't recall how we met—and we became inseparable. When the show finally closed to go on tour, Philippe accompanied us for several weeks through Belgium and Italy.

He returned to Paris, as I recall, when we played Rome. Since we were there for a month, I was able to see all the sights. The Italians were friendly and curious, following us through the streets for the first few days trying to figure out what we were. They soon learned from their newspapers and word of mouth. Our show was rather a cultural shock to them.

Milan, Turin, and Naples were depressing places to me. Wherever we went we were followed by children: dirty, rags hanging from bony limbs, hands extended, and faces full of expectations of a lira. Disappointment settled on them like shadows when coins were not offered. I felt awful. Giving is a wonderful thing, but I wasn't a rich tourist and there were so many, many begging children.

Our next stop was Switzerland. Zurich lay in a valley formed by towering mountains. We were taken to a pension, a hotel with room and board, with beds covered in soft quilts of eiderdown that melted over the body like sleep. The stairs creaked with antiquity. Everywhere there was charm: tiny streets, grand boulevards, toy shops and watchmaker shops, snow-capped peaks, the Limmat River running through the city and into the Lake of Zurich, and serene, smiling people with a heritage that made their eyes sparkle. And no sign of poverty.

We made friends quickly, mostly with people who came backstage and invited us to their homes. One of them was a young man named Peter who had gone out of his way to be introduced to "the girl on the right." Othella, we thought. Peter invited us all to a party in his home, which overwhelmed us with its luxury. The antiques. The exquisite pieces encased in glass. Rembrandts, Gauguins, Monets, Manets on the walls. The wide, winding staircase.

Peter was talking to Othella in a corner. I envied her, for I've never been much of a partygoer and I was feeling lonely. After a while, Peter noticed me sitting alone. He came over and leaned on the piano next to me, saying nothing, giving me the impression that he wanted to talk but had nothing to say. I felt his closeness and I'm sure he felt mine.

I saw Peter the next night after the show in the restaurant our company frequented. Still, nothing was said. As the days went by, I became morose. I felt empty. My conversation rambled; my words had little meaning. I ate without appetite and stared into space a lot, totally bored and wishing for something interesting to happen. I think now that I had quite a crush on Peter, but I didn't recognize the symptoms.

One night, while I was sitting in the restaurant in just such a mood, Philippe walked in. How adorable he looked, more handsome than ever. We hadn't seen one another for a long time. He took me for a walk along the river and told me how he had longed to be with me, but his father had kept him so busy that he had been unable to get away.

His words were mellow and sweet to my ears. He said all the things I wanted him to say: He loved me; he was jealous to see me with other men; he wanted to spend every moment with me. The words and the hour of night were right. The air was clear and the moon shone bright above the surrounding mountains: the city was romantic and my mood could not have been better. But it was the wrong mouth. It would have been hypocritical of me to have encouraged Philippe after this sudden revelation, so I suddenly left his side and ran-walked to my hotel a block or so away.

Back in my room, I thought of Peter and wondered if he would be a good man for me. But since he seemed uninterested, I drifted into self-pity. Would my prince come along some day? I covered myself with the comforting eiderdown that hugged me like a lover, and I fell asleep.

The following night I went to another party. Philippe wasn't there, but Peter was. I was sitting alone on a divan when he sat down beside me. "You look sad," he said.

"That's my forte."

"Meaning what?"

"To get attention," I said.

"You've got it."

We sat in silence for a moment. Then Peter said, "I made a drastic mistake, you know."

"How?"

"I wanted to meet someone, and was introduced to someone else."

My heart leaped, but I maintained my composure. "Really?" I said.

"Really."

I knew then that I was the "girl on the right" he had wanted to meet. I wanted him to continue, but instead he excused himself and went to greet a friend. When he returned, someone else was sitting beside me. Afraid that we would have no way to talk privately, I took a chance on his following me to the buffet table. He did.

We spent the rest of the evening together, sitting on the floor and talking. He told me about his country: the beauty and importance of the mountains, the food that had been stashed in caves during the war, and the tons of dynamite that had been placed there also—a pull of a lever would have sent a potential enemy, and the city, to kingdom come. He talked of the beauty of the summer and winter resorts and health spas. "I'll take you to the mountains one day, if you like."

"I'd like," I said. Then, noticing that people were leaving the party, I added, "Well, I guess I'd best be going."

"Do you have someone taking you?"

"No. . . ."

"Then I shall do so. That is, if you don't mind my little bug of a car."

His "bug" looked exactly like a beetle. It was a Renault that made today's Volkswagen bug look positively streamlined. Peter had to fold himself in half to get into it, but it was fun to ride in, quick and responsive.

A few days later, Peter took me to a resort high in the mountains. It was a two-hour trip each way, and I had never seen such magnificence. I felt minute and unimportant as we crawled along the feet of God.

The resort town was charming, with its small shops, bricked streets, and crystal clear air. At the ski quarters, Peter couldn't resist making a ski run down the mountain slope. I walked with him to the lift, then played in the snow until I finally spotted him flying down the slope, a speck at first, growing larger and larger, twisting and turning with perfect balance and astonishingly graceful body control, sending great puffs of snow into the air at each turn. Then he headed straight toward me at what seemed the speed of sound, and playfully executed a perfect stop that spattered my legs with fine powdered snow.

He removed his skis and said, "Let's eat."

We went to a hotel rooftop restaurant where a balcony overlooked the valley of ski jumpers, riders, and climbers. I ate the most wonderful meal imaginable and made myself at home in the lap of heaven.

On the way back to Zurich the sun was setting, and we stopped at Peter's favorite spot to watch it slip behind a mountain top. Then I thought Peter had taken leave of his senses, for the moment the sun disappeared, he sped the little beetle along the winding road, over another mountain peak, and down around a bend, where we watched the sun set once more.

We returned in time for the show. I didn't go into detail about my eventful day with other members of the cast; the value of it would have been cheapened by my small vocabulary.

Since Peter worked days, I spent most of them with Philippe, exploring Zurich on foot. But from that time on, Peter came to the theater each night to take me to dinner and home.

To my regret, our successful engagement in Zurich finally came to an end. Our next stop was Stockholm. Peter took me to the train and loaded me down with boxes of chocolate. As he stood on the platform, waving goodbye forlornly, I hung out of the window as far as I could, holding onto a dream that could have been—to the very last minute.

Stockholm amazed me. I was delighted to find that the city was built on little islands. The shopping district was on one, the sports and health centers on a second, the theater and amusement center had its separate island, and the oldest parts of the town were on yet another. All of them were connected by bridges.

The theater was a converted circus house, and we appeared there for a month. None of us wanted to leave. I thought Stockholm the perfect example of civilization. Though the people were reserved and I had difficulty relating to them, they were friendly. And they looked happier than any others I had seen in the world.

I was fascinated that there were no bars or pubs or nightclubs for drinking only. Alcoholic beverages were served only with food in public places. Drinking was kept to a minimum—until Saturday nights, when those who imbibed compensated for the week's deficiency. Then when you saw a drunken Swede, he was *really* drunk!

My days were spent getting steam baths and massages and bicycling into the countryside with a young man I met who devoted his weekends to touring me around. But despite my wholesome endeavors in Stockholm, I was wearing myself out for lack of sleep. For one thing, the evenings were too pleasant to sleep through, and for another, there was no night time. It was dark only from about 9:00 p.m. until midnight; then the sun began creeping up again. I found this disconcerting enough, but then I was told that just an hour or so away, in North Sweden, the sun disappeared for six months and was never out of sight for the next six. I had enough trouble adjusting to day and night in Stockholm; I couldn't imagine myself in North Sweden, awake for half the year and sleeping through the balance. Fortunately, when we got back to Paris at the end of our stay in Stockholm, we had a much-needed ten-day rest.

19

Carroll's

Before our rest period in Paris was up, I was hospitalized. It was a frightening malady I'll explain later; the doctors thought it was caused by the irregular hours and rigors of the tour. But the symptoms really scared me: I awoke one morning and couldn't get out of bed.

After a few days in the hospital, I recovered quickly, and two days later I left for Holland with the company. But I was miserable on the long train ride. We arrived in Amsterdam the same evening. I couldn't sleep all night, so I went to a doctor the following morning. He put me in a hospital for proper care, and I remained there for ten days while the company moved on. When I joined them again, everyone was delighted to see how thin I'd gotten. The greatest concern of the Dunham company was gaining or losing weight. I haven't the slightest doubt that had a dancer's right arm fallen off, the left one would have congratulated it for lightening the load.

I was back in form when we returned for six more weeks at the Théâtre de Paris. And it was during this engagement that a friend, Hugh Shannon, came to tell me about a woman named

Frede, who owned a nightclub called Carroll's on Rué de Pantheon, a block off the Champs Elysées.

"She wants to see you," Hugh said.

"Why?"

"Just come with me," he said. "She wants to talk to you. Maybe you'll be interested, maybe not. It's worth a try."

Frede's office, with its large leather chairs and its soft settee, looked more like a lavishly furnished den than a utilitarian theatrical headquarters. Only the desk reminded one that it was a place of business.

There was no one in the room when we entered, so Hugh and I sat down to wait. I felt that something exciting was going to happen. I was both elated and scared.

Our short wait seemed interminable. Finally Frede entered, tall and lean, and apologized very formally in French for the delay. She sat down at her desk, and introductions followed. I was fascinated by her extraordinary good looks. Her dark hair was tinged with gray and bobbed closely, her eyes were green and blue, with a glint of gray, and her tailored suit was beautiful. She sat with her arms resting on the desk top, her hands fondling a pencil, and paused for a moment before she said in English with a very heavy accent, "I saw your show. I wanted to ask if you'd be interested in working here for a while."

I grinned and wrung my hands nervously.

"I don't know what arrangement you make with your company," she said, "but I thought I would talk to you anyway."

I had long been a featured player with the company and had been offered jobs—indirectly—in small clubs, but this was big time, and the offer was being made to me personally, not through Miss Dunham. I looked at Hugh, as though the instructions for handling such a situation would be written on his face. They weren't.

"You don't have to give me an answer now," Frede said. "Think it over."

I said nothing. The prospect of making my first real professional decision was mind numbing. I leaned nervously from one arm of the chair to the other.

"I have a Cuban singer who is leaving in two weeks. I need someone to take her place. When I saw the show, I thought you would be perfect for the job. I cannot encourage you; this is your decision. But one can never progress if one is not seen. You can double. Your curtain's at eleven, and there is time for you to come here and be onstage at twelve-thirty."

I walked into the theater that night with a new kind of pride—proud to be alive, proud of my dancing, proud of me. When I told my roommate, Jackie, what had happened, she was astonished. I put on my makeup in a hurry because I had to talk to Miss Dunham before curtain time. I couldn't wait. In makeup and costume, I knocked on her door.

"Come in," she said.

I entered confidently trying to cover my nervousness, and explained what my visit was about. Then I added, "I'd like to double if I can—to see if I'm capable of being on my own. I have no intention of leaving the company, Miss Dunham."

She told me that in her opinion the prestige of the company would be diminished if its members were to perform anywhere else. Then she added, "However, I think you should speak with our representatives, who are responsible for our being here. See what they have to say. They'll be here tonight, Kitty."

I thanked her and went onstage to warm up. I thought of the songs I'd sing—I knew very few. I'd have to get a dress. And I didn't have music. I had been a member of the herd so long, I was afraid to take my life into my own hands. I gradually gained confidence, thinking, how would I ever know if I didn't have the guts to try? Then I vacillated between fear and confidence. By the end of the first act, fear had won. I began to remember all the advantages of being a member of the Dunham troupe: prestige, professional training, freedom from having to search for a job. I hated the thought of being thrust into the cold world all alone.

As the curtain descended on the first act, I made up my mind that if Miss Dunham didn't want me to take an outside job, I wouldn't. I'd string along as usual and let fate take its course.

After the first act, I was called to a room adjoining Miss Dunham's to see the representative who handled our European tour, an affiliate of a large, international New York-based agency. He talked to me in a gentlemanly manner about my obligation to the agency and to the Dunham company—especially since our most exciting dancer had returned to America and they could not afford to lose me. He stressed the importance of being "loyal to the cause."

Guilt settled over me for even entertaining Frede's suggestion, let alone asking Miss Dunham. The representative told me of the problems entailed in handling such a large company and how they had planned a tour of South America with all expenses paid. I felt ashamed at having thought of deserting the ship when it needed me most.

He kept talking in a way that broke my heart. I felt so badly for my sins that I began crying and picking at my fingernails. "You should be grateful for the opportunity you've had, with complete protection," he said. "I brought you here. Got you working permits. Arranged all the tours. I'm responsible for you."

Then his voice tightened, "If you *dare* accept a job in any part of this country other than with the company," he said, raising his voice, "you will not be able to obtain a working permit and I'll see to it that you never work in Europe again!"

I couldn't believe his last words. I raised my head slowly, looking him dead in the eye. I was hurt, deeply hurt. I hadn't said I was accepting a job—I had asked for permission. Without another word, I ran to my dressing room, wrote out a two weeks' notice, descended for my cue of the second act, and handed the envelope to an attendant, saying, "Please give this to Miss D."

I went on with the show automatically, thinking of all the others who had left and wound up without jobs, or who had married into a life of boredom or who had come back on bended knee. When the final curtain descended, my whole body trembled with fear. But I would not be intimidated! We were called back onstage—the usual procedure after almost every show—and Miss Dunham said softly, "Rosalie, see if you can find someone to take Kitty's place. She has given notice."

A gasp went through the company; all eyes turned to me. I

wondered for a moment if I should repent my sins and be forgiven, but I remembered the representative's threat and quickly put the thought out of mind. Jackie put her arm around me and walked me back to the dressing room. The theater was quieter than usual. Some of the company were meditating, some were rationalizing, some were disbelieving, some were glad. I could feel the various moods in the air.

I left the theater a lost soul and stayed in my hotel room wondering whether I had made a mistake, until the following afternoon when Hugh Shannon dropped by to find out what I had decided to do. We talked for an hour and finally decided to let Frede handle the situation. The thought of not getting working papers and of being deported frightened me.

"I don't believe that," Hugh said. "Frede will know what to do."

Happy to hear of my decision, Frede told me not to worry about the representative's threat. It was simply a matter of paperwork. "Instead of opening in two weeks," she said, "you can open when you like."

"I can't do that," I said. "I really don't have an act or anything to wear."

"I will see that you have proper rehearsals with the Cuban band. You and the leader can get together on ideas; he will help you. Sing the songs you know—four or five should be enough." Then she added, almost casually, "I will pay you ten thousand francs a night."

Ten thousand francs a night. My mind raced to calculate it. That was thirty-five dollars a night, seven nights a week—$245 a week! What a jump from the ninety-five a week I was getting with the company. But then the fear crept back. Where would I be in a month? Frede guaranteed me two months' work, which bolstered my confidence. She advanced me 25,000 francs to buy material for a dress, which I made myself.

With the bandleader's help, my act was as ready in three days as it would ever be—a conglomeration of Afro-Cuban and Black spirituals, ending with a little Cuban dance. I ran from the theater to the club on my opening night. Since Frede had advertised a little, some of the members of the Dunham company were in the audience, even though I had said nothing to them. Hugh Shannon joined me backstage, but didn't help much: He was as nervous as I was. Flowers of encouragement and luck—and a bottle of champagne—were in my dressing room when I arrived, and someone had thoughtfully laid out my gown. My hands were numb as I fumbled my way into the white silk gown I had made. It was strapless, with a drape on one side that was accented by a large pink rose.

I looked at myself in the mirror, thinking that I was suitably attired for a cabaret act. As I was about to go onstage, Frede came in, took one look at me, and said, *"Mon Dieu!* Where do you think you are going like *that?"* Rip went my angelic dress up the left leg to the middle of the thigh. And before I could even protest, I was pushed onstage, the music blaring and the introduction: "Ladies and Gentlemen, we present to you a new discovery, *Miss Eartha Kitt!"*

I became vaguely aware that my name had been announced. I became acutely aware that I was standing in front of people. Alone! It occurred to me that I should either account for my eccentric behavior or excuse myself and leave. It was by pure reflex that my mouth opened and began singing. The song ended. Applause. And a shot of confidence. Another song ended. More applause; not polite applause, but genuine, soul-satisfying applause that told me that I had been accepted. To that point, I think a part of me had been sulking around backstage to avoid blame. If I had bombed, that part of me could have said, "Don't look at me! The mouth did it." But encouraged by the applause, all my senses came back to me by the third number.

At the end of my act, I did a little pelvic-movement of a dance, with a Cuban twist, the hip movements getting smaller and smaller. A shrug of the shoulder brought my act to an end as the spotlight blacked out to more heartwarming applause.

I went back to my dressing room, elated. Frede came back to say how pleased she was and that I had the job for as long as I wanted. Since there was only one show a night at Carroll's for each artist, all my friends, including the few members of the company who had surprised me by coming, went with me to the Café de Paris for a breakfast celebration.

20

Clouds

In Paris, one had to depend largely upon word-of-mouth publicity to be successful, and word-of-mouth was obviously on my side. Frede helped me by placing a lot of ads, too. I was drawing larger crowds as the weeks slipped by, and I was pleased to see celebrities coming in to see my act—even more pleased to see them return to see it again. Frede began treating me more or less like a daughter. She'd stand on the stairs every night like a mother hen to see that everything went smoothly for me, and she saw to it that no one bothered me.

I moved into a little hotel in the Latin Quarter on the Left Bank, to a comfortable and more spacious room. And I made myself very much at home, for my stay was going to be indefinite—maybe even infinite. I had found a home, an appreciative audience, and many friends in Paris. Everything was going my way—everything. I had gained poise and polish as an individual artist, and I thought I need never again experience the terror of being alone in the outside world as a solo artist. It was a euphoric state. And the coming emotional plunge was to be as meteoric as the rise. George Bernard Shaw once lamented that youth was wasted on the young; I had the unbounded optimism of the young. The sky was the limit, and clear blue. There were no dark clouds on the horizon—not my horizon. And even if there had been, the stormiest clouds that nature could gather wouldn't have dampened my spirit. It never crossed my mind that anything could possibly go wrong. That's youth.

We had our neighborhood theatrical hangout where my friends would gather every afternoon. And it was there that my French agent sought me. I was laughing at the jokes and show-business anecdotes my friends were telling me when he walked in, looking worried. I greeted him gaily, trying to raise his spirits, but he approached my chair solemnly and said softly, "Kitty, we just got a call from America—someone named Wayde. They said you should call as soon as possible, that your aunt is ill."

For three days I tried to get a trans-Atlantic call through, to no avail. Finally, Mama Wayde's daughter, Bernice, answered. "Where have you been?" she asked. "We've been trying to reach you for days."

I didn't bother to explain. "How is my mother?" I asked. (I was still calling her mother, as I always had.)

"She kept asking for you," Bernice said. "Why didn't you come home?" There was a pause; the use of the past tense seeped in. Why didn't she say "*keeps* asking for you"? Then Bernice added, "Darling, your mother's been dead since Wednesday."

For a moment I could hear only the mumbling of the cafe patrons and sound of the piano in the background. Wednesday, I thought. Today is Tuesday. Why didn't they tell me sooner that she was ill? Why hadn't I gone home when she had asked me to? I held the phone from my ear, hating its invention, hating the distance between Paris and New York. I wanted to relive the past three years. I wanted to go home, to find my aunt happy, healthy, and waiting for me.

The tinkling of the piano and the laughter—bizarre and out of context, in my emotional state—drifted into the telephone booth, making me conscious of the present. I put the phone to my ear again and heard Bernice saying, "Baby girl, baby girl, are you all right?"

"Yes, I'm all right."

"We'll get money from the insurance people and send you a ticket to come home."

Bernice and Buster Wayde met me at the airport in New York. As my bags were collected, Bernice told me how my aunt had packed an overnight bag one day, paid all her bills, and checked into a hospital in the Bronx. Months before that, my aunt had mentioned by letter that she was going to have an operation, but she had led me to believe that it was nothing serious and that she was going to wait until my return before having it. I had expected to be home earlier, too, but the tour kept being extended far beyond the time any of us thought it would.

We took a cab to the apartment I had first entered upon coming north. Mama Wayde greeted me in grief. Bernice, jabbering on as people will in crises, went into detail about the problems they had faced—how my aunt should be buried, whether the dress should be this or that, whether she should have the service at Salem Methodist Church or have it down South, whether she should be embalmed by this or that under-taker. . . .

I longed for her to stop such agonizing talk of death, but I suppose she couldn't help it; death does distract one from all else. "She wanted you home so badly," Bernice said.

I felt ill at ease, thinking that it was I who had not cared enough. If I had come home, she might still be alive. I would have been with her.

"That hospital!" Mama Wayde said. "They should have known better. She had a tumor in her stomach that should have been taken out years ago! She had high blood pressure too. And when they examined her, they found she had a bad heart. When they asked her if she wanted to have the operation right away or be built up first, she said, 'Right away,' and signed her life away!"

Mama Wayde was mad at the hospital, feeling that they knew my aunt's heart wouldn't take the operation. "They say when someone packs a bag to go into a hospital, they never come back," Mama Wayde said. "She must have known she wasn't coming back—paying all her bills and everything. She even paid her hospital bill in advance."

I pictured my aunt on the boat, seeing me off to Europe. And I remembered one of the last things she had said to me, which I had discounted and which had proved prophetic: "I feel I shall never see you again."

As my aunt had requested, I made arrangements to have her taken south, to be buried at St. Peter's Church, where my mother and grandparents were buried.

21

South Again

I took my aunt's body south by train. There was a crowd of people from the town of North, mostly church people, awaiting our arrival in Orangeburg. I recognized no one as I stepped to the platform and waited for the descent of my aunt's coffin, oblivious of everything around me. It was a sensory return; I could feel it and yet wasn't conscious of occupying time and space there—it was like a bad dream in which the nervous system participates but the body rests unmoved. I vaguely recall a person or two approaching me, and although I didn't want to seem unfriendly I couldn't break through the spell that was over me, couldn't awaken to those around me.

I felt the Orangeburg station, which I hadn't seen since I was eight. And in my mind I could hear the childhood chants: Yella gal, yella gal, yella gal.... The coffin descended, a cold, black soulless box, and I watched the men take hold of it, wondering at the dispassion of their work. But this was a natural function to them. I watched until they put the coffin into a hearse and drove from the station.

I finally managed to break the spell when I was told to get

into a car, which would take me to the house of an aunt—
another of my mother's sisters. She was a stranger, although I
might have seen her as a child. The car was an ancient one that
must have run on prayer alone; the deeply rutted and dusty
backroads rocked, jostled, and jarred us as we crawled our way
to North. I tried to relate to the surroundings, the knolls and
woods and cotton fields and more woods, but time hadn't erased
my bitterness—all bad memories. It was as though I were being
lulled back into an awful nightmare from which I had
awakened.

The car eventually bumped down a narrow path, took a
bend over a creek and into open fields to an incredibly
dilapidated shack—which no doubt would have looked to me
like a haven or a palace in my youth.

A fire was burning in the hearth, its warmth dissipating
through the holes left by missing slats in the floor and through
cracks in the walls and through the croaker sacks in the paneless
windows. I went to bed early; not much more than hellos had
been said. And it's a good thing, for when we did try to talk to
one another the following day, there were great communication
problems. No one understood what I was saying. A simple
northern accent was difficult enough for their ears—my accent
could well have come from another planet as far as they were
concerned.

I rose early and decided to be useful by making breakfast.
In the kitchen I found a strong, round wood-burning stove of a
kind I had kindled countless times as a child; the pots and pans
looked as though they had been taken from my playhouse. I had
donned jeans, and the family stood with perplexed expressions,
watching me get water from the well and chop wood for the fire.
I don't know what they had been told about me, but it was
apparent that they didn't know I had done such things at age
four. Later, a member of the family came over—thinking to
rescue me, I suppose—and when she found me doing chores, she
said, "I came over to see if they were having a hard time entertaining you. You sure are a good sport."

The next day was the funeral. That morning I got up early
to go shopping with my stranger-aunt. "I ain't got nothin' to

wear to a burial," she had said. "The chillin ain't have nothin', too."

I outfitted them all for the funeral. At the same time, I bought school clothes for the children, put in a supply of canned goods that would last a month or so, and gave them $150 in cash.

"You is good," I kept hearing. "You jus' like your aunt."

The husband said, "She came down here once when the church was blowed down and built it up again. Yessir, that's what she done. Nobody forgets her for that."

I listened with pride as the husband and wife discussed my aunt's character, feeling that I was getting to know her even better in death.

We all got dressed, after heating water on the stove and washing in a foot basin. I dressed in a black suit I had brought from Paris. We were ready and waiting for the time to arrive, when Josh White drove up. I had contacted Josh in New York, and he had insisted upon attending the funeral. It was sweet of him, and nice to have a close friend with me.

I sat in the first row, looking at the open coffin. It was draped with a purple veil to hide the discoloration of her body, owing to the long period between death and burial. The little church of St. Peter's was crowded.

"We are gathered together on this unhappy occasion with tears in our hearts . . ." the preacher said.

"Un-*Huh!*" the congregation said in unison.

". . . to pray for the soul that has left us."

"Amen!" the congregation said.

"She was a *good* soul . . ."

"Amen!"

". . .she was a *kind* soul. . ."

"Amen!"

". . .and we *know* she's gone to heaven."

"Hallelujah! Amen! Un-*huh!* Tha's right! Hallelujah!"

"She rebuilt this church!" the preacher said.

"Yeah, she did!"

"She built these pews."

"Yeah, she did."

"She gave us a helpin' hand."

"A-a-a-a-men!"

I listened with both pride and sorrow. I was ashamed of not having been closer to her than I was. She had identified with these souls. In death, this is what she wanted to come back to—to be buried in North, to have them say prayers over her. She never lost contact with them and constantly let them know that she belonged. They were proud of that. They probably knew her better than I did.

They were sincere in their sorrow at the loss of a friend and a benefactor. No more helping hand from the North. Who will rebuild our church when the storm knocks it down? Who will send us city clothes? Who will donate to our school?

The preacher was reaching the end of his eulogy.

"Saint Peter, open your golden gates and let in this lonely soul who asks for forgiveness and for her soul to get cleansed and to be a child of God! Wash her hands . . ."

"Un-*huh!*"

". . . wash her feet . . ."

"Un-*huh!*"

". . . wash her *soul* . . ."

"Un-*huh!*"

". . . accept her in heaven . . ."

"Amen!"

". . . take her by the hand . . ."

"Amen!"

". . . and lead the way . . ."

"Amen!"

". . . glory hallelujah!"

"Amen!"

A song began: "A-a-a-a-men, A-a-a-a-men. . ."

The congregation sang the hymn "Amen" softly as the cries of "Glory be to God" were heard among the mourners. As the singing faded, Josh rose from his seat at the back of the church and walked down the aisle to sing a spiritual in honor of the dead. When he got next to the coffin, a wary and fearful stillness settled over the congregation. Josh was carrying his guitar.

A guitar! A sinful instrument! I didn't know Josh was going

to sing and play, or I could have warned him that the church people considered guitars evil. The mood was killed; I felt ill at ease for Josh, but I couldn't insult him by asking him not to play. This was his contribution, his gift, his tribute to my dead aunt. People looked into their laps for fear of dealing with the devil. Josh sang; he was alone all the way. But I knew that my aunt would have understood.

"Take my hand and lead me on . . ." Josh sang. And at the end of his song, the last soulful and sweet chord from his guitar was still in the air when the rinky-tink sound of the church piano smothered it—"What a friend we have in Jesus. . . ."

The coffin lid was lowered, and I saw my aunt for the last time. Her face was lovely, even in death; her body was still; her soul was gone. Since the first shock and the tears in Paris, I had remained hollow—almost detached from feeling—and dry-eyed, but when they carried her down the aisle past me, to lead the congregation to the churchyard cemetery, the tears began flowing and I couldn't control them.

And then we were in that lonely graveyard where my mother and grandparents were buried, the same graveyard I had fled through late at night when I was getting medicine for the Stern woman, knowing that my mother's spirit would protect me. Such a barren place. The few tombstones had sunken halfway into the ground. There were a few scattered flowers. Most of the graves were bare.

I stood at the head of the opened ground that was to envelop my aunt. I watched them lower her coffin with ropes, watched it sinking slowly into the pit.

"No more! No more!" someone chanted.

"Ashes to ashes and dust to dust," they said, as dirt was sprinkled on the lid of the coffin.

Perhaps it was the chant "No more! No more!" that got me. Or perhaps it was the sickening staccato sound of earth spattering across the lid of the coffin. Either or both triggered an unendurable desperation within me and I screamed, "Don't cover her up! Please don't cover her up. I'll never see her again. Please! Please! Please! Don't cover her up. . . ."

Josh and several others took me from the graveyard and put

me in the car. And it took me days to realize that my aunt was, indeed, no more.

Back in New York, I decided to seek work in my own country rather than return to France. I moved in with a friend and her mother downtown. But after three months of searching for work, I was down to just a few hundred dollars. My aunt had left me $10,000 in insurance, but that had gone fast—and it was a lot of money in 1951. The funeral expenses were exorbitant. Before I had even arrived from Paris, $2,000 had gone for mortuary expenses. And when I went to the funeral home, I was presented with another bill totaling nearly another $2,000. It didn't seem right at all, but I thought it sinful to argue over death money. Then there was the expense of the trip south, as well as the money I had given to people in the South. And although my aunt had settled all her debts before entering the hospital, there were those in New York who felt entitled to certain moneys. Rather than ignore them or haggle with them— these were "friends" of my aunt's who claimed to have helped her at one time or another, not financial help, but help that could be rewarded financially—I paid them.

Anyway, my money was nearly gone, and I finally told the New York affiliate of my French agent that I was going back to Paris.

"No, you can't do that," the agent said. "We're getting you a job."

"Really?" I said. "Where?"

"The Blue Angel."

I was ecstatic. This agent—who kept forgetting my name and who didn't have the faintest idea what it was I did—had been working for me after all. He knew only that I was a draw in Paris, and until I announced that I was leaving *for Paris*, he had ignored me. I thought I had been wrong about him until he told me what kind of job he was getting me. It was really an audition—and one of the worst kind. I was to perform one night at the Blue Angel, and if I was any good I would be given a contract. No advance, no costumes, no music—and an international act that I wasn't even sure would be understood at the Blue Angel.

I was to go in cold on a Saturday night. By Thursday I started to panic. I wasn't sure enough of myself. I couldn't face the possibility of failing in my own country. I chickened out and bought a ticket on the *Queen Elizabeth* bound for France, where I knew I was safe and accepted as an artist. If my first trip to Europe had been depressing, this one could best be described as terrifying. There was no job waiting, no Dunham troupe to depend on, no loving aunt to return home to if my career didn't work out in Europe. I was absolutely alone.

22

Mr. Welles

I had left America on a low note, my self-confidence shaken. And much as a woman will buy a new hat to cheer herself up, as soon as I hit Paris, I indulged myself by registering at the Hotel Gallia, off the Champs Elysées. The rent was far too high, but the elegance was balm for my raw-edged ego.

That afternoon, I began calling friends to let them know I was back. When I called Jessie Hawkins, one of the Dunham dancers, he said, "Orson Welles has been looking all over for you."

"Oh, I'm sure he has," I said, going along with what I took to be Jessie's sense of humor. Then I remembered that Orson Welles had seen me a couple of times at Carroll's. And it wasn't like Jessie to play practical jokes. But what nonsense! The posh Hotel Gallia must be getting to me. "Stop kidding," I said. "Why would he be looking for me?"

"You better call him if you want to find out."

I changed the subject, telling him I'd treat him to dinner at the Chez Inez despite his bad joke. Jessie picked me up later that evening at the hotel, and when we walked into the restaurant,

Inez came over and said, "So you're the little girl Orson's been searching for! You'd better get over to the theater before it's too late."

"I told you so," Jessie said.

The following morning, Jessie picked me up and escorted me to the theater.

"No more casting," the stage manager said.

"But this is the girl Mister Welles has been looking for," Jessie told him.

"Not anymore. The part's been filled. No more casting," the stage manager said, opening the door for us to leave.

We walked in silence into the square before the theater. Even the Hotel Gallia couldn't lift me from the mental depths I had plunged into. Then a cab door slammed, and I heard someone call, "Hey, Miss! Miss! Wait just a moment." We both turned to see a kind-faced gentleman with cane and derby hat hurrying toward us. "What is your name?" he asked, out of breath from his effort.

"This is the girl Mister Welles was. . . ."

"I thought so!" the man interrupted. "Your face is much too interesting for you not to be the girl Mister Welles wanted."

I grinned, and he looked toward the theater, then back at me, and said: "I know, no more casting. But I wish you would come when Mister Welles is here so that we can be sure of our decision. Say tonight at eleven? We'll be atop the theater in the attic room."

I thanked him gratefully, and he tipped his hat and went inside.

The part was cast, I knew, but His Majesty Orson Welles would be quite enough. And one never knew what plays he might be casting in the future. We arrived exactly at eleven; word was sent to Mr. Welles that we were waiting to see him. Moments later, the large, domineering-looking Mr. Welles giant-stepped toward me. I felt the electrifying waves of his personality pass through me as he drew nearer. "Where have you been?" he boomed.

"In America," I said in a voice almost inaudible.

"I thought you were in Scandinavia somewhere! Someone told me you were not to be found."

I wondered where he had inquired. Certainly Frede and most of my friends knew where I was.

"Anyway, here you are. I'm too occupied at the moment, but I'd like you to come and read for me tomorrow night. Can you?"

"Yessir."

"At eleven-thirty. Right here."

"Yessir."

At precisely eleven-thirty the following night, Jessie again escorted me to the theater. We stumbled into its darkness, down three steps, through a dim corridor, up three flights, around a corner, and there sat Mr. Welles alongside the kind gentleman who had hailed us from his cab and who, I learned, was Mr. Hilton Edwards, owner and director of the Gate Theatre in Dublin. It was at the Gate Theatre that Orson had lied his way into a starring role at age seventeen by claiming to be twenty-one and a great American star.

As I walked in, the two greeted me and gave me a chair at a table to read the part of Girl Number Three in a play called *Dr. Faust*. In the play, Girl Number Three is the co-starring role; she's a student as the play opens, then becomes Helen of Troy, then becomes Mary by the time the curtain descends. Confusing, yes. That was Orson Welles.

Orson kept his back to me, seated at first, then pacing the floor all during the reading. When I began, Mr. Edwards started to direct me.

"Leave her alone!" Orson said.

I read: "I couldn't think that God would create a man such as you."

"That's fine."

I kept reading, and reading, and reading, for what seemed like hours, progressing from youth to old age. Finally, Orson said, "All right, I don't know what we'll do about the other girl. As far as I'm concerned, you've got the part. Be here tomorrow at one for rehearsals. I'll have a script for you then."

His words struck me like a truck—with the resultant shock one experiences at such an impact: no feeling. I was perfectly calm. My spirit could have leaped the Eiffel Tower—and probably did that night—but my mind and body went back to the hotel in a daze.

The following morning, the shock wore off and I became a five-foot-two nerve ending. Girl Number Three was *the* part. I was to have scenes alone with Orson Welles—just the two of us on stage together. I'd believe *that* when it happened. Three hours until rehearsal. I dressed in my best and decided to walk to the theater—a good forty-five minutes away—hoping that would alleviate some of my tenseness. It was incredible. No singing or dancing. Straight acting. With Orson Welles! Walk...

Orson handed me a script when I arrived. "Can you learn fast?" he asked. "We open Saturday."

It was Tuesday. A major part. Onstage for the entire hour of a play that was to open on Saturday. And it was Tuesday! Thinking back on it, it was the best thing that could have happened to me. There was no time to think of my aunt, no time to think of anything but *Dr. Faust*.

All knew their parts, as I read mine. The stage manager directed me as well as he could. Fortunately, memorizing scripts comes easily to me. After the first rehearsal, Mr. Welles and I and one or two others remained to paint scenery or to go over our lines alone. Sometimes, during the rest of that short week, we stayed on stage until the wee hours of the morning repeating lines to each other.

"The word is *world*!" Orson would shout at me.

"I said *world*!"

"Speak as though you came from New York."

"I *did* come from New York. How does one from New York speak?"

"Not the way *you* speak!"

"Why should I talk like someone special?"

"Because you are."

"Yes, but I don't want you to be conscious of it."

"You win."

The rehearsal would go smoothly for another fifteen

minutes or so, then Orson would stop and say, "Why can't you speak English? You know so many other languages that you can't even speak your own."

"What's wrong with my English?"

"It's too *clear!*" he'd yell. "You don't sound as though you came from *anywhere*. Everyone sounds as though he comes from somewhere. But *you?* No!"

We got along well together, for I took his direction faithfully, and there were no problems—except for my English. The genius, strong character and vibrant personality of Orson Welles wasn't taken with a grain of salt—there was too much pepper to contend with. He could not tolerate ignorance of any kind. And if one was not quick enough, Orson lost patience. The quicker one was to receive what Orson had to give, the better his creative powers were.

Mr. Edwards worked with the rest of the cast, while Orson worked with me. I think he was pleased with me in many ways, for he didn't direct me too much; he allowed me to bring much of my own interpretation to the part. Whenever I made a wrong move, he would patiently explain the character I was portraying. One day I asked him, "What kind of a woman am I?"

"All kinds."

"How old am I?"

"All ages."

"What period of time am I supposed to be living in?"

"All periods."

At dinner time I was sometimes taken with Mr. Edwards to eat at Orson's favorite restaurant, where I was introduced to gastronomic delicacies and heard extraordinary tales and conversations.

On nights when we left the theater very late, Orson and I would walk along the Champs Elysées in silence. The sun would be coming up, and Paris would unveil herself. Paris was warm and fresh and quiet in the early morning as we strolled along her majestic boulevard to my hotel. Orson would take me to the door, ring the bell, and say, "A demain."

Opening night came. We had been in the theater all day for the last-minute touches. The curtain went up on the first half of the evening, a play Orson had written entitled *The Unthinking Lobster*, a satire on Hollywood, which I thought very funny but which few others liked. The second hour of the evening was *Dr. Faust*.

As it turned out, I was called upon to sing a little theme song in the play—once at the play's opening, and two more times in the course of the hour. It was a haunting little song: "Hungry little trouble, damned in a bubble, yearning to be, be or be free, all that you see is about me." Words by Orson Welles, music by Duke Ellington.

We took about ten curtain calls when the play ended. The audience response was so enthusiastic that we were sure it was a hit, but the decision would be in the hands of the drama critics. The next day, all the Paris papers were kind to me: "The most moving voice in the world." "Orson Welles discovers great talent." "Eartha Kitt great find for Paris. . . ."

In all the papers were pictures of Orson and me. I even won second place in the talent poll for the year 1951—an exceptional honor for a foreigner, and a neophyte at that. People from Carroll's came to the theater to ask if I'd be interested in returning. I told them that I would be, but that I'd have to wait until the play was on the way. They returned a day or two later; again I gave them the same reply. But apparently Frede wanted a more definite commitment, so she sent them around a third time. Orson lost his patience and threw them out of the theater. "Get out of here and leave her alone," he said. "She'll open when I let her!"

A week after the play opened, Orson gave me permission to double at Carroll's. My good reviews and ever-increasing celebrity had increased my worth to Carroll's considerably; I was given a substantial raise. I had become what is called in France a vedette, or star, and I was well on my way to being anything I wanted to be.

A clash between Orson and Josh White was narrowly avoided one night. Josh was in Paris and came to see the play, sitting in the front row. Orson was not himself that night. Either he was feeling his oats a little more than usual or he resented something I had done unwittingly. The scene called for him to envelop me in his a ms and say, "Helen, make me immortal with a kiss." Only this time, Orson sank his teeth into my lower lip, drawing blood and bringing me almost to tears. I could not move in his death grip, and I couldn't breathe for an uncomfortable length of time. Then he threw me aside and exited as I walked into another scene. I dabbed furtively at my lip and saw blood; moments later my lip began to swell.

When the final curtain kissed the platform, I lunged at the giant, pounding his chest with both fists and trying to scream above the audience applause, "Why did you bite me?"

I was still pounding on him when he tired of it, brushed me aside like a troublesome gnat, and said, "Oh, I was just in the mood."

After the show, I joined Josh at a sidewalk cafe just a block from the theater. Josh, who had been eyeing my swollen lip, finally asked, "What happened to you?"

I knew better than to tell him the truth, for Josh had always been over-protective of me. "I fell into a wall," I said, quite convincingly. But one of the cast, who was seated at a nearby table and who thought the incident very funny, said, "Orson bit her."

Josh had jumped to his feet and was running down the street before any of us had a chance to think about restraining him. He reached the theater just as Orson, in his chauffeur-driven Citröen, was being driven up a one-way street against traffic. Josh came back panting, and ordered me to stay away from Orson off stage. Knowing Josh's temper, I kept a low profile while he remained in Paris, sorely missing the backstage clowning and camaraderie that drives boredom from the task of saying the same lines over and over night after night.

I never knew what mood Orson was in until the moment of the kiss each performance; if it was gentle, then I knew his day had gone well. And though he never again bit me, there were times when the pressure of Orson's kiss was enough to crush a coconut. However, Orson was a delight to work with, because one never knew what he was going to do onstage. He was irrepressible. Often, when his back was turned to the audience, he'd make faces at me, trying to break me up. I remember one night in particular when the tables were turned on Orson. Actress Janet Wolfe—always a delight—came onstage during a mob scene and instead of delivering her line, "He's a horrible man, your husband," said, "He's a horrible *ham*, your husband!" Orson was surprised and delighted. The mood having been set, *Dr. Faust* became a comedy for the rest of the evening.

After a six-week run in Paris, we went to Germany. My new-found celebrity preceded me wherever we went. The show was cut—the parts of the three girls were written into one character, which I played—and retitled *An Evening with Orson Welles*, which some Germans retitled *An Evening with Eartha Kitt*. It evolved into a peanut concert; the first half was *Dr. Faust*, followed by a second-curtain opening of Orson's magic act, after which he introduced me with adjectives that I always feared I couldn't live up to, and I would sing for fifteen minutes. Then at third curtain opening, Orson did a scene from *Richard III* to end the evening.

The tour started in Frankfurt, where we made a side trip to entertain American soldiers at a nearby camp, then moved on to Hamburg, Munich, and Berlin. Munich became one of my favorite cities. My days were spent being shown the town by newspaper people, who did not fail to include lunch at the beer hall where Hitler was supposed to have given most of his speeches at the beginning of his fiendish political career.

Berlin was exciting; I was introduced to German theater, which I found marvelous. Since this was before the Berlin Wall, only posted signs separated East from West. They were written in several languages: "You are now in Russian territory," or "Long live Stalin," or "Here begins the true democracy." The "true democracy" of East Berlin showed little sign of life. In going across the invisible boundary, I saw few except Russian soldiers on the streets. It looked terribly sterile to me, and it felt like a world without God.

I was terribly curious to see what the Russians looked like up close, so when Orson and I visited a monument in honor of the Russian soldier, which was in the British sector but guarded by the Russians, I climbed the twelve or so steps and found myself eye to eye with a tiny Russian soldier. I stared at him. He looked back at me, quizzically, as though saying to himself, "What the hell is *this?*" But he held tightly to the rifle crossing his body and stared straight ahead—at me, because I was just inches away from him and studying him as though he were an inanimate work of sculpture.

It was against regulations for the soldier to move. If he was annoyed, there was a push button near his elbow. Although he looked as though he wanted to do something about me, he seemed more curious than upset.

"He's no bigger than I am," I said to Orson.

I suppose my scrutiny of the young soldier made him feel like an insect under a microscope. I finally quit my study and joined Orson, who had walked on.

Our tour was to end in Belgium, where we performed for ten days. That final night in Brussels was most uncomfortable. Orson gave a farewell cocktail party at his place, and we all sat around wordlessly, just looking at each other. We were all sorry to see the show close, but it couldn't go on forever.

23

Other Exotic Places

Upon my return to Paris from Brussels in September 1951, I was again stricken with the same illness I referred to in Chapter 19. When I wrote my first autobiography nearly twenty years ago, it was taboo to speak candidly of such subjects as female disorders. But that's what mine was. And while I don't wish to dwell on the subject, it's sufficiently important to a later episode in my career to describe the nature and effect of the illness in terms other than the euphemistic "exhaustion."

This time, again, it was a menstrual problem that resulted in a massive loss of blood, exhaustion, anemia, great weight loss, and all the other side effects one can expect from such a disorder. In each case, my normal cycle would begin, but the flow of blood would increase and the cycle would last from three to six weeks. And in each case, the only cure was complete bed rest. Actually, I had no alternative, for the condition left me so weak I couldn't stand, let alone dance, sing, or act.

I have never learned what caused the disorder. I was afflicted with it only three times. But it occurred the last time at a critical phase of my career and was reported as "exhaustion," leading a number of people to speculate that I had "feigned illness" to get out of a play. That's a terrible stigma for a performer, one that's bothered me ever since. I had to live with it, though, because in the 1950s, talk of vaginal bleeding was taboo—and certainly wouldn't be trumpeted to the press.

So after I recovered from my second bout with hemorrhaging, I went to see Frede, who had sent word that she was opening a new club and wanted me to reserve my services for its opening. She told me that the club would open in a week or so. Anxious to get started, I began preparing a new act and bought clothes for it. I had no money coming in and my hotel bill had been mounting since my illness. When, the day before the club was to open, I had not heard from Frede I went to see her.

"It will open in a week," she said. "We are having troubles."

The opening time stretched from one week to two, then to three, and my anger began rising as high as my bills. I built up my fury to temper-tantrum proportions and burst into Carroll's like Hurricane Eartha. I found Frede in the bar, and to show her that I meant business, I threw my coat to the floor and demanded a week's pay to compensate for the work I had lost while waiting for her. I also threatened to work elsewhere.

"Don't accept another contract," Frede said. "We will open any day now."

"I won't wait any longer," I yelled. "My expenses have gotten too high waiting for you."

I could tell from Frede's casual attitude that she thought she could talk me into waiting a little longer, so to impress her with my anger, I picked up a chair and threw it into a corner of the barroom. "You've made me wait three weeks without any money coming in!" I said. "I must eat in order to be alive when your club opens. I demand 100,000 francs to pay my bills, or I accept another contract."

"Oh, Kitty, Kitty," Frede said. "Don't lose your temper. I will give you fifty thousand."

"One hundred thousand!" I screamed. "I could have been working by now. I don't believe that place will ever open. I won't leave until I get what I asked for!"

Frede retreated to her office for half an hour. When she returned, she handed me an envelope containing 100,000 francs.

The following Friday, the new Perroquet opened. Every celebrity in town was there. I played the cabaret for a while, then went back to Carroll's for a two-week engagement before accepting an offer from London. When I returned to Paris from London, my agent had offers from all over the world—including one luring bid from Turkey. I had a strong urge to return to America, but got cold feet and rationalized that Turkey and Greece were exotic places that I might never again have an opportunity to visit. So I decided to delay my homecoming a little longer.

My tour began in London at a club called Churchill's, where I was received with great enthusiasm and was made very happy by the thoughtful owner. The club was frequented by royalty and other important figures, many of whom became friends. When my engagement ended, I took a plane back to Paris, where I spent a few days before continuing to Istanbul.

Friends in Paris thought I was crazy for accepting the offer from Turkey. "No one hears of you in Istanbul," one of them said, meaning that the engagement couldn't possibly advance my career—on the theory that if I was a smash, only the Turks would know.

"I don't care about that," I said. "My main interest is to go there." And as it turned out, my engagement there not only was self-fulfilling (the dream of a little cotton picker from the South traveling to the exotic East), but it also contributed to my career a few years later when I recorded a Turkish song that became very popular.

The flight to Istanbul took seventeen hours and we made many stops along the way. The world became stranger to me the farther East I went: the language became more tongue-twisting; the eyes narrowed; the cheekbones became more prominent, and the hair and skin darkened.

At a fairly modern airport outside Istanbul, I was met by two representatives of the Karavansary, the club where I was to appear. Neither spoke English but one of them spoke French, so we had no difficulty communicating. One presented me with a bouquet of flowers while the other took my baggage tickets. They saw me through customs and then took me by car to my hotel. In front of the hotel waiting for me were the Nicholas brothers, Fayard and Harold, whom I had known since my early Dunham days in New York and who were appearing in another room at the Karavansary. I jumped from the cab and threw my arms around them. What a delight it was to see familiar faces in such a faraway land.

The Nicholas brothers accompanied me to the hotel to see that I was comfortable and to give me a few hints as to the do's and don'ts in Turkey. I was to open the following evening, but since Fayard and Harold were working the evening of my arrival, I decided to tag along and look over the club.

While we waited on the sidewalk for a cab, I was chattering away about our times in New York when Harold directed my attention to the fact that people were gathering around us in increasingly large numbers and staring at us as though we were from another planet. Then we realized that they were all staring at me, and with a good measure of awe.

"Funny, we never had that happen before," Fayard said. "It must be because you're a strange-looking woman." I thought he meant it as a joke, so I laughed. But I later realized that he wasn't joking. I was happy to get into the cab and away from the crowd; it was a disconcerting experience.

As we entered the club, I got the same reaction from the patrons. All eyes were upon me as we walked through. A table in the balcony was reserved for artists every evening, so I joined the people seated there to watch the show. The moment I could be seen from below, all eyes went up to me. And I wondered all kinds of things about myself. I was dressed no differently from many of the women I had seen. So it wasn't my clothes; it had to be me. I wondered if they thought me weird, exotic, funny, mysterious, ugly, beautiful, or what? I learned not to be surprised by anything in the weeks that followed. And my opening night was the first lesson.

As I stood onstage at a pencil microphone, the room went dead silent. Ordinarily I would have thought this the reaction of a very pleased and attentive audience, but I sensed that something was wrong. Not a cough. No rustling of clothing as people got comfortable. Absolute silence. The music began, and I sang. Halfway through my song, a soft whispering began. A few bars later, the whispering built to a murmuring. They were talking as I was performing. All of them! My hands began perspiring. I wanted to walk offstage, but I stayed with the song and went immediately into the second one. Talk about bravery!

The second song was a French one. Again the murmuring began—until a loud male voice, speaking in Turkish, boomed out at the audience from stage left. The murmuring stopped. I kept singing, thinking that someone had told the audience to shut up, but as I finished a phrase, the voice said something in Turkish, and the crowd roared with laughter. I sang another phrase; the voice cut in at the end of it, and the crowd laughed again. I looked toward the door in search of consoling eyes—where were the Nicholas brothers? It continued throughout my second song: the voice went on; the crowd roared; I persevered.

It seemed the longest song I had ever sung in my life. When it ended, there was thundering applause—apparently for the comedian who had mocked me throughout the number—and I walked quickly off the stage and past the tables toward the door that led to safety. Mr. Kibar, the owner, was standing in my way.

"You don't have to tell me," I said. "Just give me my ticket back to Paris where I belong. I won't even ask to be paid, just the ticket."

"What are you *talking* about?" Mr. Kibar said. "They *love* you! They talked all through your songs."

I looked at him for a moment, thinking: They love me. "That's why they *talked* all through my songs?" One of us had definitely gone mad, and I was sure it wasn't me.

"That was to show they were complimenting you," he said. "Can't you hear the applause? They want you back."

"But that horrible man . . . ?"

"He was telling them that you could do no wrong, that you are beautiful, and he wishes he were fortunate enough to have you, to take care of you. Go back and finish your act."

Much to my relief, the vocal "compliments" had run their course and I was able to finish my act in peace. When I finished, Mr. Kibar asked me to make the rounds; I was introduced to practically everyone in the audience, and they were charming. They returned to the club time and time again. In Istanbul, when the people like you, they become ardent and even fanatical supporters. To show my appreciation, I learned several Turkish songs and incorporated them into my act. One of them was "Uska Dara," which I later recorded with great success in America.

It was about two weeks later that I learned why I was causing so much commotion whenever I appeared in public. When I first arrived, someone—I think it was one of the escorts who met me at the plane—cautioned me never to go into the streets alone. I didn't think to ask why; I just assumed that perhaps there were muggers in the streets (which was not at all the case). And in the first couple of weeks, my days were spent sightseeing with the Nicholas brothers. Whenever I decided to go somewhere and the Nicholas brothers were otherwise occupied, an escort was always furnished me—which I thought a courtesy, not a precaution.

Signals got crossed, though, when the Nicholas brothers' engagement in Istanbul ended and I saw them off at the airport. On my way back to the hotel by cab, I decided to go on a shopping spree. I discharged the cab and began walking, peeking into the shops along the way. To my astonishment, traffic became snarled and finally stopped, doorways became jammed with people, and passersby began mobbing me. Some dropped to their knees and tried to kiss the hem of my skirt and my feet. Others, who couldn't get to my skirt hem or feet, touched me, felt my clothes, stroked my hair. Men and women were flocking from nowhere; the crowd got larger and larger, making it impossible for me even to walk. And although no one was trying to do me harm, I became mystified, then terrified, as perhaps forty or fifty people surrounded me, all trying to touch me or wrestling with one another to kneel at my feet.

I was on the verge of becoming hysterical; the whole world around me had gone mad. Then a stranger came charging into the crowd, yelling at them in Turkish—apparently ordering them to disperse—and grabbed me by the arm. He shoved his way through the crowd, put me into his car, and drove me back to the hotel. I had never seen him before, nor did I ever see him again. And the most bizarre part of the incident was that he didn't speak one word to me from the time he pulled me from the crowd until he dropped me off. I had thanked him for helping me. No reply. I had asked him why the people had mobbed me like that. Eyes straight ahead as he drove, as though I weren't even in the car with him. And I didn't even tell him the name of my hotel; he just took me there. He knew.

That evening I was taken to the opera by a Turkish family I had met socially. I told Aykut, the head of the family, about my strange experiences, about people gathering around to look at me when I was escorted, and about how they had mobbed me when I had gone shopping alone. Aykut said that I should have been informed: From the moment I had entered the city, the Turks had thought me an Egyptian princess. Kibar verified this later. "As a matter of fact," Kibar said, "I thought the same thing when I first saw you at Carroll's in Paris."

As to the mysterious man who had rescued me from the admiring crowd, I may have stumbled across what he was, if not who. In casual conversation, one of the escorts assigned to me by the Karavansary told me that he was a member of the secret police and that members of his department had followed me for two weeks because I had dated the son of the Admiral of the Turkish Navy. I had no doubt that he was telling the truth, for he told me every move the son and I had made on every date. That would account for the mystery man who had whisked me away from the crowd. If so, it must have been terribly embarrassing for him. No wonder he didn't speak to me. There we were, riding together in his car, while he was supposed to be following me undetected. Secret police, indeed!

Turkey was wonderful, but I grew homesick. And I had never felt farther from home than when I picked up the phone one day at the hotel and said, "I'd like to make a long-distance call."

"Yes. Where to, Miss?"

"New York."

I nearly fell out of my chair when the operator replied, "I'm sorry, Miss, but one cannot call America from here."

Turkey works in mysterious ways. I had been at the club for two weeks or so when I received a letter informing me that I was being sued by the Turkish government for illegal entry. I had come as a tourist and had obtained work, which was against the law. I didn't know what the government was talking about. No one had told me that I was entering the country as a tourist.

Off to court I went at nine in the morning with an attorney. "Don't worry about a thing," he said. "This is the regular procedure."

"You mean this is the way you get artists into the country?"

"It's the only way we can do it. They expect it. No matter what the judge says, say yes."

We waited for more than an hour for our case to be called. Nine in the morning for a club entertainer is like four or five for a person with normal working hours. I was half-asleep. Turkish words flew back and forth between the lawyer and judge for fifteen minutes. Then silence. More words. Finally the lawyer took his coat and hat, helped me with mine, and took me back to the hotel. "Meet you at eight-thirty in the morning," he said as he left me in the lobby. "The case isn't over yet."

Back to court the following morning. I had worked into the wee hours as usual that morning and had gotten even less sleep than the night before—a fitful, worried sleep—for I was sure that, despite the lawyer's assurances, they were going to put me on a Turkish chain gang. More Turkish words between judge and lawyer. More silence. More heated words, it seemed to me, then the judge finally addressed his remarks to me as my attorney interpreted. I was reprimanded strongly and sent back to my hotel with a work permit—after being fined five dollars for being a bad girl.

Then there was the problem of getting out of Turkey. When my engagement ended, Kibar asked me if I would stay for six months. I told him no, but the engagement was extended anyway. I needed a certain paper to get out of Turkey, a paper that should have been presented to me the day I requested it. It wasn't. I later learned that an admirer with considerable influence was trying to keep me in the country. It was only at the intercession of Mr. Constantino, owner of the club in Athens where I was scheduled to appear after my engagement in Istanbul, that I was finally given the piece of paper ten days later.

My engagement in Athens was a wonderful experience. It was decided that I should present an act suitable for the club's clientele—all the old standard American songs that everyone knew and loved. The Americans who frequented the club were glad to have a reminder of home. And I was glad to put together a less Continental act, one suitable for American clubs, for I had decided to return home after our tour.

After I closed in Athens, I went back to Paris for a few days, then on to London, the last engagement of my European tour before going home. Europe had been good to me; its people had given me the opportunity of developing my art as a dancer, singer, and actress—I even starred in two foreign films that have never been shown in America—and the audiences were marvelous. But there's no thrill comparable to being recognized as a worthy artist in one's own country. Indeed, there's no place like home.

There is one sad postscript. While I was in Europe, Philippe had proposed marriage to me a number of times, and each time I had refused him. But I loved him dearly as a friend and told him so. Meanwhile, he had gone into the French army and was put on orders for overseas duty. He made a date with me on the eve of his departure, and after walking for two or three hours, he came to the point: He wanted me to wait for him; he wanted to marry me when he was discharged from the service, and he asked me to wait.

Under the circumstances, I didn't have the heart to tell him that the chemistry wasn't there, that I didn't think a marriage would work between us. I told him again that I loved him as a friend, as a brother, but he insisted that he could change my mind if I'd only wait. The only commitment I could bring myself to make in truth was that I had no intention of marrying while he was gone. He said he would be satisfied, knowing that.

Shortly thereafter Philippe was killed fighting with the United Nations forces in Korea.

24

An American Flop

There was nothing set for me in America. But Ed Robbins, a friend from school who had become an artists' representative with a major agency, had kept in touch, asking me to let him know when I could come to New York. A number of clubs were interested because of my European reputation—which had crossed the Atlantic with New Yorkers and other Americans who had seen me perform.

I reached New York on the *Queen Elizabeth*, nearly broke. Before coming home, I'd spent a few weeks in Paris saying goodbye to friends and being too generous and living too grandly for my pocketbook. But mostly I had depleted my savings by helping less fortunate friends who had gotten into one financial scrape or another. The idea of returning without a definite commitment, and without enough money to sustain me for very long if I had to move into a hotel, was frightening. My first call when I arrived was to my friend Roxie Foster, who had dared me into auditioning for Katherine Dunham and who had always been my number one cheerleader. What an enormous relief it was when Roxie came on the line and said, "Come on home. We're waiting for you."

I moved in with Roxie and her mother, and within a day or two an audition was arranged for me at La Vie en Rose, where I met the agency representatives and Monty Proser, who wanted to give me a contract. The agency made the arrangements. Opening night was set for December 11, 1951.

Things went smoothly. My Parisian gowns were worn to a frazzle. I needed new ones, and Roxie made them for me—she still makes many of my gowns, and we still get together whenever I'm in New York. Meanwhile, the agency started a very clever ad campaign to publicize a "new sensation," first time in America. The ad said: "Learn to say Eartha Kitt." It ran in New York papers for ten days, up to the opening day, with the print getting larger each day until the final day, when it said in huge bold letters: EARTHA KITT.

It was a very clever ad. I was told that people were talking about it because it was so unusual. And they were saying such things as: "What's an Eartha Kitt?" "Is it a liquor of some kind, or a product?" There was even a rumor that it was "a Continental singer who doesn't know a word of English." It was scary enough to be opening on home grounds, but that ad was really getting to me when I realized that it was causing people to expect something so "different."

During rehearsal one day at the club, Mr. Proser asked, "How many languages can you sing in?"

"Seven," I said.

"Then sing in seven languages."

As a result, my program was made up of German, Spanish, Turkish, French, African, English, and Italian songs. And as I ran through them with the Cuban drummer and the club's trio, people kept coaching me to "be sexy," which meant to them pelvic movements of all sorts. Mr. Proser was staging me, somebody else planned the choreography, and the agents were telling me how to sing. I followed their suggestions and orders without question. All of them were involved with American show business, and I thought that they surely must know better than I what an American audience wanted to see. It was certainly different. No doubt about that.

Opening night arrived. The room was packed. My nerves

were shot. And I was too numb to feel anything. I was putting everything on the line—in my own country and on my own stomping grounds. To me, this would prove whether I was good or not. Proof was success at home. I don't even remember descending from my upstairs dressing room. Suddenly I was walking across a dimly lit stage in a darkened room, and I began my act.

There was a blonde seated at ringside whose reactions told me how my act was going, and she was seated so close to me that I couldn't avoid her opinion. It changed with each song. During the first foreign song, she leaned back in her chair. The next language, she slumped. Another, she folded her arms, her face impassive. Still another, she looked at the man who sat with her. My English song took her by surprise. The German one made her exclaim, "Now, *really!*"

I knew I was a flop before I went into my last song, which was Afro-Cuban. I felt like a multilingual Christian being fed to the lions. And I knew that I wasn't the "different, new sensation" the ads had been promising when I heard the blonde say loudly to her escort, "She's just another nigger!"

I walked offstage after my one and only bow. I wanted to cry, but I couldn't find a strong enough reason. I was too scared to show anyone that I knew, and I refused to feel sorry for myself until I was alone. A few friends came in: "How wonderful you were!"

Why do they say that? I thought.

Roxie came in and took a chair without a word. After my room was emptied of the few who came to see me, Roxie said, "You weren't you, Kitty." I knew what she meant, but how could I find myself? I was too frightened and confused to know who the real me was anymore.

The thought of having to do a second show that night almost petrified me. I almost prayed for something dreadful to happen—anything to keep me from having to do another show. But I made up my mind it had to be done. One can will oneself into almost anything if the desire is strong enough. I was ashamed to face the public and, most of all, those who had hired me, those who had had great expectations and confidence in me. How could I have failed them?

My performance for the second show was a little better. I had gone on stage in a semiconscious state and was therefore more relaxed. But it still was not what I was capable of doing. After the performance, I went downstairs into the club to meet some of the celebrities who had come to see the advertised "sensation."

Judy Garland made a special effort to console me. How warm she was to talk to. And how comforting her words. "You'll be all right," she said. "You're afraid now, but you'll find your way." Artie Shaw, who sat at the same table, said, "You've got something. I don't know what it is, but you've got it." Kay Thompson also gave me encouragement that night. "Look for your own path," she said.

I accepted the fact that I was a flop. I didn't read the reviews to find out how much of a flop. The fact I knew; the degree wasn't important. Thinking back on it now, I know that I had placed too many chips on the opening. I was all, or I was nothing—no good. And it occurs to me now that perhaps the La Vie en Rose engagement was the one time in my career that I left Eartha Mae backstage, cowering in the dressing room from the incredible pressure I had put upon myself. Maybe only half of me was out there: poised, polished, technically proficient—but hollow. Perhaps Eartha Kitt is the instrument and Eartha Mae the heart and soul that lends the necessary depth and dimension. Maybe that's what Roxie sensed but couldn't analyze when she had said, "You weren't you, Kitty." Perhaps she was saying, in effect, that only half of me was appearing at La Vie en Rose.

For the next five days, I went through absolute hell trying to fulfill my obligations. Whenever I was alone, I exuded self-pity: no home, no mother, no aunt, no money—and a flop! It pained me to know that everyone in New York knew I was a failure. Who would give me a job? I felt sure that it was back to the factories. My confidence was so shattered that even going back to Europe was out of the question.

Each night onstage I insulated myself. I saw nothing. I felt nothing. I was ashamed to look at the owners' faces; therefore, I never saw them. I'm sure they were there all the time, but I honestly didn't see them. One night I was going through my act automatically, until the last song. I haven't the faintest idea what happened. All I know is that I suddenly found myself on the floor. And I scrambled to my feet still singing, like a veteran prizefighter who, knocked nearly unconscious, bounces from the canvas and continues purely on reflex.

I ended the song, walked offstage and sat down, too emotionally upset to cry. I felt as though there were needles sticking in my heart, as though I were being punished. And I had a sudden overwhelming hatred for show business. It wasn't for me. I wanted out.

The producer, Marshall Edgar, came to me. "How do you feel?" he asked.

"I can't describe how I feel."

"Well, you better do something about that chin."

"Chin? What about my chin?" I felt my face. There was a piece of flesh hanging from it. Blood was dripping on my white satin gown. Had I done this deliberately, to escape? I knew that the only reason I hadn't been fired was because no one wanted to hurt my feelings. How could I possibly have fallen face down without reacting to protect myself? How could my chin have hit the floor without some other part of my body hitting first and cushioning the fall?

I was taken to the hospital within the hour, and six stitches were sewn into my chin. My agent, Eddie, and the stage producer waited for me, and when I came out, they laughed to keep me in good spirits. "Can you work tomorrow?" Eddie asked.

"I'll try."

The next night, I removed the bandage, put makeup over the stitches, and went onstage. Because of the swelling and pain, my mouth wouldn't open very far, but I did my shows. Two days later my contract was cancelled. What had been my American dream had become an American flop. I had taken it on the chin in more ways than one.

25

Reflections

I was driving through Harlem in my huge white Cadillac with black upholstery. My mink stole was thrown casually over one shoulder, and I was deliriously happy. All my friends were crowded into the car. We joked and laughed. We were carefree and prosperous—living each moment to the fullest.

The daydream continued until my eye shifted from the white Cadillac to one of a different color on the Broadway showroom floor, but I was distracted by my own reflection in the window, and embarrassed by it too: straggly hair, dungarees, and a jacket. I looked the part of a bedraggled orphan, a victim of the La Vie en Rose war. But defiance rose in me for a moment, and I pretended that it didn't matter—until I noticed the reflection of a man approaching, standing behind me and a little to the side, and looking into the showroom. The face was familiar, and I remember hoping he didn't know me. Please, I prayed, don't let him know me. And in the reflection I saw the familiar face turn toward me; I knew the face well but I couldn't connect it with a name—perhaps I didn't want to, for I was a flop and the last thing in the world I wanted was to be recognized. No, I said to myself. Please, no.

"Miss Kitt?"

I turned toward him but avoided looking into his eyes. It was a face from the past, so out of context that I couldn't place it. But I was trapped. "Yes?" I said.

He had taken his hat off. "I want you to know that I was at La Vie en Rose on your opening night, and I know how you must feel because I have read about it. And I want you to know that I think you're a wonderful artist, and you mustn't give up. Your turn will come again, and it will not be as difficult as you're finding it now," he said.

I was astonished to hear such praise, and I kept trying desperately to think who he was. I kept thinking, he thinks *you're* wonderful? *You?* But I found myself saying, "Thank you. I wasn't as I would like to have been." And then I mumbled: "But I'm glad that I managed to please you—if I did at all . . . ."

"Which way are you going?"

"Uptown."

"I'll walk you to Fifty-ninth Street," he said.

I don't remember our conversation, just casual small talk, I suppose. And all the while I kept trying to remember his name. Apparently he sensed this, for when we reached Fifty-ninth and Broadway and he bade me *adieu*, he turned to me for a moment and—almost as an afterthought—said, "Oh, by the way, my name is Jose Ferrer," and was gone.

He had done it again. Jose Ferrer wasn't embarrassed to be seen walking and talking with me on Broadway. And he had said I was wonderful, that I had brought him joy with my work! On the corner of Fifty-ninth and Broadway, my spirit began to soar, I didn't hate show business any longer. If Jose Ferrer said I was wonderful, then there was hope. How incredible it was that the man who had inspired me to enter show business (how long had it been since I had seen him as Cyrano de Bergerac—five, six years?) should suddenly enter my life for a few minutes and rekindle the inspiration when my career was at its lowest ebb!

So the inspiration was there again. And hope. Maybe I could pull myself together: maybe I could prove my worth again. But where did one begin? Especially after flopping in spectacular fashion at a place like La Vie en Rose.

My agents were no help at all. After La Vie en Rose, I didn't have the nerve to visit the agency in person. Finally, when I needed money for rent, I called the agency to ask if I could borrow twenty-five dollars. "What is your name again?" the secretary asked.

"Eartha Kitt."

"How do you spell that?"

I told her, and she put me on hold. The agent I was calling wasn't in, and they couldn't seem to find anyone who had heard of me. Okay, it was a big agency, but I *had* opened at La Vie en Rose with a good deal of promotion. And if nothing more, they should have remembered the bad reviews. Perhaps they did. Perhaps they didn't want to know me. They finally found someone who recognized my name, and I was told that I couldn't borrow anything. I never saw the agency people again, until I had secured work without them and they came around for their percentage of my earnings.

Shortly thereafter, though, I got a call from Virginia Wicks, a publicity girl whom I'd met a few days before I opened at La Vie en Rose. She worked for the club and had done some of the publicity for me. "Would you be interested in working the Village Vanguard?" she asked. "It's not La Vie en Rose, but I thought you might be interested. It's up to you."

I was cautious. No more rejections. "Have you spoken to them?" I asked.

"Yes. Max Gordon remembers you from the Dunham days and is willing to give you a contract for two weeks, with options."

The contract was signed, and I gathered my music for the first rehearsal. It was a closed rehearsal; no one but the trio and me. This time there were no agents or producers to put the show together or to tell me how to act. The musicians were enormously encouraging and helpful, and together we assembled a program that was nearly the same as the one in London and Paris.

I wasn't the calmest person in the place on opening night. The boys from the agency were there—so, too, were about two hundred other people. I was announced; the music started; the crowd was warm and responsive; and I went out this time with the confidence that at least I had it all together and with the hope of acceptance. I was accepted.

My two-week engagement stretched to fourteen weeks—the last four with John Carradine, who did marvelous dramatic recitations. I became financially solvent once more. We drew good crowds. The newspapers rediscovered me, and I gained popularity by the day. One day I got a letter from Leonard Sillman, whom I had never heard of. He wanted to talk to me and asked that I call him for an appointment. When we finally got together, I learned that he had seen my act at the Vanguard and that he wanted me to audition for the backers of a show he was going to produce called *New Faces of 1952*.

It was a typically horrendous theatrical audition in a big barn of an echo-chamber place: ugly bare stage, dim lighting, and out in front of you, a dank, dark cave, with unseen figures—enemies?—seated somewhere, holding your fate in their hands, like something cold and slimy that they'll let slip to the floor at the drop of a note. No brilliant lights and costumes and lavish props and full orchestra to make their magic. You have to belt them into the void and hear your hollow-sounding voice ricochet back at you from the empty theater as though it were bouncing off the darkness, as though it were not penetrating and couldn't be heard out there. By whom?

And you begin thinking: What am I, crazy? I should be standing here in this big stupid box yelling at the darkness? This is show business? I could be home. I could be at the dentist's having my mouth amputated—anything's better than this. Why am I doing this to myself? Why are they doing this to me? And who are *they*?

It would be nice if you were to walk onstage and one of the figures in the darkness said: "Thank you for coming to the audition. I know that you can't see us, but there are nine of us out here, and each of us is human. We hope you'll be right for the part. You may begin whenever you're ready." But that's not the way it works. It's an old show-business tradition. What you generally hear from the darkness is silence. The silence screams at you, intimidates you: *Silence!*

So I sang into the darkness. Apparently I got through to

someone. The debate on my contract started. Soon I went into rehearsals with sixteen other new faces—against the advice of almost everyone I knew: It's a long shot; the odds are against it. Look at the money and exposure you'll be losing by not working the clubs. Rehearsal money won't even pay your rent. And what if the show closes on opening night? Look at all the time and money and publicity lost. You need another flop?

Reasonable arguments, but. . . "I have a feeling," I said. "I can only follow it."

Everything went well until we got to the choreography on a song of mine we thought could be a show stopper. The choreographers stood around for about three hours one afternoon trying to figure out what to do with the number.

"Let's hear you sing that song again," they'd say.

"I met a rather amusing fool. . . ." June Carroll's lyrics; Arthur Siegel's music. June and Arthur had talked to me about the places I'd been and the people I'd seen—including my adventures in Turkey—and then had written the song, "Monotonous." The choreographers listened, and at the end of the day they were still scratching their heads.

That evening I went up to Mr. Sillman's apartment to talk about rehearsals—particularly "Monotonous." "Why don't we use six chaise longues for that number?" I said. "Let me slither from couch to couch."

Mr. Sillman thought about it for a moment, then said, "That's a good idea."

The next day the chaise longue idea was introduced, and the choreographers stood looking at me blankly. Finally they got six chairs and scattered them across the stage and blocked out my movements. I was to run to a couch, settle into a position awkward for singing, sing about three lines, then run downstage, sing a word or two to the audience, run to another couch, lie down, sing, run, sing, recline, sing, run.

I rehearsed it that way, feeling that it was all wrong. The audience wouldn't hear half the words and I'd be worn out by the time the curtain went down. It seemed illogical to me, but I didn't feel in a position to argue about something I couldn't prove. Rehearsal was one thing, opening night quite another.

26

New Faces

We opened in Philadelphia to excellent notices. Mine were good, but I couldn't afford to be good—I had to be better than good. At the celebration party that night, all were happy with themselves except me. I got next to Mr. Sillman when he was feeling mellow. "I want my spot changed, please," I said.

"What do you mean? You did a wonderful job."

"I'm capable of doing better."

Prior to our opening in Philadelphia, we had made a bet. He was sure the spot would stop the show; I felt that it wouldn't—not the way it was arranged.

"You'll stop the show in New York, don't worry," he said.

"I want to be sure. Please change it."

"Okay, okay," he said.

We played the City of Brotherly Love for two weeks, then took the show to New York. We had three days to work out the rough spots, including restaging my number. Our director, John Murray Anderson, watched me run through it. I finally worked out the choreography myself, with the experts' approval.

On opening night the spot stopped the show. Afterward,

Mr. Chrysler, our main backer, gave us a party in the Metropolitan Opera House ballroom, where we waited for the reviews. The show was a hit. I was singled out by reviewers as one of the show's most promising personalities: "weird," "strange," "can make a song burst into flame," "feline," and so on.

I was signed for the run of the show in New York, and I was signed to double at the Blue Angel, where I would open a week after our Broadway opening night. It looked as though *New Faces* would have a long run. How I wished that my mother and aunt were alive. Often during those early days I used to fantasize about how my aunt would quit working as a domestic in hotels and private homes and forget the beautician courses she was taking and just retire with me. Success would have been so much sweeter if there had been somebody to share it with. Not that I wallowed in self-pity—with both engagements going, I hardly had time for anything but work and sleep—but I dreamed of my aunt often.

My engagement at the Blue Angel was a long and successful one—twenty-five weeks, to be exact. It was also frantic. When the final curtain dropped at the theater each night, I'd start running. I had just enough time to go from the theater on the West Side to the club on the East Side, change clothes, and walk onstage. If it rained, I was usually late, because that slowed traffic. I'd always find the Blue Angel's owner, Herb Jacoby, at the entrance, pacing back and forth.

"Where have you been?" he'd say. That was my greeting for twenty-five weeks. And to complicate matters, the Blue Angel had only one entrance. So once inside, I had to crawl on my hands and knees down a side aisle of the club to keep from being seen and perhaps detained by the customers. The Blue Angel held about 200 customers, and every night was Saturday night.

When I had settled into my frenetic routine, I began looking for an apartment to call home. Through a friend, I heard of a three-room, ground floor apartment being vacated by two young men. The location was ideal, so I went to see them. There was one problem: The place had never had a black tenant. "Maybe you won't have any trouble," one of the young men said, "but just in case. . . ."

They gave me the number of the housing commission and somebody else to call—just in case. Then they helped move in my luggage. I bought their furniture from them, a studio bed and one chair. Period.

As the young men left, one said, "Just act as though you're our guest for a while. Say we're away and you don't know when we'll be back."

I slept in the nearly empty apartment until I could find time to buy furniture. About two weeks after I arrived, at about eight in the morning, someone knocked at my door. I knew it couldn't be anyone but the landlord or manager. I stumbled sleeply to the door, figuring I might as well get it over with. It was the manager.

"Who are you?" he said.

I told him.

"What are you doing here?"

"I'm a guest."

"Where are the boys?"

"Away."

"When will they be back?"

"I don't know."

"How come *you're* staying here?"

"I had no place to stay, so the boys loaned me their place."

I'm not a very convincing liar, and I could tell from his next question that he guessed what was happening. "Do you intend to keep this place?" he said.

"I wish I could. I've been trying to find a place for months, but no luck. You know how hard it is to find a place these days."

"Well, if you intend to keep this apartment, you're mistaken. There are some buildings in New York that don't allow Negroes in, and this is one of them."

I looked him in the eye. I could sense by his actions and the way he spoke that he didn't really want to say those words, but the words had to be said.

"I'll give you a week to find another place," he said, and walked away.

I thought of calling people, but figured it would only aggravate the situation. I didn't think I could force my way in and be tolerated. I'd have to use my head to make it *his* decision that I stay. Besides, the landlord had a right to throw me out; in order to legally sublease, the owner must be notified.

I stayed on.

He came back about a week later. "Well, have you found a place?"

"No, sir. I've tried but there isn't an empty apartment in New York."

"Why don't you try to find a place in Harlem?"

I invited him in, and he stood ill at ease, leaning against the living room wall.

"Why shouldn't I be allowed to live anywhere I please, if I can afford it? Would you like to be refused a decent place to live for no other reason than the color of your skin?"

He didn't reply. I offered him a glass of milk, and he accepted.

"You and I are more or less in the same boat," I said, recalling his last name. "You and I have a lot in common—you many more generations than I. It's a pity to fight each other, don't you think?"

There were other words, leading me to think he had moved to a softer mood. But after finishing his milk, he opened the door and said, "You must find some other place. If anyone asks what you're doing in the building, say you're a maid." He left, closing the door behind him.

I didn't expect *that* from him. It stunned me for a moment, but I held on, thinking, don't weaken your own will, weaken his. He can't be so terrible as all that. He wouldn't have accepted the milk or have listened to you.

I knew I had to handle the problem with intelligence and dispassion. If I won, fine. If I lost, at least I would lose without creating more hatred.

A few days later he was back, knocking softly at my door. "So you're still here, eh?"

"Yes."

"Were you thinking of staying here indefinitely?"

I didn't know if he was trying to trap me somehow or not, so I decided not to answer him. I'd let him rephrase the question or try a different approach.

"Would you like to have this apartment?"

Still not knowing what he was up to, I said, "Well, this isn't the greatest apartment in the world."

"Huh? What's wrong with it?"

"The ceiling in the kitchen is torn. The pipes in the bathroom are rusty, and they leak."

"I'll get all that done for you," he said. "Not only that, we'll paint the place, clean the floors, give you a nice comfortable place to live in—as long as you insist."

"That's very nice," I said, warily, "but to whom are you giving the lease?"

He pulled a document from his coat pocket. "Here's your lease for two years," he said. "Sign here."

I read it and signed.

I never knew exactly what changed his mind, or how he had influenced the building owner or the tenants or whoever it was he had to influence. It wasn't the fact that I was an entertainer. He knew my name, but he didn't know I was on Broadway or at the Blue Angel until three months later, when he came and offered me the penthouse, where I was to live for four years.

New Faces was going well, and my engagement at the Blue Angel brought me exciting, happy moments as well. I was leaving the club one night when the maître d' stopped me. "There's a young man over there who's longing to meet you," he said, nodding his head toward a table next to the wall. "He's been in every night for ten days with a request to meet you."

I glanced at him. "He looks so young. Should he be drinking?"

The maître d' laughed. "Please go over and say hello. He's a very nice young man, very reputable. We know him well; he comes in often. And he's wonderful to us."

I didn't want to. It was late and I wanted to go home. I was afraid he'd start a conversation, making it difficult for me to break away.

"He's always alone," the maître d' said. "Orders the same drink every night, and sees both shows. Then he comes into the bar, sits and waits until you leave, then he leaves."

I had a feeling that he'd drive the maître d' crazy if I didn't go say hello. And if he sat through both shows every night, it was the least I could do to thank him. "All right," I said, "I'll meet him."

The maître d' made the introduction: "Miss Kitt . . . Mr. J. B." Actually, the young man was introduced by his full name, but owing to his social prominence let's call him J. B.—for his sake, not mine.

"Hello," he said.

"Hi."

"I like your work."

"Thank you."

'Uh, I'm putting on a show sometime soon. I wanted to meet you to ask if you'd be interested. It's . . . uh . . . a musical. Would you be?"

He was awfully young, and I sensed that he was just making conversation. "You can talk to my agents about it," I said, telling him the agency name.

"I know them," he said. "How can I get in touch with you personally about it?"

"Through them." He was nice, but very young, I thought. "Good night," I said.

"Good night," he said softly.

I took a cab home as usual. The following night, he was sitting at a front table. I said hello with a smile, and he nodded back. He was sitting at his usual place at the bar when I was leaving. I nodded good night. He smiled.

This scene recurred for several nights until the maître d' came to me again. "We think our friend is very lonely," he said. "Why don't you have a drink or something with him. It won't hurt you to sit for a while."

I went over to his table, and he got up to greet me. "You should know my act backwards by now," I said.

"I do." We both laughed. I ordered spaghetti; he ordered champagne. I ate heartily because the Blue Angel had good spaghetti. He drank heavily because presumably he was lonely, although he didn't seem affected at all by the wine when the bottle was empty.

"May I take you home?" he asked.

"I suppose."

He escorted me to an expensive car parked in front of the club and drove me home. When I said good night to him at the door, he said, "I'll meet you at three in the afternoon, okay?"

"Okay."

At three the following day, he rang my doorbell. I was moving furniture and hanging curtains at the time. He entered and immediately began helping me. After a while, he said, "I have something to do downtown. Would you like to come along? It won't take long."

We drove down Madison Avenue, pulled around the corner on Fifty-something Street and stopped. He helped me out of the car, then took me into a jewelry store on Madison Avenue and introduced me to the owner.

"Let me see something unusual," J. B. said.

The owner brought out some antique pieces and laid them on the counter. J. B. looked them over carefully, then turned to me and said, "Which piece do *you* like?"

I figured that he wanted my help in choosing a gift for someone. I pointed out a ring holding a large pearl with a cluster of sixteen diamonds around it, telling him that I thought it the most beautiful of the pieces. I couldn't believe the price tags. The ring was $1,000. J. B. nodded, seemingly pleased with my choice.

"Shall I wrap it?" the owner said.

"No, give it to her as it is," J. B. said, smiling. I looked at him, dumbfounded. "It's yours," he said.

I was too surprised even to thank him. And I didn't think it proper to discuss whether I should accept such an expensive gift with the owner standing there watching my reaction.

Back in the car I asked, "Now why would you want to do a thing like that?"

"Maybe because I know what kind of life you've had and I like you," he said. "You're a great artist, whom I appreciate. I want to make you happy. I don't want you to want for anything."

His words made me ill with contentment—inexplicable to those of you who haven't experienced the flood of joy that assaults the senses so suddenly that one feels a queasiness in the pit of the stomach. Whether he truly meant them or not, I wanted to believe that someone really wanted to make me happy. I don't mean to be melodramatic about it, but maybe in the back of my mind J. B.'s interest in me as an artist and a person represented to me someone with whom I could share my success.

Thereafter, J. B. met me every night at the club to take me home. Sometimes he came over to help with the apartment. We were soon inseparable. And in his quest to make me happy, the gifts never stopped. Such gifts! Every week it was a new piece of jewelry or clothes or furniture for my apartment. I soon had a completely new wardrobe, including minks I had never dreamed of owning at that age. Santa Claus had always passed up my house in my youth; J. B. became Santa personified. Viewed from an angle, one would have thought, a-ha, the kept woman! But it wasn't that. He had won me forever, as far as I was concerned. His motive for giving was the joy of giving. Nothing ulterior.

One night at the theater, Ronnie Graham said, "How do you like my friend J. B.?"

"He's a wonderful person," I said.

"You sure know how to pick 'em."

"What do you mean by that?"

"He just inherited something like eight million dollars about six months ago. He belongs to one of America's richest families."

New Faces ran for a year in New York, and I doubled at the Blue Angel for six of the twelve months. J. B. was with me the whole time, and for the first time in my life I had the security a woman looks for in a man. I had loved Charlie, but dependability wasn't his forte. I began to depend upon J. B. for everything: My moods were determined and affected by his moods; every move I made, everything I planned was connected with J. B. But like Charlie, J. B. was white; I became acutely aware of this and began to fear that awful abstraction, society, and the color barrier.

J. B. was everything I had looked for in a man—and pigmentation be damned! We often spoke about what society would call our "color differences." And although I don't think either of us really considered the consequences, J. B. would always say, "Don't worry about it. I can handle myself in any situation." He had always assured me that he knew what he had gotten himself into; he had a mind of his own. Meanwhile, it *was* the early fifties, and our being together angered even complete strangers we'd pass on the street. One can imagine how the uppity social circle in which J. B. moved regarded the "scandal."

We got a taste of it even from the press. I was reprimanded by the black press for my relationship with the "downtown" world. And we were both scorned by the downtown press for not conforming to society's game. Oh, they weren't as candid as the black press, and that made them even worse. It was a problem, but one we chose to overcome by ignoring.

When I closed at the Blue Angel, J. B. met me each night at the theater. Sundays were our days together, when no one could interfere or interrupt. We would usually stay in my apartment, reading, talking, watching television, or playing—we played like children. Each Sunday became more enjoyable than the last, and we always looked forward to them. Until one week when our Sundays came to an abrupt stop.

"I can't be with you this Sunday," J. B. said.

"Why not?"

"I must have dinner with my family."

After that our relationship was never the same. We began seeing less and less of one another, which I didn't thoroughly understand at the time. Then suddenly J. B. went abroad and stayed for quite a while. When he returned, he saw me only once, saying something like, "Whether I love you or not has nothing to do with it. We cannot be as we have been."

What hurt most was that he had sold out. Had I written this chapter in those days, I would probably have disguised his name as S.O.B. rather than J. B. But then again, probably not. I truly loved him, and he must have been under terrific pressure. I don't think that even at that young age I really expected to be invited to his parents' mansion for Sunday dinner, let alone be welcomed into the family. The film *Guess Who's Coming to*

Dinner would have been considered science fiction in the early fifties. And when it was screened in the sixties, it was still fantasy—or at least a fantasized case history in abnormal sociology. It still is.

Okay, I should have known better. But love often makes one stupid as well as blind. I was broken up to the point that everyone in *New Faces* moved closer to comfort me, and friends spent hours trying to make me realize that everyone has disappointments in life. I tried to be rational about the situation. But emotion overruled reason, and, having lost the one who had been everything to me, I was again gripped with the feeling—indeed absolute belief—that I was unwanted, uncharming, unattractive, uneverything. It didn't take much to bring Eartha Mae to the surface, with all her anxieties and insecurities.

27

Son of New Faces

A few weeks later, *New Faces* went on the road. In the meantime, I had made a number of records with RCA Victor, and one, "Uska Dara," the song I had learned for Turkish audiences to show my appreciation for their kindness toward me, was making my name better known across the country. I was getting offers for club dates from coast to coast, dates that I couldn't accept while committed to the play.

My contract with *New Faces* was for the run of the Broadway engagement only. Now they wanted to renegotiate the contract to take the show on the road. I had not thought beyond Broadway; it hadn't even occurred to me that they would take the same cast on the road. I had mixed feelings, for I was anxious to get back to the clubs.

"You must be with the show," I was told. "The Shuberts won't give us a theater without you."

I owed much to the other new faces and didn't want to be responsible for the show losing an opportunity for the road.

"Three weeks in Boston, four weeks in Chicago, and we close," I was told.

Fine. I would accept the Hollywood Mocambo contract offered me by its owner, Charlie Morrison; three weeks in Boston, four in Chicago, then I'd take a four-week vacation and open at the Mocambo. But it didn't quite work out that way.

Our three weeks in Boston were a cinch. But our four weeks in Chicago turned into eight months! "C'est Si Bon" was released while I was in Chicago, and now I was becoming really known across the country. The club offers were pouring in.

Charlie Morrison began calling periodically about my contract with him.

"I can't come until the show closes," I told him.

"But your commitment was fulfilled weeks ago. You have no business with that show now; you've outgrown it."

"But I can't leave. There are too many who say that they depend on me. I can't leave in midstream."

Feeling terrible about disappointing Charlie—even though, technically, I wasn't to open the Mocambo until *New Faces* closed—I would go to the management each time Charlie called and ask them how much longer. "In about a month," was the reply they gave me for months. As a result, my club engagements were cancelled about five times in that ten-month period.

The clubs kept calling the agency, and I kept putting the dates off as the producer kept saying we were going to close. Meanwhile, I began hearing my records on jukeboxes and radio, and disc jockeys were talking about the new "up-and-coming songbird." It seemed very strange at first hearing my voice in restaurants and on passing car radios and portables at the beach. It gave me a tremendous feeling of accomplishment. "C'est Si Bon," people would say to me as I walked down the street.

There had been talk of filming *New Faces* after the Chicago engagement ended. My producer said that I just had to do the film because they wouldn't do the picture without me. I doubted that, even though I had heard it from other sources. When our eight months in Chicago ended, my contract was up, and again the producer came to me. We'd been offered three weeks in San Francisco and two weeks at the Biltmore Theater in Los Angeles, following the filming, and he asked if I'd stay on for those five weeks.

"Five weeks?" I said.

"Yes. Five."

"You told me we'd be through after Broadway. Then you told me three weeks in Boston and *four* in Chicago. We've been in Chicago *eight months!* And now the movie. . . ."

I didn't know how much the other new faces really depended on me—if, indeed, they felt they needed me. But this was always the pitch I got from management, and always I decided not to take a chance on disappointing them. Mostly I did it for me; I didn't want to lose the love the company had for me.

Toward the end of our run in Chicago, the fan mail began getting out of hand, so I hired a secretary. Three days before we left Chicago, I sent her on to Hollywood to make arrangements —hotel, publicity for the club, and disc jockey promotions under the supervision of Virginia Wicks's New York office. The secretary rented a two-bedroom bungalow at the Garden of Allah. And what a delight it was to live in that mecca of international celebrities and intellectuals. Five years later it would be torn down and its place taken by a savings and loan building and parking lot at Sunset Boulevard and Crescent Heights. All that remains of it is a little park that shelters an encased replica of the famous Garden.

The night of my arrival at the Garden of Allah, my secretary and I went to the Mocambo for dinner, where we met Mrs. Morrison and the people from the club. Before I had left Chicago, Charlie Morrison called to ask if I would double while doing the film. "That would be difficult," I had said. "Our studio call will be in the early-morning hours."

"You can do it. I need you. I'd like you to work for three weeks. You'll be here for that amount of time."

"I don't know, Charlie."

"Please, Eartha, you don't know what this will mean to me."

I knew Charlie Morrison to be an honest and considerate person; I think he was one of the finest people ever to own a club. I felt really terrible that he had been put off for months because of the unexpectedly long Chicago engagement, so I had told him that I'd see what I could do. But it wasn't unusual, while working on a picture, to report to the make-up department as early as 6:00 A.M., and working the Mocambo until 1:00 or 2:00 would give me only about three hours' sleep a night.

As it turned out, it wasn't quite that bad, but it was bad enough. My call for the film was 8:00 A.M.; my call for the Mocambo was from 11:30 P.M. until 2:00 A.M. After I wound down from each evening's performance, I could get about four hours' sleep. But, in truth, I would have gone without sleep for Charlie Morrison and his Mocambo patrons. Everyone was wonderful. And fortunately, my part of the filming only lasted ten days.

A few days after we started shooting the film in the fall of 1953, I opened at the Mocambo. Charlie Morrison had outdone himself advertising. And I was met with even a greater surprise when I drove to the club for opening night. Stretched across Sunset Boulevard was a banner several feet high. In huge letters that ran nearly the width of the street, it read: EARTHA KITT! The marquee said the same. And already there was a double line nearly a city block long of patrons waiting patiently to get in.

I had been nervous enough at the prospect of opening. But the banner and all of those people scared me so badly that, in my downstairs dressing room, I couldn't even apply my makeup properly. The dressing room was filled with flowers, and there was champagne. I kept drinking hot tea, hot coffee, hot water, anything hot to calm my nerves. Nothing worked. Just before I was to go on, I got sick to my stomach. Charlie Morrison came down to the dressing room to console me, bringing a glass of brandy with him. "Here," he said, "take a sip. It will calm you down."

I took the tiny glass and downed the brandy in one gulp, stinging my throat and vocal chords. It took my mind off my nerves, all right. For a moment I thought I was going to strangle; I was still trying to catch my breath when I stepped onto the stage that was just large enough for the mike and me.

The room was packed, and I was astonished. I had played only a few clubs—none on the West Coast—and had made a few records. I really hadn't expected to be a draw on the Coast, for I had spent nearly two years in New York and Chicago with the play. But there I was, standing before a capacity crowd.

They looked at me expectantly.

I looked at them. Applause went up to welcome me. I searched the audience for a smile to comfort me; there were many. The applause eased me into my opening song. Arthur Siegel, who wrote the music for "Monotonous," accompanied me on the piano. I was glad he was close by, for he had a quick, easy, carefree laugh that always reassured me. Whenever I was a little uncertain during the show, I'd look at Arthur and he'd laugh as though nothing mattered. That always cheered me.

"Santa Baby," my most recent record release, was received with delight—so was "C'est Si Bon." The more serious numbers, like "Lilac Wine," written by James Shelton, were appreciated for their change of mood. There was thundering applause when I finished the act. Charlie Morrison met me backstage and shouted, "You're a star!" The applause continued for an uncomfortable length of time.

"What do I do now?" I asked Charlie.

"Go back and sing some more."

"I don't *have* any more!"

"You must have more songs."

"I only rehearsed ten with the orchestra."

"Doesn't your pianist know any?"

"To tell the truth, Charlie, I'm scared to go back. I might spoil what I've created."

I went back to my dressing room on the verge of tears, so happy to belong. I had felt it in the theater, but at the Mocambo it was even stronger because I could communicate more intimately. I could see every face in the audience, every smile, every expression of love. And I went back to the dressing room in love with the world. Why couldn't my mother and aunt have seen this? Champagne flowed in my room as friends and fans crowded in to congratulate me.

When all had left me so that I could take a breather before the second show, I sat down with a cup of hot tea. I was tired, but I couldn't allow myself to be. My secretary, Rennie, sat with me, saying nothing and turning away visitors so that I could rest for a while. She was used to my quiet moments.

The second show that night went just as well. My fatigue disappeared as soon as I met the audience. I was as happy as a child when I went back to my bungalow at the Garden that night. I took a hot bath to calm down, but sleep didn't come easily. I kept thinking about that banner stretched across Sunset Boulevard just a few blocks away, and about people driving under it at that very moment and seeing my name. I marveled at what had happened to me in the five short years since I had sailed to Europe with the Dunham Company. I lay awake wondering why people become what they become. Or, I should say, Eartha Mae lay awake wondering. . . .

Who was this Eartha Kitt? When did she begin exerting influence on my life? In South Carolina? In Harlem? In Europe? And what drove her? Was it a lack of something like bread, or a mother and father? Lacking nothing, would there still have been that same drive? And how much of it is luck? All questions and no answers. Eartha Mae knew only that the South Carolina cotton picker would have to arise from her bed at the Garden of Allah in a few short hours and drive down Sunset Boulevard, perhaps with Eartha Kitt's voice coming from the car radio, to Twentieth Century-Fox, where she was making a film.

It was almost like Shirley Temple—with a few script changes, of course. Shirley would have to learn to pick a little cotton and hoe beans. But at movie's end, Shirley could dispatch her chauffeur to the nearest market for a bunch of bananas, sit in a rocking chair beside the lotus-shaped pool at the Garden of Allah, and eat all the bananas she wanted. It was obviously time for Eartha Mae to trade her fantasies for slumber.

At seven the following morning I went to the studio to be made up for call. I dozed in my cabin between takes. I had had only two solo spots in the Broadway show, but the film producer, Eddy Alperson, gave me five spots in the picture. He also had my wardrobe specially made. I felt very strange before the camera, because one's movement is restricted. But I didn't mind filmmaking at all. I had made two French films and, of course, had appeared in the film with the Dunham dancers. And in the near future, I'd be making others as well.

After my ten days of filming and doubling at the Mocambo, I was nearly exhausted—even though I hadn't had to go into the studio on two of those days.

The banner hung across Sunset for ten days too. Every time I passed beneath it, or saw it from a distance, I was filled with a tremendous feeling of pride—and fear. The fear was from the realization that the name on the banner really didn't belong to me; it belonged to a friend, someone I loved and wanted only the best for, someone for whom I'd want everything that I'd want for me. But I feared for her, feared that she might not be able to live up to that banner, to be deserving of it, and I felt impotent because I couldn't help her. And that was terrible, because she was taking such good care of me.

28

Paleface and Other Problems

While I was appearing at the Mocambo, I was asked by the head of a committee to participate in a star-studded benefit to be given by Mayor Paulson of Los Angeles in honor of the King and Queen of Greece. The event was to be held at the Ambassador Hotel's Cocoanut Grove, and I felt honored to be asked.

"Which songs do you want me to sing?"

"Oh, 'Santa Baby,' 'C'est Si Bon,' 'Evil'—anything you are known for will be fine," I was told.

"How many songs?"

"Two is what everyone else is doing, but be prepared for three or four."

Conscious that I would be appearing before royalty, I purposefully chose a tasteful and conservative gown to wear for the event. It was so high-cut that my neck could barely be seen. A car was sent for me, and I was escorted by my accompanist, Arthur Siegel. We sat with June Allyson and Dick Powell. Dick sensed my nervousness and said, "You don't have a thing to worry about. Just remember that they're nervous too." He made me feel a little better, but I don't know why: Dick seemed just as nervous as I was.

When the dinner was over, the drum rolled and Harry James came out to lead the orchestra as Dick Powell walked to the microphone. He began by reading a delightful poem to Her Majesty, and we all laughed our tensions away. Then, because it was nearing my show time at the club, he introduced me. And what an introduction. He made my spirit soar when he said, "One of our great artists, Miss Eartha Kitt."

June Allyson looked at me with the kind of warmth that only she has, and it put me completely at ease as I sang my first song, "I Want to Be Evil."

I was startled by the burst of applause when the song ended. I had expected the audience to be reserved because of our royal guests. My second song, "Santa Baby," was received with more of the same.

I started to return to my seat but was applauded back to the microphone. I did Duke Ellington's "Blues" and ended with "C'est Si Bon." I said goodnight to June and waved to Dick as I fled the room to my paying audience waiting at the Mocambo. They were still applauding when I left.

That evening I did my second show to a full house, with standees. The streets were jammed. And I was happy. (As a matter of fact, during my engagement I broke the thirteen-year house record at the Mocambo—which made me as happy for Charlie Morrison as I was for myself.)

A few days later I called a rehearsal at the club to add a few new numbers to my act. I was onstage when someone said there was a telephone call for me. It was a member of the press.

"Eartha, what did you do at the King and Queen's ball the other night?"

"What do you mean?"

"There was a meeting Tuesday at the mayor's office. You were called down as un-American."

"What?"

"The subject of the benefit came up, and the mayor said you did not represent good American art. Can we come over and take some pictures?"

"What have I done? I only did what I was told to do."

"Well, the mayor thinks you were risqué."

"Risqué!"

Before I left the rehearsal, several photographers arrived to photograph what the mayor had called risqué. For several days, headlines made everyone on the West Coast conscious of Eartha Kitt. Mr. Rio, then head of the American Guild of Variety Artists, came to my defense. "If this is the way an artist is treated after a benefit performance, no more benefits," he said. "We contribute a million dollars' worth of talent and they call us names."

Hollywood backed us up. "The mayor obviously doesn't know what American is." "What does he mean by risqué?" "Invite the mayor to see the show, Eartha." And we did invite him, but he never showed up. The feud went on for days.

I was on the spot and in the spotlight. My record sales went sky high. I received a contract from El Rancho Las Vegas and a million dollars' worth of free publicity—and found a million friends. Hollywood was really wonderful to me during that episode. I was especially grateful to Jack Benny, who, characteristically, had a long talk with the mayor a few days later and apparently set him straight. Mr. Benny was not only a legend in his time, but he was also a great humanitarian. He's irreplaceable and unforgettable.

The only bad effect of the incident was the crank letters I got—I was still getting them a full year later. But one message I received put all the crank letters out of mind. It was a telegram from the royal couple that read: "We don't know what all the fuss is about. We thoroughly enjoyed the show."

On the Tuesday night of my last week at the Mocambo, the company of *New Faces* came to see me, and we were sitting upstairs with Charlie and Mary Morrison. I noticed a young man come into the club; I think it was his unusual pallor that arrested my attention. His expression was warm, but he looked tired and pale. He looked directly at me as he entered. The time was right, the face was right, and the man. . . .

"Who's that man standing in the doorway?" I asked Mary.

"Oh that's. . . ." She never finished, because Charlie jumped up to usher him to our table. The pale-faced man sat down and ordered a drink. He was introduced by his first name;

out of deference to him, let's call him Paleface. I was then signaled that it was show time. And as I got up to leave, Paleface grabbed my arm.

"Don't go away," he said.

"I have to. I have to change for the show."

"Come back."

"I have to come back up to work," I said.

"I mean here. Come back and have a drink with me," he said, holding fast to my arm.

"I'll come back," I said.

During my act I saw him sitting alone at the long table. Mary, Charlie, and the others had left because it was late. When I ended my show I went downstairs to my dressing room, and Paleface came knocking on my door, smiling. "I didn't think you'd come back," he said, "so I came down to be sure."

We went out for hamburgers and coffee, he telling me that he'd been waiting a long time to meet me, and I wondering if he were sincere. When he took me home, I said goodnight. He said, "Don't go to bed. Stay and talk with me."

"I'm tired," I said.

He went in and sat down on the sofa, not taking no for an answer. "Well, I'm going to stay right here," he said.

I was too tired to argue, so I went off to bed. I didn't worry about his presence; he was well known and of good reputation, and besides, my secretary occupied the bedroom next to mine. I figured when he saw I was serious he'd leave. But the next morning I found him asleep in the living room. I awakened him and fixed him coffee, and he left for home in the early-morning mist. That afternoon he was back to pick me up and take me somewhere. For the remaining seven days of my engagement at the club, we were constantly together.

Shortly before I left for San Francisco, Paleface gave me the first birthday party I ever had, at the Mocambo. When I arrived, our mutual friends were seated at the long table waiting for me. It was beautifully arranged with a magnificent floral centerpiece. At the head of the table lay a bouquet and a small gift-wrapped box from Paleface. I opened it nervously, and a tiny angel, riding three clouds formed by fresh-water pearls, looked up at me. The attached card said, "You may want to be evil, but I think you're an angel."

Paleface was charming and witty and thoughtful, but I expected our relationship to end when I left town. I was wrong. A day or two later when we opened in San Francisco with *New Faces*, he called. I was happy to be missed, and every day for the first week or so he called me. Then, on the following weekend, he came up to San Francisco, and we did up the town. Ronnie Graham, a few other members of the cast, the producer, and I went with Paleface to call on Hoagy Carmichael. And when Ronnie and Hoagy got together, I was sure I had never witnessed such zany madness. What a comedy team they'd make. It was complete bedlam, evoking the kind of laughter that has you begging for them to stop, because the muscles of your face, ribs, and abdomen can't stand the punishment.

It was during our run in San Francisco that I first met Sammy Davis, Jr. At that time he was still working with his father and uncle as a trio, and I didn't know who he was. I walked backstage one day and saw him talking to one of the girls in the *New Faces* cast. I thought he was a stagehand or a prop man. The girl stopped me as I was passing and introduced me.

I said hello. And then as an afterthought, still thinking he was a stagehand, I said, "Would you mind getting me a cup of coffee, Mister Davis?"

"Not at all," he said.

I got money from my handbag and handed it to him, and off he went to a nearby restaurant for coffee. The girl he'd been talking to was aghast. "You sent *Sammy Davis Junior* to run after coffee for you?"

I looked at her blankly. It was common for stagehands to get coffee for the entertainers who couldn't get away from the theater. She told me that he was appearing at the fashionable Fairmont Hotel, and a few minutes later, when Sammy returned with my coffee—and my change—we all had a good laugh.

After that, I went to the Fairmont to see his act and was most impressed with his talent—to say the least. Several times Sammy and I had lunch in one of San Francisco's fine restaurants. Invariably the maître d' would greet me by name but ignore Sammy. He would sit down muttering—not mad, just frustrated—and say, "I just don't understand it! I mean, I've been in show business all my life. Some day my name's gonna be just as big as yours, Eartha. You just wait and see. Some day. . . ."

I forgot all about those restaurant incidents until one day Sammy and I were walking along the street and for some reason had to part, going in opposite directions. I hadn't gotten thirty feet when I heard Sammy shouting behind me. I turned, and there he was, standing in the middle of a busy intersection, waving his fist in the air and yelling, "Some day my name is gonna be as big as *yours*, Eartha! You'll see! One of these days, my name. . . ."

Passersby were staring at the stranger as though he had gone mad. . .stopping traffic, poking his finger into the air, and yelling. They didn't know they were staring at a prophet, that one day he'd be stopping traffic by just *walking* down the street.

After our San Francisco engagement, we returned to Los Angeles for our two-week stay at the Biltmore Theater. Paleface and I went everywhere together, and our friends were wonderful to us. He was his usual charming self. He had a house in the Hollywood hills overlooking Sunset Boulevard and the Mocambo, and he told me that we had been fated to meet.

"I went all through Switzerland with your voice haunting me on the radio," he said. "I made up my mind to look you up when I got home. What could have been more surprising than to look down the hill and see the name I had been looking for?"

Our times spent together were glorious. I believed once more that I had at last found the right man, and that we'd live happily ever after.

Charlie Morrison again asked if I would double at the Mocambo. "It will be too difficult," I told him at first, "especially on matinee days." But I couldn't turn Charlie down. He had been too wonderful to me during my engagement at the club. He had thrown a going-away party for me on my last night there. He had come down to my dressing room before show time and given me a pounded-gold cigarette case with my name on it; a diamond dotted the *i*. And before the last show, he reappeared, giving me a gold medallion of the Virgin of Guadaloupe, the Virgin of Mercy, to protect me in time of need. Charlie was always giving me expensive gifts, claiming that I had helped renew interest in the club at a time when he feared it might go under.

As if the gifts weren't enough, that same night, when I had finished the first three songs of my act, a line of waiters filed on stage, each presenting me with a bouquet of roses. Overwhelmed, I looked to Arthur for support. As usual, he laughed, which got me giggling, and then the tears started flowing. I put the flowers on the piano and began another song. I choked up and the tears began rolling again. The audience was silent. Then applause started. I cried some more. People in the audience began sniffing. Handkerchiefs were being taken from purses.

The music started again. I wiped my eyes, and then I laughed and the audience laughed with me. I turned my back to them, composed myself finally, and continued the show.

Charlie Morrison. There was the time I was sitting in my bungalow with my secretary on Thanksgiving Day, feeling kind of sorry for myself—no family, and the depressing idea of having Thanksgiving dinner in a restaurant among strange families. Enter Charlie Morrison, leading a couple of waiters around the Garden of Allah's lotus-shaped pool, each carrying a tray. He came into my bungalow with a bucket of champagne on ice and a bottle of wine under each arm. One tray held turkey and trimmings, and the other, a yard long, was covered with autumn leaves and Indian corn and orchids and gold-painted grapes and fruits of all kinds. How could I possibly turn Charlie down when he asked me to double while we were at the Biltmore Theater?

Every night when the theater curtain went down, I changed to street clothes, jumped into a waiting car, and sped across Los Angeles, arriving just in time to slip on my evening gown and walk onstage. The cold and rain didn't stop the crowds, but a virus finally stopped me. One matinee I was too weak to walk, too stubborn to lie down, and too hoarse to sing. My doctor came. "You've got a bad infection and should be in bed," he said.

I did half the show but was sent home. I was perspiring

with fever and vomiting every ten minutes. The doctor gave me a sedative. Naturally, I didn't go to the Mocambo that night, either. Charlie Morrison was understanding and thoughtful, but as far as *New Faces* was concerned, the newspapers were apparently given another story. One said, "Eartha Kitt's walkout on *New Faces* gained her no friends." Another said, "We don't mind anyone trying to make money while the making is good, but Miss Kitt should realize she has sixteen other kids to think about."

I was very tired and looked forward to a vacation after the show closed in Los Angeles. I had been with *New Faces* for more than two years. But just before we closed, our producer came to me with the proposal that we return to San Francisco for five weeks, then go on tour back toward New York.

"But you said you were closing," I told him.

"I know, but business has been good. We can go on for a little longer if you're with us."

"I've made other commitments because I expected this to be over long before now," I said. "I'm awfully tired, and besides, my engagements are overlapping each other. Buffalo says they won't let me out of my contract again."

I was told that if I left, there would be no tour. As usual, I was given the distinct impression that the other new faces were totally dependent upon me—as though they would each plummet into obscurity if the show folded. This, of course, was nonsense; many of the new faces are still active and famous. Such talented people certainly didn't need me.

I didn't think we should return to San Francisco, but the others disagreed. I consented to the tour—except for the eight days I had to be in Buffalo. The producer offered to put my name on the marquee, but I refused, thinking it unfair to the rest of the cast. We had started as a family, and we should wind up that way.

We played San Francisco again, took two weeks off before the next engagement—I went back to the Mocambo for those two weeks—then continued for a short while. On April 1, 1954, *New Faces of 1952* finally closed on the road.

29

Sweet Dreams and Nightmares

A week after the play closed, I opened at El Rancho Vegas in Las Vegas, Nevada, where I was headlined in letters even larger than those that had stretched across Sunset Boulevard. And there were billboards on the outskirts of town advertising the star who was to appear at the El Rancho. They do everything big in Las Vegas.

I began rehearsals the afternoon of my arrival. Bill Loose, whom I asked to accompany me at Henri Rene's suggestion, led the orchestra with the arrangements he had made for me. He knew my work because he had done some of my arrangements when I recorded with RCA. Beldon Katleman, the El Rancho boss, came into rehearsal to greet me. I was in the middle of a song when he said, "Hello, there." I looked at him and completed the song before returning his greeting. We hit it off at that very first meeting because, as one of the musicians said, "You are two of a kind. When you like, you like, and when you don't, there's no pretending." Later I met Mr. Katleman's wife, Millie, and we too made friends quickly. And she's still a close friend.

A few days after the opening, Paleface came to Las Vegas to

be with me a short time. I couldn't have been happier. Everything was going well, and a new Broadway play, *Mrs. Patterson*, was being prepared for me by the producer of *New Faces*. I was looking forward to doing a drama because, although I was known as an actress in Europe, I had become popular in my own country only as a singer, and *Mrs. Patterson* would give me the opportunity to prove my acting ability as well. I was advised not to take the chance: "Don't press your luck too far," I was told. "Be satisfied with what you are. You're making a good living as a club artist." It was the same old advice that had warned me against going into *New Faces*—but from new faces.

My Las Vegas debut was highly successful, as was the Buffalo appearance before it. I continued fulfilling my commitments across the country, including the Latin Casino in Philadelphia, where I found two other people of the Charlie Morrison caliber in Dave Dushoff and Dave Dallas. But all the while I was eyeing—and avoiding—the big challenge, the scene of my American debut flop: La Vie en Rose. I kept chiding myself for letting a bad experience get the better of me. It was like getting back on the horse after being thrown, skidding on one's chin, a country mile. It was a standing offer from La Vie en Rose, and although I didn't know whether I was being brave and pushing myself toward it, or being drawn like a moth to flame, I finally agreed.

I walked out onstage exuding absolute confidence, but inside I was so filled with fear that I thought my teeth would chatter. The house was packed, for which I was grateful, and after the first three songs my fears were gone. The audience was with me all the way. I was bursting with happiness when I walked offstage to encore applause. It was perhaps the sweetest success of all, for I had conquered not only a professional but also a very personal fear. Whether I remembered Jose Ferrer's words at the time, I do now: "...I know how you must feel... you mustn't give up...your turn will come again...."

I worked my way back to the West Coast again, and after an engagement at the Cal-Neva Club in Lake Tahoe I returned to Hollywood to see Paleface and to rest before the new Broadway show. "You're never here," he lamented. "Three months away, two weeks here." We began making plans for my moving permanently to California after the closing of *Mrs. Patterson*. I had mixed feelings. There was no telling how long the play would last, and we didn't want to be separated. But *Mrs. Patterson* was something I wanted to do and had committed myself to, despite my emotional entanglement.

Our rehearsals were in New York, but we would open out of town—three or four weeks in Detroit, then eight weeks in Chicago before the Broadway opening. The play was about a traumatic experience similar to the real-life encounter with which I opened this book. In *Mrs. Patterson* I played a fifteen-year-old southern black girl who was in tears (it seemed) through half the play. On a conscious level, it took me back to my early days in the South, whether I liked it or not. And I didn't. Subconsciously, Eartha Mae's ever-present fear—that I could one day return to eating bread and sopping molasses and being hated—helped stimulate my soul to re-create my own experience. This, together with the strenuous physical activity demanded by the part, left me physically and emotionally exhausted and threw me into an almost constant state of depression, which was alleviated only by the twice-a-week phone calls from Paleface.

We opened in Detroit to fair reviews. Thanks to the angels that guide me, which I will always believe to be the spirit of my mother, my personal reviews were wonderful. But to improve the play as a whole, we worked on it every day throughout the Detroit run.

One morning, close to the end of our stay, I was awakened by the phone at 4:00 A.M. It was Paleface's voice: "Hello, Earthie."

"What's the matter, are you ill?" I asked.

"No."

"Why do you call me at this hour?" I said, glad to hear his voice but a little irritated that he had frightened me.

"I want to tell you something." I could hardly hear him, and I was sure something was wrong. I waited, pressing the phone against my ear hard. "If I tell you something," he said, "will you remember it tomorrow?"

"Yes... what is it?" There was a long pause, and I caught

myself holding my breath, afraid of what it was he would say.

"I love you!"

I relaxed and let his message settle within me, feeling its comfortable warmth sweep through my body. I said nothing for several seconds, not wanting to interrupt the glow of it. Then, a slight doubt nudged me cautiously into my protective shell again. "You're drunk," I said laughing.

"Yes, I am." A long pause, then: "If not, I probably wouldn't be able to tell you. But I've loved you for a long time...afraid to reveal how I felt."

"Why didn't you tell me when I was *there?*"

"I didn't know how to. It was easier to say nothing."

"You won't remember this tomorrow," I said, teasingly, hoping I was wrong. "You're too drunk."

"I know what I'm saying, and I'll say the same thing tomorrow."

"All right. Call me tomorrow. If you say the same thing then, I'll believe you—providing you're not drunk again."

I couldn't go back to sleep for a long time. And I went to the theater that evening feeling high-spirited. My performance, I thought, was better than usual, for my creative powers were bursting within me. When I returned to the hotel I expected a message, but Paleface hadn't called as he said he would. A day went by, then two, and I convinced myself that he hadn't meant what he said, or at least that he hadn't meant to tell me. On the third day he called: "Yes, I love you," he said across three thousand miles. That was all I wanted to hear.

"What do we do now?" I asked.

"I don't know. I've never been in this situation before. I love you, but I'll never be able to marry you."

I understood. I wasn't happy about it, but I understood. He was from a prominent and influential family that was dead set against his marrying a woman of color. Never mind that I am a human being first, then a woman, then—if one must be concerned with fine distinctions (but really not so fine)—part white and part black and part Indian, in no particular order or degree of parts.

Over the years, I have been asked thinly veiled questions

about the loves of my life, with emphasis on color and the implication that, perhaps (amateur psychologists all), I was searching for my lost white-father figure. In truth, on society's skin-color scale, my relationships would register about fifty-fifty, or at least sixty-forty. And considering the ratio of white to black in the West, it's a wonder that I haven't registered a ninety-ten. But I haven't. Some of you will understand when I say that I don't see people as white or nonwhite. I see them as human beings, male or female, friendly or hostile, and so on. If Paleface, for example, had gone into the sun and, for some strange reason, turned a *permanent* flaming red or blue or...I would have loved him no less.

This is, of course, the story of my life to date, not the story of my love life. But to leave love out of it would be dishonest. That is what human *being* is all about, as I've pointed out in the dedication. That's what we all seek. So it should come as no surprise that I'm a human being with a full complement of needs and desires and drives. And needs and drives are colorless. Color has to be learned by rote, not reason. Reason always gets in the way of my learning it; I have to keep being reminded. I forget.

If we forget about Alex, my Puerto Rican first love, and a few others whom I've mentioned in passing and who were black, it will be noted that the five with whom I've dealt in detail—Charlie, Philippe, Peter, J. B., and Paleface—were white. There are two reasons why I have singled out these five, to the exclusion of others. First, my relationship with each of them occurred during critical and lonely phases of my life. And, second, each of them had one thing in common that caused me to be attracted to them: They were haunted. Like James Dean, they were loners—lonely and driven by the furies, lost, without roots. Each of them, in his own way, touched my soul, just as Jamie Dean did.

So Paleface loved me, but couldn't marry me. It was understandable. But understanding the source of pain doesn't render it less painful. This was the early fifties; mixed marriages or cohabitation were rare and seldom spoken of. Society would wage war more vigorously—and effectively—against them than against its deadly enemy cancer. Despite the aggravations surrounding our relationship, we still made plans for me to move to California, and I intended to arrange my club engagements so that I could be home, near him, more often than I was. No, I didn't like the idea, but we were in love, and among other things love meant a willingness to sacrifice. I wouldn't go so far as to live with him—was I not a good girl, despite my love? I would get an apartment or house to be near him. But the plans were never carried out. Society won when our relationship was cheapened and broken by slanderous insinuations.

Mrs. Patterson played Chicago for two months, and again the play was getting bad reviews while I was on safe ground. For the most part, I was happy in Chicago. We believed that the play's ills could be remedied before New York, and I had my dreams of life ever after with Paleface. I went nowhere, saw no one, and stayed in my room with my books and my thoughts, although I had no idea when the play would close and allow my dreams to become reality.

Toward the end of our eight-week run, I began hemorrhaging again, but not badly enough to put me on my back. I couldn't let illness get the best of me, for it would close the show, losing the producer and backers lots of money and me a chance to prove myself as an actress on Broadway. I took vitamins and watched my diet, got plenty of rest, and tried to talk myself into being well. But before we got to New York, I had to seek medical help again.

There was a hospital across the street from my hotel, so on my way to the theater I stopped by. I knocked on the first door I saw bearing a doctor's name and told him what my problem was. After checking me, he said, "My God, woman, I know who you are. Why in the world are you walking around? Your blood count is one-third that of a normal human being. I don't know *how* you're walking around, even!"

He was ready to admit me to the hospital. "You have to go right to bed," he said.

"I can't go to bed," I said. "I've got this play to do. I have to be there."

"I understand what you're saying, and I appreciate that you have responsibilities to fulfill, but I've got to talk to your producer, director, whoever is responsible for you."

"Please, no, you can't do that. I don't want them to know that I'm ill," I said.

The doctor reluctantly agreed to treat me with injections of vitamins and iron, which he gave me almost daily, and he continued checking my blood count until finally we were about to close Chicago. Then he became more adamant: "I don't think you should take this responsibility of opening in New York, not now. I must talk to someone connected with your company."

I pleaded with him not to do it. After all, I was an adult, and such a decision should be in my hands. But he said that it would be unethical for him not to do so. "Your health is in jeopardy. If you keep going around like this without a two-week rest, you'll be flat on your back for a much longer duration than you would be ordinarily," he said.

It was determined that it would cost $20,000 a week for me to take such a rest and that the company couldn't afford it. The doctor raised his hands helplessly and said, "Then I am no longer responsible." We opened in New York as planned.

Earlier, during the year's run of *New Faces* when I had had the same problem, I had been taken to a doctor who was famous for his miraculous treatment of celebrities in and out of show business. Let's call him Dr. Wonder. And wonderful he seemed. He had put me back on my feet for *New Faces*, and I had heard nothing but praise for the man—go to him, and he works miracles. So when we got to New York with *Mrs. Patterson*, I gladly went back to Dr. Wonder. Again he injected me with some kind of miracle drug—it could have been B-12 and iron, for all I knew then—advising me that if I didn't come to him twice a week for the injections he wouldn't be responsible for my health. I got my strength back and began feeling good again. My hair, which had been turning yellow with my condition, returned to its normal coloring.

We opened to a glorious house and thundering applause. I could feel the presence of the critics in the first two rows, and I left Eartha Kitt standing guard in the wings as Eartha Mae drew from the depths of her life. I didn't really find my bearings until the third act, when I tapped directly from the well of experience. When the final curtain went down, I was so drained that I barely made it back to my dressing room. I remember my favorite stage manager, Morty Helphurn, saying to me, "Take it easy; don't give so much! You'll wear yourself out."

Just as I had gathered the strength and determination to take my makeup off, the door burst open. A seemingly endless line of theatergoers had formed: You were great! You were magnificent! You were this, you were that. Some were still crying from the last act. Morty opened the champagne that had been sent by a friend, Bob Collins. I was toasted; I was kissed; I was hugged. I was happy. Judging from the reaction, I thought surely we'd get good reviews. Finally, when everyone had been persuaded to leave me alone so that I could change for the theater party, the letdown came, and I put my face in my hands and cried.

The party was a good distance from the theater, and when I arrived everyone was waiting nervously for the papers. When the reviews were read aloud, it was jubilation time. Everything became so jumbled that I don't recall hearing any of the words, only Virginia Wicks saying to me, "You should be a very happy young lady." But I really didn't realize exactly how happy I should have been until a few days later, when I went to the theater and saw the printed signs of what the critics had said about me—or, rather, what they had said about Eartha Kitt. She had become a Broadway star, and later she would be nominated for Broadway's coveted and prestigeous award, the *Tony*. She didn't win, but the nomination was reward enough.

Meanwhile, my involvement with Paleface was crumbling long distance. His mother was exerting great pressure on him because she didn't want a black daughter-in-law. Jamie Dean, who was in constant touch with Paleface on the Coast, was calling me all the time to tell me how Paleface was reacting. Jamie was trying to help, but the outcome was inevitable. So, emotionally, I was really broken down. Although I had no way of knowing, I wasn't faring well physically either.

By the time the play had opened, Dr. Wonder had me feeling in the best of health. I was feeling so well, in fact, that I stopped going to him; I couldn't be dependent upon Dr. Wonder the rest of my life, I reasoned. All went well until one night when I walked out on the stage and just stood there, silent, staring out at the audience. And I felt myself just standing there. I heard Morty saying the words to me from the wings, thinking that I had forgotten them. But I knew them. And I kept talking to myself saying, Eartha, please, please, come on! You know the the words. Just say them! They would not come out. I just stood there, staring at the jammed theater.

Finally, I saw the curtain come down, and I think two people came and took me to my dressing room. I don't recall much of what was going on around me, but I remember hearing my maid saying, "Miss Kitt is ill, Miss Kitt is ill, Miss Kitt is ill! Call a doctor. I'm going to call a doctor." Within about fifteen minutes Dr. Wonder arrived, looked at me, and said, "Don't worry about a thing. I'll have her back onstage in five minutes."

He took my arm, and something within me knew that if he put one more needle in my arm I would never be the same again. And I fought him, screaming and yelling, "No! I hate you! You're a monster. I hate you, hate you. Don't *touch* me!"

Naturally everyone in the room thought that I had gone mad. *Mrs. Patterson* closed because I was physically unable to continue. But I would have no more to do with Dr. Wonder. It wasn't until years later that he lost his license and was, I believe, sent to prison. I never knew exactly what he was giving me in those hypodermics, nor did anyone else. But it certainly wasn't vitamins.

30

Kindred Spirits

Someone once described me as having the hand of God on my shoulder, saying that the whole of my talent and being is larger than the sum of its parts and that, after all is analyzed, there is something about me that is illusive and indefinable. Whether this is true of me, I'll leave to more objective critics. But there were two people I had the good fortune of knowing, to whom that phrase would most definitely apply: James Dean and Marilyn Monroe. Certainly the hand of God was on their shoulders.

Jamie (as I called him) and Marilyn were remarkably alike in a number of ways. Both were loners and lonely; both were hard-driving and sure of their career goals; and both were frustrated at the exploitation, misuse, and waste of their talent. Also, both send out vibrations from the movie screen that are gripping and awesome, as though somehow the film has captured not only their sounds and images, but their unseen auras and energy fields as well.

Since their deaths, at least a dozen books have been written about each of them. And at this writing, there are three new

books about each of them on the market. No doubt their un-
timely deaths contributed toward the establishment of the cults
that have made them as newsworthy and controversial in death
as in life. But their deaths only accelerated the inevitable. Their
presence on film does it: They transcend the parts they're playing
to send out spiritual darts that pierce you deeply, if your
receptors are tuned in. Since then, Kirlian photography has been
developed—a photographic method whereby the body's visible
energy field seems to change colors with each emotional
variation. I wouldn't be at all surprised to learn that Jamie and
Marilyn radiated a powerful energy field that even ordinary film
processes recorded. Perhaps we have yet to develop the means to
detect it or measure it.

Another thing Jamie and Marilyn had in common was their
penchant for using the telephone—particularly during the wee
morning hours. I was often the recipient of such calls, from
Jamie more often than Marilyn, for I really didn't know her that
well. And being a day person, I was always shocked and
irritated to be awakened by the phone ringing at 3:00 or 4:00
A.M., fearing terrible news of some kind. But relief and pleasure
would follow when I heard Marilyn's timid, soft tones or Jamie's
loud voice, which was almost always accompanied by laughter.

In the spring of 1975, author John Gilmore interviewed me
for his book *The Real James Dean* and jogged a good many of
my memories of Jamie. John had known him too, and in fact
had met me one night when I was with Jamie, in an encounter so
brief that I had forgotten it. We have the same literary agents,
and a few weeks after they had turned over John's book to his
publisher, I completed work on the chapter in this book that
begins with seeing my reflection in a window on Broadway.
When the agents read that, one of them became curious about a
remarkable and coincidental experience he remembered from
John's book.

Jamie had been moderately successful in New York but was
still unknown when he went to Hollywood. He was down on his
heels, sleeping in unlocked cars and making the rounds of studios
on foot. One day as he was leaving a network television station
(having found no work there) and was crossing Vine Street, he

caught sight of his raggedy, run-down reflection in the window of a restaurant and stood staring at himself in disbelief and frustration—just as I had stared at my own unkempt reflection on Broadway in either late December, 1951, or early January, 1952.

John had not mentioned Jamie's experience when he interviewed me. I, of course, had written about mine in my first autobiography, which was published in 1956, but John had not read my book. When my agent read my account, he called John to ask when Jamie's experience had occurred. "I'm not sure of the month," John said, "but it was either late 1951 or early 1952."

I wonder if perhaps Jamie and I were standing on opposite coasts and looking at our reflections at the exact same moment.

I don't remember when Jamie came into my life or where. I guess that we met in Hollywood in 1953, for we were each doing a movie—*East of Eden* and *New Faces*. At the time we were introduced, I didn't even know him by reputation. But it seemed as though he had always been a part of my life, or as though I had known him in a previous life. He'd make light of that last statement, I think. I can hear him now, in my mind, chuckling and saying, "Kitt, you're runnin' one of your spiritual numbers on me again."

Jamie and I were like brother and sister. He told me, in fact, that he thought of me as a sister. Our relationship was strictly platonic and spiritual; we had wonderful times together, both in New York and on the Coast. I wish I had kept a diary in those early days, but it never occurred to me to do so; we were all young, and we would never forget any of those wonderful moments, and we would live forever. I did write poetry then—and still do—but it was epigrammatic and introspective. Nothing of Jamie there.

When we were in New York, Jamie joined a dance class I taught, but not to learn how to dance. He was a consummate artist, always striving to improve himself. He wasn't satisfied to schlepp across stage; he wanted to move, to learn body language so that his movement, too, would communicate. After class we'd stroll in Central Park for hours, eating popcorn or hot dogs, often walking for fifteen or twenty minutes in complete silence. We were so attuned to one another that there was no need to fill the silence with small talk, as strangers or casual acquaintances do because they find it awkward.

I don't even recall how we happened to be in New York at the same time. I was working—maybe it was the time of my second appearance at La Vie en Rose—and Jamie might have been visiting old friends between pictures. I remember one incident vividly. I had a date with a casual acquaintance who shared my love for dancing. Just as I was leaving my room, Jamie arrived. I told him that I was going to the Palladium ballroom—we had often gone there together to listen to the good Cuban band and to watch the dancers—and suggested that he join us there later.

I forgot all about it, and an hour or so later I was sitting at a table with my date, Mr. George Abbot, and with Marlon Brando and his date, when Jamie showed up saying, "Hi! Here I am," and plopped down at our table. George looked at the interloper with considerable disdain. I introduced them, and within minutes they were having a heated argument. I don't remember what it was about, but it soon died of natural causes. Jamie stayed, listening and watching. He loved to watch people, and since I'm a people watcher too, I understood what he was doing. We very often received the exact same vibrations from people. Jamie absorbed experience like a sponge. One could almost see him mentally cataloging and filing everything away to draw upon for some future role.

Many of those who knew Jamie describe him as a solemn, intense, and troubled young man. I rarely saw this side of him. When we were together—mostly in Hollywood—it was play time. I think we were so close because each brought out the child in the other, and we didn't have to play the adult games or put up with the adult problems.

The phone would ring, awakening me, and I'd grope in the darkness for it.

"Yes?" I'd say.

"Hi!"

"Oh, Jamie."

"Yeah, How about going for a ride?"

I'd switch on the light and squint at the clock. "Do you know it's 4:00 A.M.?"

"Un-huh."

"Okay."

"Pick you up ten minutes."

In a child's world, 4:00 A.M. is as good a time as any to go riding. I loved it. I'd put on dungarees and a sweat shirt, grab my helmet, and be waiting when Jamie rumbled up to my place on that silly motorcycle of his. And off we'd go to cruise Sunset Boulevard. Sometimes we'd stop for coffee, or for talk at a park or bus stop. I remember one night, sitting and talking, when a drunk came weaving by. Jamie laughed and watched him closely, and when the drunk had gone from view Jamie got up and did an enormously funny imitation of him. Or sometimes he would relate conversations to me, imitating the voices perfectly. Most people don't know it, but his talents were such that he could have made his living as a stand-up comedian and impressionist.

Although we were so very close, Jamie and I had few mutual friends. John Gilmore thinks it was by Jamie's design, and perhaps he is right. In his book John describes a chance meeting in the early-morning hours when I was riding on the back of Jamie's bike and John was cruising Hollywood on his. Thinking back, I have a feeling that it was Eartha Mae and the real James Dean whom John discovered that morning. I learned from John that those small hours were what Jamie's crowd called the Night Watch. They would gather at a coffee shop, or cruise the streets on their bikes and clown around while the rest of the world slept.

I can't remember Jamie taking me to one of his haunts. Perhaps, as John suggests, Jamie blocked out that part of his life when he was with me. Maybe he sensed that Eartha Mae was too shy to meet groups of people. We'd often stop for hamburgers or coffee, but never where the Night Watch congregated.

Our early-morning treks were frequent and, for me, exhausting. I often wondered when Jamie slept but never asked him. I learned only recently from John that often Jamie didn't sleep. He'd show up at the studio with deep, dark rings beneath his eyes, and the studio makeup man would skillfully cover them. If one of us was out of town, Jamie would call me in the middle of the night and we'd laugh for hours. When I was on the nightclub circuit, it would be my turn to cover dark rings.

Occasionally, Jamie would call about matters important to him, particularly when he was troubled. Sometimes he'd ask my advice about a relationship with one girl or another. At other times he'd talk about professional problems, but he never asked my advice on these; he knew what was wrong and how it could be remedied. Such calls seemed a release valve for his anguish; he would talk it out. Jamie's biggest personal trial came while filming *Giant*. He'd call almost every night, so upset with the film—and apparently so at odds with the director—that each day he dreaded going before the cameras. He vowed that when the film was completed, he'd never go to see it.

Jamie felt that he was not being allowed to develop the character he portrayed in *Giant*, particularly his change and growth during the second half of the film. He felt that he was being restrained from using his full acting potential. I had never known him to be so distraught and troubled. He felt a bit insulted, too, at being sandwiched between what he referred to as "surface actors" and "two of the weakest actors in the business": Elizabeth Taylor and Rock Hudson. Jamie said that he couldn't carry his character "under the surface" with such weak supporting actors, and his frustration erupted in arguments with the director and others. He didn't see *Giant* as just another Hollywood film. He wanted to give it his best, and it hurt me to see him suffer. It was a slick epic film, and Jamie knew it could have been much more than that. As it turned out, he never lived to see *Giant* released.

I don't recall ever dressing up to go out with Jamie. We always wore dungarees and sweat shirts or tee shirts, unless we were attending a party; even then, we never went formal. Most of them were what we called drum parties. Besides teaching Jamie the exercise and body movement of the dance, I also taught him to play drums. He loved the intricate rhythms of

Cuban and Afro-Cuban drum patterns. And we often brought percussion instruments to someone's house, where we'd play records and drum to the music. Nothing stronger than wine or beer was served, and I can't recall anyone ever getting drunk. This was a far cry from the notoriously wild Hollywood one reads about, but that's the way our drum parties were.

In his very private life, Jamie was aesthetic. He wrote poetry, loved music and art, and lived to act. His wants were few and his tastes simple. He lived in a small, inexpensive apartment, which he used primarily for making phone calls and changing clothes—he seemed always to stay at someone else's house or guest house. He seemed to have no desire for creature comforts, for big houses or swimming pools or fancy clothes. He had only three passions, I think: motorcycles, sports cars, and acting. He seemed to have little regard for money—unless he had his eye on a new sports car. But the things I found most fascinating about Jamie were his childlike shyness, his wit, his extraordinary intelligence, his philosophical bent, and his uncanny psychological insight. He studied people constantly and knew more about their psychological makeup than any other layman I have ever met.

In 1955, just five days before Jamie's death in an automobile accident, I returned to Hollywood for a few days' rest between engagements. I went over to see Paleface and was surprised to find Jamie opening the door for me. As was our custom, we hugged one another, and I felt a strange emptiness in Jamie.

"Jamie," I said. "What's happened to you? Something's wrong. You're not here."

Jamie grinned and shook his head. "Oh, Kitt, you're running one of your spiritual numbers on me again."

I had had the distinct impression that his spirit had already left him. I know that sounds weird, but it happened. As I said before and as I used to tell him, I felt as though he had always been with me. Yes, I was stunned but not surprised to hear of his death. But I never felt the loss of his presence, except for that one day when it seemed that his spirit was passing to the other side. I don't believe he has ever left me. I debated setting this part of my story down, because I'm sure that some of you will think I'm whacko. But it happened.

I was never close friends with Marilyn Monroe, but like Jamie, she seemed drawn to me. I first met her at a party many years before her death. And since neither of us cared for large gatherings, where it was impossible to get to really *know* people, it was probably natural that we two wallflowers would strike up an acquaintance. Marilyn used to spend an hour or two psyching herself up for parties, and I suppose, in a way, I did too. I've often wondered who approached whom, because Marilyn was as shy as I was. Maybe we both chose the same corner to hide in that evening. From then on, whenever we were trapped at the same party, we'd find a quiet place where names weren't being dropped and we'd sit and talk. Marilyn was a very good conversationalist and a most intelligent woman. After we told each other what we had been doing since we had last met, we'd discuss current events or music or books.

I never visited her home, nor did she visit mine. In fact, I didn't even know her phone number. But not long after we'd met she began calling me—usually at odd hours of the night or morning. It never occurred to me to ask how she got my unlisted number. By that time I had grown accustomed to Jamie's 3:00 A.M. calls, and it was common knowledge that Marilyn often called people late at night.

I remember something from an F. Scott Fitzgerald novel to the effect that in the dark night of the soul, it is always three o'clock in the morning. We confront ourselves at such times. Perhaps Jamie's Night Watch served to guard against such confrontations—I don't know. But Marilyn's Night Watch was a lonely vigil, and her link with others was the telephone; I think it saw her through many frightening nights. Marilyn never had a specific reason to call me. She'd say, "Hi. This is Marilyn. How are you?" As though I couldn't recognize that distinctive voice. But that wasn't the message I received. What she was really saying, I think, was, "Tell me you're out there—that someone is out there. Reassure me that I'm not the only one in the entire world who's awake tonight and alone."

There was nothing momentous about any of our conversations. It was small talk, mostly cheerful, about everything and nothing. We didn't know each other well enough for Marilyn to confide in me. For this reason, I had the impression that I was her last resort. If she could reach no one else she'd call Eartha. Or, if she had already talked to everyone else she knew closely, she'd call Eartha.

I think Marilyn Monroe was a very gifted actress, but she was cursed with both great beauty and natural sensuality—a curse many women would love to bear. But if you're a truly gifted actress, beauty and sensuality can destroy you in a place like Hollywood, where lust and sex are synonymous with love —or are mistaken for it. Thus, beauty and sensuality are exploited at the box office. Marilyn's talent was thrown away as she was miscast in one silly, superficial sex-bomb picture after another. There were a couple of exceptions, but if one has the gift and burning desire to act, one has to die a little each day when the gift and desire are sacrificed at the box office.

Unfortunately, Marilyn allowed the commercial world to devour her. She was a very frightened person. I don't think she was able to differentiate between her *self* and the marquee. I have Eartha Mae, who doesn't identify with the name on the marquee in letters taller than she. Somewhere along the line, Marilyn lost Norma Jeane. I suppose it's what psychologists would call an identity crisis. If so, it was a tragic one. How does one go about treating or helping a marquee?

In his book, John Gilmore tells how James Dean entered the studio commissary one day to find a huge blow-up photograph of himself hanging on the wall. In rage, he ripped the photograph down and screamed at the studio brass nearby that they had no right to hang his picture on the wall. That wasn't his home, and they didn't own him. His action was considered eccentric, but in light of what happened to Marilyn, one can see that Jamie's action was very rational indeed. He was fighting to keep his personal identity, to keep from being swallowed up by something commercially bigger than himself.

31

Before the Exile

There's a movie being re-run on television these days called *If It's Tuesday, This Must Be Belgium*, which deals in part with the frantic pace of group tours, where the tourists are herded like cattle from one country to another, trying desperately to see as much as they can in the little time allotted—something like fifteen countries in eight days. The film reminds me very much of my personal life and career from the mid-fifties to the mid-or late sixties. My professional itinerary looked like a bilingual crossword puzzle, and was nearly as challenging and confusing.

It would have been relatively easy to keep my American commitments in some semblance of order, but I kept getting offers from Europe, Asia, and South America that I couldn't refuse. So I hopped back and forth, logging millions of air miles and entertaining in 92 countries besides my own. At home, I continued my work in legitimate theater, which I love. I co-starred with Eddie Bracken in the Broadway production *Shinbone Alley*, a musical version of *Archy and Mehitabel*. I toured the Straw Hat circuit in *Mrs. Patterson*, and played the La Jolla, California, stock company production of *The Skin of*

Our Teeth, with James Whitmore, Cloris Leachman, and Dennis Hopper. And I toured cross-country in *The Owl and the Pussycat*.

Aside from the films I did in Europe, I co-starred with Sidney Poitier and Juan Hernandez in *The Mark of the Hawk*, filmed in England and Africa and released by Universal Pictures; did *St. Louis Blues* with the late Nat King Cole, for Paramount; and co-starred with Sammy Davis, Jr., in *Anna Lucasta* for United Artists—yes, Sammy had even exceeded the prophetic declaration he had shouted above the traffic noises in San Francisco, and I doubt that he was any more delighted than I was.

It seemed that I spent half my life on television in those ten years or so. I guest-starred frequently on every variety show, including "The Ed Sullivan Show," "The Colgate Comedy Hour," and "The Steve Allen Show," to name a few. I did all the talk shows and numerous straight dramatic shows, such as starring in the "Omnibus" presentation "Salome" and the critically acclaimed "Wingless Victory" for "Play of the Week." I appeared as guest star in dozens of series, winning an Emmy nomination for a segment called "The Loser" in the "I Spy" series, starring Robert Culp and Bill Cosby. In addition to these and many other television shows, I became a regular on a daytime celebrity quiz show and a semi-regular as the Cat Woman on the "Batman" series, which also featured the wonderful actor (and my very close friend) Cesar Romero as the Joker and Pierre Salinger, who had been John F. Kennedy's press secretary. "The Batman" series was great fun to do, and was considered very campy and in at the time; some of the biggest names in show business vied for spots on the show.

During this period I was nearly as active in European theater and television. I starred in a number of plays, including *Bunny*, which ran for more than a year in England and *The High Bid*, which played for six months. And I did nineteen television specials for the BBC and other European networks, including "This is Eartha," a variety special filmed for Swedish broadcasting, which won the Golden Rose First Place Award in

1962 for the best special of the year against entries from fourteen other countries in the Montreux Film Festival.

I wasn't quite so active in records, but I was doing well. I had three hit singles in America and five RCA albums that fought each other for the top four places on the national charts for about two years: "Eartha Kitt," "That Bad Eartha," "Down to Eartha," "St. Louis Blues," which I recorded with Shorty Rogers, and "Thursday's Child," which took its title from my autobiography and was released at about the same time. I also recorded a number of albums in Europe. Three of them, "Love for Sale," "Romantic Eartha," and "Sentimental Eartha," are still in release in England.

Then there were concert tours through Australia, the Middle East, Scandinavia, and the rest of Europe; several Command Performances before the Queen in London; benefits in America, England, Israel, and other countries; the writing of my first autobiography, which took me nearly three years, as I hopped around the globe; and the club dates. Besides some of the clubs I've mentioned, I had the pleasure of breaking gross and attendance records at London's Talk of the Town, (three years in a row), at the Chi-Chi in Palm Springs, at the Sahara Inn in Chicago, at the Shoreham Hotel in Washington, D.C., and, during snowstorms, at New York City's Latin Quarter. There were other memorable club appearances in Lake Tahoe and Reno, in New York at the Persian Room of the Plaza and at the Empire Room of the Waldorf Astoria, at the Americana in Miami Beach, and many others.

Interlaced with my concerts, tours, films, television, writing, benefits, nightclub engagements, recording dates, and plays, was my private life, which was going as marvelously as my career. Fortunately, I returned to El Rancho in Las Vegas every year for seven years. This afforded me the opportunity of being near home once in a while, for I had purchased a home in Beverly Hills that had once been the stables and livery room of a huge estate. Someone had joined the two structures by adding a kitchen, family room, and bedrooms at one end and a bar, dressing room, master bedroom, basement office, and pool dressing room at the other. I have been decorating it and modifying it to suit my own taste for more than eighteen years, and I'm still not finished. For, unless I force myself to take a vacation, I'm seldom home more than three or four weeks at a time.

I had no sooner moved into my new home when I installed an assortment of dogs and cats, some doves, and about twenty-five chickens. Then I planted a large garden, which I keep planted the year around—collard greens, beans, and all the good stuff. I'm a nut on organically grown vegetables and seldom buy canned or frozen. It wasn't long before the city tried to take my chickens away from me. One can't keep chickens in Beverly Hills, they told me. But I've never believed in the adage that you can't fight city hall. I collared the mayor and had heated discussions with him, and it was finally discovered that according to the statues, any land that had housed livestock before 1954 was exempt from the ordinance prohibiting animals. My house had once been a stable, so I got to keep (and still have) my chickens.

So I finally had a home to call my own, no more apartments and hotels. And soon I had a husband to call my own, then a daughter—a family at last. But the marriage didn't work out. What can be said of a failed marriage? No one likes to dwell on failure. Bill and I were married in 1960; our daughter, Kitt, was born in 1961 and we were divorced in 1965. To avoid raising unanswered questions, I'll add that my ex-husband was a student when I met him, and he's white. Our marriage was going to last forever, but like more than half the marriages in this country today, ours didn't last.

I can't speak for Bill, but I was immeasurably enriched by our union: I have my daughter, who's truly the sunshine of my life, and I found a close friend in my late mother-in-law, whom I adored.

I continued to work until the last few weeks of my pregnancy. I wasn't very big, and I had gowns designed that made my condition almost undetectable. My last engagement before my baby was born was "Sunday Night at the Palladium" in London. On the final night, I was onstage before a live audience, but the show was being televised as well. I was in the middle of my performance, and about to seat myself on a tall stool before the microphone, when my baby gave me a kick that would floor a mule. She had been kicking a lot, but never that hard and never onstage. I was so startled that I tripped and nearly lost my balance before I grabbed the stool for support. I also instinctively grabbed my stomach, then realized that the show had stopped momentarily and that I was bent over, one hand on the stool and the other on my stomach, while the audience and television camera stared at me in wonder.

I had been calling the baby Junior, thinking that I would have a boy. So when I regained my composure and had partially recovered from the stupendous kick, I looked down at my stomach and said something like, "Don't worry, Junior, I promise this will be our last show until you are born." The audience laughed. I laughed and the show went on. But to my amazement, the BBC's telephone started ringing immediately, and for days afterward the station received a flood of mail from irate viewers complaining that I had made reference to being "with child" on their home television sets. How times change!

Being a mother is the most natural thing in the world to me and the most joyous experience of my life. Six weeks after Kitt was born, I went back to work at the Chi-Chi in Palm Springs. I was breast-feeding my baby and, unfortunately for me and for my gowns, mother's milk became an all-too-apparent part of my act.

I was booked to appear at the Talk of the Town in London several weeks later. The doctor wouldn't let Kitt travel until she was three months old so I had to go ahead without her, but my sister-in-law, Norene, brought her to me before my engagement ended. I took a nurse, Mrs. McCullogh, during my London stay, but I haven't had one since. I didn't believe in nurses raising children and I wouldn't be without Kitt; consequently, she traveled around the world with me several times before she was even of school age.

I enrolled her in private schools when she was old enough, and we traveled with tutors until she got into junior high and began forming the friendships that are so important to her. Then

I determined to focus my career in America so that we could stay at home and live a more normal life. But something happened that forced my career into exile. To make a living for us, I was forced to work abroad whether I liked it or not. The force was political and subtle and absolutely overpowering. And, ironically, it was exerted by invitation.

32

The Washington Tea Party

In January, 1968, I was invited to participate in the year's first Woman Doers' Luncheon, instituted and organized by our then First Lady, Mrs. Lyndon Johnson. The subject for the meeting was to be "Why is there so much juvenile delinquency in the streets of America?" I thought the question a good one and the opportunity to exchange ideas and points of view most worthwhile, so I accepted the invitation and even paid my own transportation expenses.

The guest list included fifty women, some of whom were leaders concerned with anti-crime activities. At the time, I had no idea how my name had gotten on the list. I later learned that Congressman Roman Pucinski, chairman of the House Committee on Juvenile Delinquency, had recommended me. According to Liz Carpenter, Mrs. Johnson's staff director and press secretary, as reported in her book *Ruffles and Flourishes*, Congressman Pucinski apparently was asked "...if any famous personality from Hollywood [a guest who always stirs interest] had ever done anything in the field." Congressman Pucinski is reported to have replied: "Yes, Eartha Kitt has testified in favor of the President's anti-crime bill. She was articulate. And she's done a good job in Watts, teaching ballet classes." (I taught dance, not ballet.)

Despite the incredible furor that resulted from my participation at the Woman Doers' Luncheon, Congressman Pucinski's intentions in recommending me were most honorable, for the Illinois Democrat and I had worked together on a project a year or two before the luncheon. I was touring in *The Owl and the Pussycat*, playing Washington, D.C., when representatives of a youth group calling themselves Rebels with a Cause approached me for help. Their organization was taking kids off the streets—mostly youngsters without jobs—and channeling their talents and energies into constructive endeavors, particularly cleaning up the back streets of the capital. They had gone as far as they could go with their own resources and were seeking government aid to continue projects that they had initiated using their own funds. They had sought out members of Congress and anti-poverty personnel, but no one would listen to them. They needed a spokesman.

The Rebels with a Cause took me on a tour of four or five areas, showing me dirt streets that had never been paved since they were built in the thirties, crowded apartment buildings without the luxury of hot running water, and other conditions one would expect to find only in the very worst ghettos. Our national showcase looked like a movie lot: millions, even billions, of dollars in magnificent buildings and monuments, and behind them, Tobacco Road.

Ironically, at about the same time, a public relations representative of the anti-poverty program was showing me around town too, pointing out what the program was accomplishing—which wasn't much. The anti-poverty money was being horribly mismanaged. Most of it was siphoned off, and what little money finally trickled down was being used to treat the symptoms rather than the malady. But they were trying. The public relations man wanted me to speak kindly of the program whenever the opportunity arose. I didn't object to his suggestion. That was his job, and it wasn't his fault that much of the money wasn't getting to the people who sincerely wanted to get the job done. And if enough people like me praised the program, he thought, it would ease the task of getting money from Congress for its continuation. The public relations man was not aware that Rebels with a Cause existed, and it seemed to me that the intelligent move would be to get the two groups together.

I tried to call Adam Clayton Powell, but he wasn't in town. Then I remembered having met Congressman Pucinski, who had impressed me as being sensitive and concerned. He agreed to meet with the Rebels with a Cause, and I asked if he would bring along representatives of the anti-poverty program, which he did.

The meeting went well, and afterward Congressman and Mrs. Pucinski joined me in the lobby of my hotel, where we talked until nearly daybreak. When we finally parted, we did so as friends closely joined by a common goal. The congressman mentioned that he was going to take the matter up with Hubert Humphrey. He said: "I'm ashamed of myself, Eartha. I'm a public servant, and I'm afraid my eyes have been closed. I was not aware of what is right here under my own nose. Maybe I'm not curious enough, maybe I've been too busy, but I had no idea that there were areas like these in Washington, D.C., or even that the people think the way they do. Thank you very much for making me aware, and I will do whatever I can to see that these things are corrected."

Roman Pucinski kept his word. The Rebels with a Cause received the funds they needed, and their most pressing problems were remedied.

The point in my relating the Rebels with a Cause story is that I do not take such causes lightly. So when I was invited to a meeting at which "Crime in the Streets" was the topic, I accepted with a grave sense of personal commitment. It was no secret to anyone that the highest incidence of crime involved ghetto minorities in the urban areas of the country. And these were the areas about which I was the most knowledgeable. The Rebels with a Cause episode wasn't an isolated incident; countless such groups—both youth and adult—have approached me for help over the years. I have been visiting ghettos and talking to people in every city where I have worked, and not only did I have a dance workshop in Harlem, when I lived in New York, but I formed the one in Watts when I moved to California. It's still going, after more than ten years.

So I keep in touch with people—particularly the young. And before leaving for the Washington luncheon, I talked with a group called the Mothers of Watts about crime in the streets. The consensus was that the war in Vietnam was one of the biggest problems—both economically and morally. The Mothers of Watts were concerned with the disproportionate numbers from minorities who were fighting the war, and with the drain on the economy from the $80 billion a year that the war was costing us. And, perhaps worst of all in their view, the good were indeed dying young: If a young man was law abiding, he was rewarded by being given a gun and the opportunity to kill or be killed in Vietnam. But if he had a record, the armed forces wouldn't take him, and he was deprived of this "privilege." There were few black men—or poor men of any race or color, for that matter—who had the cultural background and money to get a college draft deferment. But they could (and many did) get a *crime* deferment!

Was this cowardly of them? Many will think so. But not the people with whom I talked. They could understand an enemy like Hitler, a madman who had built a war machine that had not only crushed other countries but also had been rapidly gaining the capacity to storm American shores. Now *that* was an enemy! But the Vietnamese? They were farmers fighting among themselves who were unable to build an air force, let alone a navy, that could storm our shores.

Their reasoning was valid regardless of one's point of view. These were sweeping generalizations, yes, but contributing factors nonetheless. Vietnam was only one of many issues I wanted to raise at the luncheon, if given the chance. But things got a little out of hand—to say the least.

I flew from my home to Washington at my own expense, and a limousine took me to my hotel. The following day, a car from the White House drove me to the luncheon. But rather than joining the small reception that was being given prior to the luncheon, I was directed instead to a room in which three men sat with a tape recorder, and I was questioned and cross-examined regarding my views on the day's topic and other related matters. As I recall, the three men represented themselves as members of the president's anti-crime committee or something like that. All I know is that they were in a White House office of their own and therefore obviously represented someone in the White House.

I was the only woman in the room. I don't know if the other forty-nine luncheon guests were questioned or not. But the point is, I aired my views candidly, just as I was to air them at the luncheon—though with more passion, under the circumstances—so that these people knew what I was going to say if the opportunity presented itself. After the questioning, I was escorted to meet and be photographed with Mrs. Johnson. We chatted for a moment before adjourning to the dining room.

In her book entitled *Lady Bird Johnson: A Whitehouse Diary*, Mrs. Johnson emphasized that several of the guests were late, but named only one of them: me. One could gather from the way she singles me out that my tardiness was indicative of my seeming audaciousness. I was, in fact, not late. I arrived in the White House car that was sent for me and was detained by the three men with the tape recorder. I was then taken to meet Mrs. Johnson.

Mrs. Johnson writes in her book that, because of her nervousness, she ate very little. She also notes that I too ate very little, and she was right. I eat infrequently and very lightly, and only when I'm hungry. I wasn't hungry and, besides, the prospect of participating in a seminar on "Crime in the Streets" wasn't conducive to a hearty appetite. She also stated in her book that I sat and smoked a great deal—which would be unusual for me, for I'm a light smoker; but I didn't count. One gathers from her account of the luncheon that she was paying an inordinate amount of attention to me. Perhaps my chagrin at the way the luncheon was developing was apparent to her; it was beginning to take on all the overtones of the Mad Hatter's tea party.

In all fairness, I should say that many of the ladies around me acted with a good deal of dignity. But most did not. No one at my table seemed at all concerned with the topic at hand. Most were taking menus as souvenirs, tasting the wine and jotting down the brand, and marveling about the table settings (some even *sketched* the table settings), the furnishings, the carpeting, even the chandeliers. But most of all, there were the excited whispers—even during the talk by one guest speaker—about the rumor that Lyndon Johnson would make an appearance: "Do you *really* think he might?" "Someone said that they heard someone else say that the president. . . ." And on it went.

Then there were the television cameras, the newspeople. As a show business person, it was obvious to me that the luncheon was being carefully staged for the president's appearance. And in my opinion, most of the people there were more concerned with the decor, the television cameras and newspeople, and the prospect of seeing Lyndon Johnson in person than they were in discussing crime in the streets. I was most definitely getting upset. I hadn't flown from Los Angeles to Washington, D.C., to watch a show.

And Mr. Johnson did make an appearance. Right in the *middle* of the first speaker's talk! As Mrs. Johnson reports in her book, ". . . when Mrs. Moore was speaking, suddenly Liz [Carpenter] had risen and said, 'Mrs. Moore, will you yield to another speaker?' And in walked Lyndon." Forget that Mrs. Moore may have been building to a point in her speech. Whatever she had said would be forgotten. "Will you yield to another speaker?" was not cute; it was rude. It would have been a nice gesture for President Johnson to have met the ladies at the reception before the luncheon. But there were no television cameras then. Now it seemed contrived, a purely political move, a dramatic entrance that stopped the "show."

The president's opening statement carried the implication that we fifty were the chosen ones and that we were fortunate to have been selected out of 200 million people. Then he talked in platitudes: Support our police; Combating crime starts in the home. He closed by relating how each night he and his family listened to a particular radio program in which the announcer signed off by asking, "Parents, where are your children tonight?" When he finished speaking, it seems to me that I raised my hand

and rose to ask him a question. Mrs. Johnson's account has me blocking his path between the podium and the door. I don't recall doing so, but I was certainly angry enough.

"Mr. President," I said, "what are we to do about delinquent *parents*—those who have to work and are too busy to look after their children? Don't you think it might be more appropriate for the children to ask, 'Parents, where are you?' Because taxes are so heavy, both parents often have to work and are forced to leave their children alone."

"We have just passed a Social Security bill that allots millions of dollars for day-care centers," the President replied.

I was momentarily bewildered by his reply. Our subject was crime in the streets; day-care centers were for small children, not teenagers who were forming gangs and terrorizing neighborhoods. I was concerned with lower-income families in which both father and mother have to work and combine their wages just to make ends meet. But his non sequitur effectively threw me off stride. "But what are we going to do?" I asked.

"That's something for you women to discuss here," the president said. Then someone took his arm and whisked him out of the dining room.

Mrs. Johnson says that I then stubbed out a cigarette and tossed my long hair, and from that point on she watched me, waiting for something to happen. She didn't know, she says, what to expect of me. I suggest that she might have expected me to participate; that's what I had been invited for. I hadn't flown several thousand miles to hear Mr. Johnson tell us how privileged we were to be there or that we should support our local police or that crime-prevention begins at home or which radio program his family listened to each night. She also mentioned that I didn't applaud any of the speakers. Is that all she did during the luncheon, watch me?

I don't know whether I applauded or not. I'll take her word for it, since she was apparently studying me closely and I wasn't taking notes on my own actions. Certainly there was little to applaud. There were long speeches, one about street lights—this from a decidedly upper-class lady (by Mrs. Johnson's admission) who had waged war on her city for more and better street lighting. Ghetto areas can't even get the cities to pave or repair their streets, let alone spend thousands or millions to light them. Then, of course, there was talk of more police, higher wages, better training, and pensions. Fine; they're deserving of it. But what about getting some of them out of those black-and-white tanks and onto the beats, where people can get to know them as human beings? What about looking at causes rather than treating symptoms?

One lady told about the more articulate policemen in her area visiting junior and senior high classrooms in an effort to bridge the gap between the students and the law. Fine, but what of the drop-outs? Well, that was being taken care of too. There was a campaign under way to find Saturday and Sunday work for them: rounding up clothes. Mrs. Lyndon Johnson liked the "hopeful, 'can-do' tone" of what was being said. She also liked Martha Coe, a VISTA worker in the slums of Atlanta, who looked "young and fresh, well scrubbed and enthusiastic."

When the meeting was thrown open to the guests, I was even more appalled. One woman told how she fought crime in the streets. When she saw a small child with a rock that might be thrown, she would take the rock from the child and say, "No, no! You mustn't do that. Naughty, naughty!" I thought we were going to discuss *causes* of crime in the streets. I thought we were going to concern ourselves with motivation, with the frustration, the anger, the needs that were perhaps contributing to our ever-increasing crime rate. Maybe even the moral (or immoral) climate in the country that might well spawn crime. I thought we were there to talk substance, to dig, to explore. Why were more and more of our children—rich and poor—turning to dope? Why were we apparently becoming more violence-prone? If we knew the solutions to such problems, we might be able to effect counter-measures. Street lights? More police? But what of the *causes?*

Mrs. Johnson tells in her book about how she noticed that my hand was up. Actually, I raised it after practically every speaker. The further afield the discussion went, the more frustrated I became. Mrs. Johnson says: "I noticed Miss Kitt's hand go up and I knew I must, in turn, get to her. I did not know what to expect—only I sensed that she had come to say something and that it would not be good."

That's a very telling remark on Mrs. Johnson's part. In her book she praises a speaker who had formed a group to install 9,000 street lights in Indianapolis; she liked her hopeful tone. She had been told that my interest was particularly in the ghetto areas. The discussion was supposed to be crime in the street, and yet she sensed that what I had come to say would "not be good"! She herself had begun the luncheon by stating that crime was a grim subject for a "pleasant meeting such as this...." Well, it hadn't been a grim meeting at all. The subject was as pleasant as the lunch. And every time an opinion was given and it occurred to me that the other side of that opinion should be explored, I'd raise my hand and Mrs. Johnson would say, "Yes, Miss Kitt, you'll have your turn." And I waited and waited.

When I was finally recognized, I tried to speak candidly about what I felt (that's why, I thought, I was invited) and to express the opinions of the many people with whom I'd talked prior to the luncheon. Unlike some of the other ladies there, whom Mrs. Johnson found remarkable because "...they walk out of their comfortable lives and barge head first—unafraid apparently—into the problems of the ghettos, learning about them firsthand by working with the people," I had lived there. I don't remember my exact words, but those who know me understand that when I speak about something that truly concerns me, I speak passionately. My delivery is very rapid, staccato-like. And I raised my voice so that all in the room could hear, not just Mrs. Johnson. This was mistaken by Mrs. Johnson as anger directed toward her. Looking back, I can understand how she might have misinterpreted my remarks. But I wasn't upset with the first lady or the lady of the street lights or any of the others. I *was* upset that the meeting seemed staged and that we weren't getting down to the nitty-gritty of the problem.

The thrust of my opinion was that crime in the streets might be related to the moral climate of America and its seeming preoccupation with violence. We raise our children at home and in school with guidelines: the golden rule and, hopefully, other philosophical principles of Christianity and the rest of the religions. Then we show them the double standard of reality. Thou shalt not kill, unless you don't have a police record. I was concerned about women I had talked to who feared they were raising a fresh crop of youngsters for the war we couldn't win and that would never end. I talked with young men across the country who felt that it didn't pay to be law-abiding; with a record they could avoid Vietnam. I was concerned about the countless young men who approached me whenever I appeared professionally in Canada and the Scandinavian countries, young men who had fled the United States to avoid the draft. Each of them said essentially the same thing: Please tell the American people that we're not criminals or cowards, but that we can't fight in good conscience in a civil war in which our country continually establishes corrupt dictatorships in the name of democracy.

All right. It was an extemporaneous expression of one point of view. I don't recall, but I may well have said, as Mrs. Johnson reports, that I knew the feeling of having a baby "come out of my guts," and that I didn't go through such labor to have the baby one day snatched off to a war like Vietnam. Such graphic remarks apparently didn't set too well with the peppermint ice cream dessert. But I was speaking from the depths of my heart. And in retrospect, it seems to me that at least it brought the subject down from the street lights in the sky to earth, where it belonged.

With God as my witness, I had no intention of launching a diatribe against the war in Vietnam. But the reaction to my statements precluded my saying much more. I wanted, for example, to discuss such things as the Los Angeles supermarket chain that took all of its dented and labelless cans and other damaged merchandise from its middle and upper-class stores and shipped them to Watts, where the price of each item was *raised* before being put on the shelves. (This is a matter of public record.) Well, that was good business. Many of Watts' people don't have transportation to shop outside their own area. The supermarket chain had a captive clientele.

So I said my piece to Mrs. Johnson. Right or wrong, eloquent or not, it was my honest opinion. I expected her to discuss my remarks. Instead, she stood up straight as a board, fists clenched, and said, "Miss Kitt, just because there's a war going on doesn't mean that we cannot be *civilized!*" Then she sat back down and put her face in her hands, elbows on the table. I was astonished. She had quite obviously taken my remarks personally. And I couldn't understand why. I wondered, what is this all about? Hadn't the implied question been: What causes or contributes to crime in the streets, and what can be done about it? Couldn't my point of view be recorded, passed on to the president and to Congress along with the views of the other women? Was this a sounding board, or was it simply a theme luncheon to no end?

At this point, Mrs. Johnson and I differ as to what was said. A woman in the back corner of the room suddenly stood up, glaring at me as though I was the lowest creature that had ever crawled the earth, and said, "Miss Kitt, I'll have you know that I have *eight* sons, and I would be glad to donate each one of them to Vietnam any day!" But according to Mrs. Johnson, who apparently knew the lady, she said, ". . . I have eight sons. One of them is now in the Air Force. None of them wants to go to Vietnam. All will go. They and their friends. . . ."

In my heart I wondered, what have I done? What did I do wrong? I was invited here to express my opinion—whether anyone agreed with me or not—and I honestly and earnestly had done so. They apparently didn't want to communicate. And I said to the woman, "I'm sorry, but I don't think I can talk to any of you, now."

As I sat down, the lady seated next to me patted me on the thigh and said, "Thank you for saying that. We all want to say the same thing, but, unfortunately, you see, most of our husbands work for the government."

In her book, Mrs. Johnson says that she felt a surge of gratitude that Bennetta Washington, an experienced and responsible "Negro," spoke up to me, saying that we were gathered to release constructive, not destructive, energies. That was pretty much the tenor of the meeting: no exploration of the causes, but rather an elaboration of the cosmetic treatment of symptoms.

Mrs. Johnson does tell of another "Negro" woman's complaint that there's a double standard of justice, that if a black kills a black, the murder is not pursued as vigorously as it would be if a white person were involved. And Mrs. Johnson felt that there was truth to that statement.

Politicians' wives seem to have been well represented among the "chosen fifty." There was the woman who told me, ". . . our husbands work for the government." Mrs. Johnson says she was comforted by a senator's wife, who had been one of the fifty. Liz Carpenter wrote that the woman with eight children was the wife of a governor—in her book Mrs. Johnson named the lady, but neglected to mention her first name or the fact that she was the wife of a governor. No wonder it was so cold in there.

Of the two books mentioned, Mrs. Carpenter's *Ruffles and Flourishes* is the more charming and witty. She wasn't any easier on me, but she was less shrill and put the incident in more rational perspective. She says that I "left without the usual thank-you, and no one delayed her departure." True and false. It's true that there were no thank-yous. No one would speak to me; in fact, no one even came near me (afraid of guilt by association?). But I was delayed. The car that was put at my disposal apparently got lost. I was left alone on the White House steps until a kindly doorman and a pretty White House aide finally came to my rescue and tracked it down.

Mrs. Carpenter also relates another incident that shows how clearly the administration, from top to bottom, misunderstood the Vietnam war dissenters. She points out with great irony that probably the most surprised man in Washington was Colonel Rowland Beasley, who was head of the USO performers and who was startled at what Mrs. Carpenter calls my White House "performance." The colonel was supposed to have been waiting all afternoon for me at the Pentagon (when I was scheduled to be at the White House all afternoon?) because I had asked earlier that morning for him to make arrangements for me to entertain the troops in Vietnam. They simply could not understand how I could be against the war in Vietnam and want to entertain our troops over there. They simply could not understand that one reason I and millions like me were against the war was that we were interested in the safety, welfare, and happiness of our American soldiers in Vietnam.

This kind of thinking infected every administration that served during that seemingly endless war: If you were against the war, then you were un-American. Yet it was President Johnson who gained office by promising to end the war and by saying that he didn't believe that American boys should be sent to fight Asian boys' wars!

The White House car returned me to my hotel. I immediately took a cab to meet the leaders of Rebels with a Cause, who were to take me on a tour of what they had accomplished with the aid of the anti-poverty program. And on the taxi drivers radio, I heard the news: "Eartha Kitt, at a luncheon with Mrs. Johnson this afternoon, brought the first lady to tears." I couldn't believe what I heard. I hadn't been away from the White House for more than two hours. First, it wasn't true. Mrs. Johnson was not in tears—she emphasizes this in her own book. Second, even if it had been true, how did that radio announcer find out? The newsmen had left with their television cameras as soon as President Johnson had concluded his brief talk to us. It wasn't until I read Mrs. Johnson's book that I learned there were newswomen among the fifty invited guests. They didn't help clarify matters at all.

The Rebels with a Cause showed me newly paved streets, swimming pools that were open now to minorities, recreation parks completed or under construction, and all kinds of other wonderful accomplishments. Then, at ten o'clock that night, we all went to dinner. I decided to call home, because I had told my daughter that I'd be home that evening and it was apparent that I wouldn't be returning until the following morning. There was still more to see, and I had another appointment or two that I had put off. My housekeeper answered and said, "My God, where are you? Jordan [my business manager, Jordan Carlin] has been calling every ten minutes. He's worried to death!"

"Why? What's the matter?" I said.

There was a long pause, and Evelyn Lynch, my late mother-in-law's sister, came on the line. "Eartha!" she said, panic stricken, "Where are you?"

"I'm in a restaurant. I haven't eaten all day, and I've been so busy. . . ."

"Don't move! Don't say a thing. Don't talk to anybody. You get right on a plane and come home!"

"Why? What's wrong?"

"What's wrong? Are you serious? You're all over the news—radio, television—and they're saying terrible things about you. Kitt's worried, I'm worried, Jordan's worried. You never know what some kook might do. You're not safe there!"

"But I didn't *do* anything except voice my opinion," I said. Their fear was contageous.

"Who are you with?"

"A few boys and girls from the anti-poverty group."

"Well, have them escort you to the airport and catch the next plane out of there."

I was astonished. It wasn't just local news; it was already a national cause célèbre, and it was soon to be international. Whatever happened to free speech?

I went directly to my hotel, but couldn't get a flight until early morning. Stokely Carmichael, whom I had run into on one of my afternoon visits, escorted me to the hotel and then to the airport. In between we debated (as we usually do) how to go about correcting the problems that plague our country. I have always subscribed to the late Martin Luther King's philosophy and had worked with Dr. King and his wife, Coretta, in many ways. And whenever I got together with Stokely or with Malcolm X, I would argue that Dr. King's approach toward solving the nation's injustices was the right one. My most intense debates were with Malcolm; the last one occurred at the BBC studio in London the Sunday before his death. (Dr. King, by the way, called me the day after the White House luncheon, saying that I deserved the Nobel Peace Prize and that he and every other black person in America were proud of me.)

When Stokely put me on the plane in the wee hours of the morning, we were still debating. And then he said, "Girl, you don't know what you've done. Those people don't want to *hear* the truth! You sure are brave."

I had forgotten all about seeing Stokely that night until I

saw my dossier in May of last year, wherein the National Security Agency had advised: "that subject [me] was seen talking with Stokely Carmichael at the Washington National Airport the evening she had been at the White House."

Were the National Security agents tailing me or Stokely or both of us?

Was it 1968 or 1984?

33

"Eartha Kitt, CIA Target"

The White House luncheon had ended about 4:00 P.M. By 5:45 a special agent for the United States Secret Service was calling the FBI requesting information about Rebels with a Cause. At 6:30 he was again on the phone to another FBI agent requesting a "subversive name check" on me and the youth group. Four and a half hours later, no less than ten agents representing the Secret Service, the FBI, and the CIA were doing their thing: combing files and tying up phone lines in a frustrating effort to gather "intelligence" on an entertainer and a bunch of kids who were cleaning up the slums of Washington, D.C.

The result of the evening's sleuthing: Eartha Kitt had never been arrested; the Rebels with a Cause were not thought to be of a subversive or violent nature. One department filed individual names, but no groups; another department filed groups, but these would take time to check. It was finally decided that the files were "across town" and that locating them would be difficult, so the FBI would probably get back to the Secret Service the following night at ten o'clock.

The intelligence gathering would continue for a week,

culminating in a dossier from my FBI file, my Secret Service file, my National Security Agency file, and my CIA file, none of which I knew existed.

On January 25, 1968, a week from the day of the White House luncheon, my dossier was sent to the White House. A government form in my dossier noted the "directions of interest": Lyndon Johnson and Lady Bird Johnson.

I had become "subject number" 00292, case number CO-2-39,700. *Case evaluation:* not dangerous. *Threat activity:* none reported. *Modes of expression:* previous behavior.

Among other things, I learned from reading the dossier that I had been under surveillance since 1956 and that the CIA had written its own version of my biography, which I am going to reveal here in its entirety. I am doing so for two reasons: first, I have a passionate reverence for truth, and, second, I want you to know the "quality" of the information with which our intelligence agencies concern themselves. As a taxpayer, you helped pay for my dossier (so did I); I'll let you decide whether your money was well spent.

Before going into the chronology of how I obtained my dossier, I want you to know that I had completed all of the chapters of this book before I even knew that the dossier existed. Sixteen chapters were already at the publishing house. In chapter one, I had already mentioned my professional exile and had given details. It had occurred to me at the time that the claim needed documentation, for I wasn't simply playing the role of martyred performer. Now, in light of the contents of the revised chapter you are reading, I think you'll see that my exile had a very firm foundation and was not at all a figment of my imagination.

After the White House luncheon and the press it received, I became persona non grata in my own country. I wasn't alone. Club and television artists, such as the incomparable Mort Sahl and the Smothers brothers, suffered similar career setbacks. In my case, club contracts were canceled or "lost," with the contractors refusing to draw up new ones. The television quiz show on which I was a semi-regular never invited me back. And the phones stopped ringing. Agents were no longer interested in

Eartha Kitt because they couldn't book her. Except for the talk shows, there were no television or film offers. Record companies weren't interested either. Was this a conspiracy on the part of the administration? Did the White House get on the phone and say, "Don't hire that woman anymore"?

The television celebrity quiz show was a good example. It wasn't until 1974 that I learned the true reason I was never invited back. One of the show's producers decided that my participation wasn't worth the risk. Despite the fact that Lyndon Johnson had been re-elected on the promise to end the war in Vietnam, only kooks publicly protested the war in 1968; it still wasn't in vogue. The producer decided that the public was sufficiently outraged at my broaching the subject with Lady Bird that my appearance on his show *might* cause controversy and protest, risking the loss of sponsors.

Thus, I was effectively stopped from performing in the United States. There were a few talk-show hosts who weren't intimidated. Mike Douglas has had me on his show. I've been on Johnny Carson's "Tonight" Show several times with guest-hosts Joey Bishop and Don Rickles. And Merv Griffin not only kept his door open to me, but rolled out the carpet and *called* me to be on his show whenever I was home. Unfortunately, I wasn't home often. This was particularly hard on me because of my daughter, Kitt. By this time she was old enough to need a normal childhood. There were many times that I had to turn down much-needed work abroad—two-and three-month concert tours, for example—because I couldn't bear being away from Kitt for such long periods of time, and I couldn't keep dragging her away from home, friends, and school.

To keep a career going and to be in demand, a performer must stay constantly in the public eye or be forgotten. Few can afford to simply drop out of sight for seven years without being considered a has-been in the entertainment industry. In mid-1974, I began getting club dates in America again—not many, but it was a beginning. New, young captains of the entertainment industry vaguely remember the name Eartha Kitt from their youth. They're not quite sure what it is she does, and some believe she retired. All, I think, consider her a has-been. It's a tough image to fight against, but fight I will.

In January, 1975, I was at home, resting from a four-week engagement at the Mandarin Hotel in Hong Kong and a two-week concert tour in Australia, when I received a phone call from Seymour Hersh of the *New York Times*. He said that Washington columnist Jack Anderson had disclosed the fact that I was the subject of a CIA dossier which, to that day, I had known nothing about. The *Times* newsman wanted to know if I would mind their running a story on the dossier. I was astonished. Why would the CIA possibly be interested in me? I told Mr. Hersh that I had nothing to hide or be ashamed of, so he could print whatever he wanted.

I was working on this book at the time, and that same evening an ABC-TV newsman called me and asked if he could come to the house for an interview regarding my CIA file. I agreed to the interview, and as the ABC crew were setting up their cameras, my literary agent called. "Have you seen the evening edition of the *Los Angeles Times?*" he asked.

"No, why?"

"Your name is in the headlines, in 120-point bold hysterics!"

"There are TV people here right now. Can you bring a copy of the paper over to me?"

"Yeah, I'll be there in twenty minutes."

When he arrived, the interview had not yet begun, and he handed me a copy of the paper. I looked at the headline, and it was indeed huge:

EARTHA KITT A CIA TARGET!

The accompanying story revealed only parts of my CIA file, and I was appalled at what I read. It was slanderous gossip about my character, personality, and morals—all of it second- and third-hand hearsay quotes from "reliable" and "other" unnamed sources. I could well understand why Mr. Anderson's office and the media were so interested in my files. Like me, they found it incredible that the Central Intelligence Agency would concern itself with such nonsense—true or not—and that it would operate illegally to gather such information.

A few days later I was invited by Carol Hemingway to appear on her KABC radio talk show in Los Angeles. It's a nightly three-hour format in which listeners are able to call in and talk to her guests on the air. I was delighted that I had accepted her invitation, for before the listener-participation part of the show began Miss Hemingway placed a call to Joseph Spear, an associate of Jack Anderson's office in Washington, D.C.

On the air, by telephone, Mr. Spear explained how it was discovered by Jack Anderson's office that government intelligence agencies had been keeping files on me as far back as 1956. "Back in 1972," Mr. Spear said, "we managed to obtain, through some wonderful sources, information from the files of the FBI and the Secret Service. One of the Secret Service files was on Eartha Kitt. It contained information from the FBI, the CIA, and one little thing from the National Security Agency . . . and was accumulated when Eartha stood before Mrs. Johnson and decried the war in 1968. The Secret Service sent out urgent calls for information, and the government bureaucracies responded, which is how this file came to be put together.

"One of the things," Mr. Spear went on, "was Eartha's CIA report. We took this file and wrote a column in 1972, which began like this:

> For years we've reported on the alarming trend toward government by investigation. The federal bureaucracy is crawling with investigators who, if they are under salaries, must investigate someone.

"So forth and so on. Then we got down to the specific Eartha Kitt file without identifying Miss Kitt, quite frankly because we felt the information was (a) salacious, and (b) totally unfounded, based upon rumor and gossip, and we didn't see any reason for spreading it by identifying the person about whom it was written. So we treated the individual—Miss Kitt—anonymously. We went through her Secret Service file; we went through her FBI file, and then we wrote this:

> Even the CIA submitted a confidential run-down on the lady's sex habits with this cautionary note, "Because of the sensitive nature of this information and the method by which it was procured, it is furnished for lead purposes only and should not be utilized for any other purpose, quoted or

disseminated further without the permission of the originating office."

Having cleared its conscience, the CIA proceeded to spell out its unsubstantiated charges about the singer's sex life: "A confidential source," declares the three-page memo, "advised that her escapades overseas and her loose morals were said to be the talk of Paris. The source stated that the Subject had a lurid sex life in Paris, and described her as a sadistic nymphomaniac."

The memo went on and on about her sex activities, with these added comments, "Another informant described her as having a very nasty disposition, a spoiled child, very crude and having a vile tongue. The informant states the Subject was not well liked by most actors and actresses working with her. The informant states that she is a very selfish, shallow person, who deliberately upstages and miscues actors working with her."

"Continuing to quote:

"The informant [and the informant here refers to the CIA informant] states that the Subject did not associate with very many Negroes, and often bragged that she had very little Negro blood. The informant states that those who work with the Subject know from experience either to play up to her or to keep their distance to avoid the Subject's treachery."

"And then we wound up by saying:

that this illustrated how promiscuous the traffic in unproved allegations has become inside the government."

I asked Mr. Spear whether in his opinion it was the CIA's job to gather this kind of information (true or false) on American citizens.

"No. Absolutely not," Mr. Spear replied. "In fact, this kind of activity—depending upon your interpretation of the law—is proscribed by the charter that established the CIA. They say that because they were covering your activities overseas they had a right to collect this kind of information. I personally think this is a pretty weak cover. It turns my stomach, as I'm sure it would turn any fair citizen's stomach, that a government agency would be doing such a thing."

I told Mr. Spear that I'm very grateful to the news media in America for its efforts in keeping government honest and for protecting our freedom and, yes, democracy, for I think democratic freedom the most marvelous concept ever devised by man. Ironically, however, the individual is relatively powerless, and our representatives are too often lulled into apathy.

Both Carol Hemingway and Mr. Spear congratulated me for my courage in letting such things about me be read openly. Mr. Spear said, "I don't know that were I in your shoes I could personally permit such things to be read about me openly, whether or not they were true." My reply to them was that I'd rather lose face than freedom.

Mr. Spear mentioned that actress Jane Fonda's file was far larger than mine, and that Miss Fonda was taking legal action. Afterward, a number of listeners called in to urge me to take legal action as well, pointing out that people in the limelight, who have the means to fight such flagrant and illegal violations of individual rights and privacy, have a moral obligation to do so in the name of all those who might never know that such files are being kept on them and who, even if they did, might not have the means to take action. Today I am acting upon their advice.

Before the show ended, Carol Hemingway mentioned Merle Miller's marvelous book *Plain Speaking*, an oral biography of Harry S Truman. Miss Hemingway pointed out that in the book Mr. Truman was quoted (in the early sixties) as saying that he would never have created the CIA if he had known that it was going to become a government in itself and totally secret.

If you haven't read Merle Miller's book, I urge you to do so. It will help you keep the faith. In *Plain Speaking*, Mr. Truman, who had been out of office for ten years or so, was clearly worried about the CIA. He talked about it spending billions of dollars stirring up trouble so that it would have something to report. And Merle Miller quotes him as saying this about the CIA's secrecy and its having to answer to no one: "That's a very dangerous thing in a democratic society, and it's got to be put a stop to. The people have a right to know what those birds are up to. And if I was back in the White House, people would know . . . when you can't do any housecleaning because everything that goes on is a damn *secret*, why, then we're on our way to something the Founding Fathers didn't have in mind."

In Mr. Truman's day, the president was getting as many as a dozen intelligence reports. It made sense to have an organization—a central one—whose job it was to gather all that information and put it into a single report for the president. That's why Mr. Truman created the Central Intelligence Agency, and as far as he was concerned, that was to be its sole function. But as Mr. Truman lamented years later, there's nobody to keep track of it.

Thank heavens for the news media.

Now it's time to look at my CIA file in its entirety. Bear in mind that what follows is a synopsis of documents from my CIA file that were sent to the Secret Service for inclusion in my dossier, which was requested by and given to the White House. It's an unauthorized biography of Eartha Kitt, written by the CIA. And I present it here verbatim, deleting only salacious and unfounded characterizations of *others* with whom I've come in contact. Here is the "intelligence" gathered by the CIA:

KITT, EARTHA MAE
(aka Mrs. William McDonald—married 1960, divorced)

Subject, a self-employed singer, actress and dancer, was born in January 1928 (listed variously as 1 January and 26 January) at Columbia, S.C., the daughter of William and Anna Mae Kitt. Her parents were self-employed on their own farm. About two years after Subject's birth, William Kitt died and the mother attempted to continue the farm's operation. When Subject was about eight years of age, her mother sold the farm and moved to New York City. (Subject has variously indicated that she was an only child and that she was one of many children.)

It has also been indicated, variously, that she quit school at age 15 and that she graduated from the High School of Performing Arts in New York City.

At some time in her mid-teens she became employed as a seamstress in a Brooklyn garment factory. At age 15 shortly before her 16th birthday, a friend arranged her audition before dancer Katherine Dunham. Miss Dunham . . . reportedly asked Subject to join the Katherine Dunham Troupe, for which Subject soon became a featured dancer and vocalist. For the next four years she appeared regularly with the Dunham Troupe, and in the Spring of 1948 accompanied the troupe on a tour of Mexico, England and France.

Dunham and her troupe regularly appeared during this period in Communist fund-raising and testimonial meetings. During the same period, and thereafter, Dunham served as a sponsor or endorser of a number of Communist-front activities. According to the *Daily Worker*, 21 November 1948, for example, the Katherine Dunham Dancers were to entertain at a "Free Spain Rally to stop Franco."

Subject left the Dunham Troupe in Paris and moved into a small hotel along the Seine. She then took a singing engagement at Carroll's, a Paris club described by one source as a "homosexual hangout." She subsequently entertained in Turkey, Egypt and Greece.

A confidential source advised in 1956 that her escapades overseas and her loose morals were said to be the talk of Paris. The source stated that Subject had a lurid sex life in Paris and described her as a sadistic nymphomaniac. Another source who also questioned her moral life stated that her moral reputation has not suffered in the United States, but this was because of the morals clauses in theatrical contracts in this country. The source stated Subject's behavior was somewhat less discreet overseas. Both sources indicated the Subject only consorts with white men and both indicated subject to be a nymphomaniac.

In the summer of 1951, Subject returned to the United States for the funeral of her mother. She was signed by Orson Welles to appear as Helen of Troy. Following the tour of the play in Europe, Subject starred in two French films before returning to the United States. Upon her return to the United States she was signed by showman Monte Proser to star at his East Side club, La Vie En Rose [sic]. She attained success when she appeared in Leonard Sillman's hit musical "New Faces of 1952." This was followed by a starring role in Guthrie McClintic's production of "Mrs. Patterson [sic]. Since that time she has been a successful singer and actress. She has made a number of successful recordings. She is booked through the . . . Agency . . . New York City, and serves as president and secretary of Eartha Kitt Enterprises, Inc., which was formed to take care of all her activities. ———, New York City, an attorney and CPA, was described in 1956 as handling Subject's financial affairs. Her residence at . . . New York City, was noted in 1956 as being owned under the corporation name. The corporation bank account in 1956 was maintained by the Manufacturer's Trust Company, 43rd and Fifth Avenue, New York, N.Y.

Copies of Subject's applications for a cabaret license to appear at Sack's Music Room and a [sic] application for renewal to appear at the Village Vanguard were noted in 1956 to be on file with the Cabaret Bureau, Division of Licenses, New York City Police Department. The discrepancies on Subject's birth date appear in these records.

During 1956, a confidential source discussed the Subject with a number of past co-workers and others familiar with her activities. One informant, in addition to questioning Subject's morals, described Subject as an extreme egotist. Another informant described her as having a very nasty disposition, a spoiled child, very crude, and having a vile tongue. The informant stated Subject was not well liked by most actors and actresses working with her. The informant stated she is a very selfish, shallow person who deliberately upstages and miscues actors and actresses working with her. She reportedly feigned illness to break her contract for "Mrs. Patterson" so the show would close, her informant stated. The informant stated that Subject did not associate with very many Negroes and often bragged that she had very little Negro blood. The informant stated that those who work with Subject know from experience either to play up to her or to keep their distance to avoid Subject's treachery. The informant stated Subject is an atheist, and recalled her telling a well-wisher who indicated praying for Subject's success: "Don't waste your time, you don't believe that God stuff do you?" Another informant stated that

Subject is regarded as intelligent, but having a nasty, arrogant and insulting disposition. Yet another informant stated at the first mention of the Subject's name: "I wouldn't trust her behind a tissue paper curtain." The informant stated that Subject was a very confused woman and because of her lack of emotional stability could not handle success. He stated she is known in trade circles as extremely temperamental, of nasty disposition and of having alienated many of her friends. The informant also commented on Subject's unfavorable moral reputation in regard to men other than those of her own race. The informant recalled one incident, the opening of "Porgy and Bess" at the Ziegfeld Theater in the early 1950's when Subject was seen throwing her arms around ——— and gushing over him in front of numerous people. The informant was disturbed by this because of———'s regular appearance in May Day parades dressed as Abraham Lincoln. (——— has also been associated as a close associate of———.)

The *New York Times*, 29 March 1960, carried an advertisement of the "Committee to Defend Martin Luther King and the Struggle For Freedom in the South," of which Subject was a signatory. Among the names of many persons not identified with the Communist movement appearing as signatories were also a number of persons identified in the past with the Communist Party, Communist Party fronts and left-wing movements.

The *New York Times*, 19 January 1968, featured a UPI story captioned: "Eartha Kitt Denounces War Policy to Mrs. Johnson." According to the article, Subject "angrily told Mrs. Lyndon B. Johnson that American youth was rebelling because of the Vietnam war," and "delivered a tirade against the war and high taxes. [sic] At a later well-timed press conference she defended her conduct stating: "I see nothing wrong with the way I handled myself. I can only hope it will do some good." The same evening she appeared for one and a half hours on Washington radio station WOL and again defended her conduct.

So much for my CIA biography. Coincidentally, my autobiography *Thursday's Child* was published the same year (1956) that most of the CIA's "intelligence" was gathered. In addition to my pseudobiography, the CIA enclosed in my dossier four Xeroxed pages from the 1963 *Celebrity Register* (in which my photo and brief bio appear just below Henry Kissinger's) and the *Dictionary of Current Biography*. What is remarkable here are the passages the CIA underlined: "A 'conservative Democrat,' she is interested in politics, but takes no active part." And, "When Miss Kitt made a $10,000 contribution to the North Side Center Home for Orphans in New York, she told an official of the organization that the dream of her life was to meet Albert Einstein. The official arranged it. As the seventy-five-year-old physicist received her in his Princeton home, he said 'My dear, you are so young.' Over teacups, as reported in *Newsweek* (January 31, 1955), they talked. When she asked a question about reincarnation, Dr. Einstein did not know the English word, so she spoke in German. Later she said: 'He was warm and affectionate. I didn't feel like an idiot, as I thought I would.'"

The CIA works in strange ways. Also, it's interesting to note that the CIA has no letterhead stationery. The FBI does and the Secret Service does, but not the CIA. With all the airlines and other businesses it owns, one would think it could afford letterhead stationery. I can think of a number of appropriate insignias or logos for its letterhead: a double-cross, or a vise gripping little miniature symbols of Congress, the Senate, the White House, and the American public, or, better yet, something simple, like a dunce cap.

The National Security Agency didn't contribute much to my dossier. Presumably it has more important things to do. It did supply a Xerox of a Hanoi press release that told about my actions at the White House luncheon. And it supplied one other bit of information: ". . . advised that Subject was seen talking to Stokely Carmichael at the Washington National Airport the evening she had been at the White House."

In the previous chapter, I mentioned being questioned by three men at the White House. After writing that chapter, I received my dossier and learned that it was the Secret Service who had questioned me, or that at least one of the three was a Secret Service agent. I even learned his name. The following, except for names, which I have deleted, is my Secret Service record verbatim, dated January 19, 1968 (SA stands for special agent):

Eartha Mae Kitt

Reference is made to information furnished this division by SA ——— concerning Kitt's remarks at the White House Luncheon on January 18, 1968. Reference is also made to Miss Kitt's statement to him that she came to Washington, D.C., not only to attend the luncheon at the White House but also to work with an organization known as the "Rebels With a Cause." She stated she had organized this group on the West Coast and now the group is in Washington, D.C., and several other cities throughout the country.

Eartha Mae Kitt is a Negro, female, born 1-26-28 in either North or South Carolina. Her parents are John and Anna Kitt.

Inquiry with the FBI revealed Miss Kitt has no arrest record on file. Their files do reveal that in February, 1960, the February 12, 1960 edition of "El Mundo", [sic] a San Juan, Puerto Rico, newspaper, in an article captioned "Eartha Kitt Against Statehood," Kitt is quoted as being opposed to Puerto Rico having statehood, stating "Puerto Rico should keep its African and Spanish culture without mixing it with the rest of the world, even if this is done to benefit the United States." [sic]

In June 1966 Eartha Kitt reportedly expressed an interest in joining the march in Mississippi protesting the shooting of James Meredith.

An individual named Eartha Kitt, residing at 261 West 143rd Street, N.Y.C., was listed as an affiant in support of a passport application in 1950 of ———, a guitarist and ballad singer who had performed at meetings and rallies supported by the Communist Party and Communist front organizations and who has sponsored various Communist Party front groups.

Movie actor ———, in August 1963, furnished a list of movie personalities who planned to participate in the March on Washington on August 28, 1963. Eartha Kitt was among those listed.

The group known as "Rebels With a Cause" is made up of teen-agers from Southeast Washington whose members number in the hundreds. The group obtained funds in 1966 from the United Planning Organization and administrative help from the Southeast Neighborhood House. The "Washington Post and Times Herald" [sic] on May 8, 1966, said that the Rebels were so dedicated to democratic discussions that a meeting of four Rebels seemed to border on anarchy. ———, a full-time staff member of the Rebels, was described as "a high school dropout who spent her time running the streets with a gang of children, the kind of kids who start riots." [sic]

On August 16, 1966, Detective ———, Juvenile Bureau, Metropolitan Police Department, Wash., D.C., advised the "Rebels With a Cause" is a branch of the Southeast Neighborhood House. ——— said there is no information that a disturbance that took place in Wash., D.C., on August 15, 1966, was organized by the Rebels: however, ——— was among those arrested.

In October, 1966, information was received from a reliable source that ——— was suing her husband, ——— principal owner of ——— for divorce as a result of ———'s catching her husband in bed with Eartha Kitt. If additional information is received, you will be advised.

Special Agent in Charge

The last document in my dossier is an FBI report (on very impressive letterhead), which I won't reprint because it proved to be the source of the Secret Service information printed above—except for the first paragraph, which was the Secret Service's own doing. Again, I'll let the documents speak for themselves. But I must comment upon the FBI's "reliable source" that Mrs. ——— was suing her husband for divorce because she caught me in bed with him. There is no more truth here than in all the other lies and half-truths gathered by the several agencies to make up my dossier. But this last statement is perhaps the most ironic. The fact is, Mrs. ——— is now and has been one of my closest friends for more than twenty years. She did get a divorce. But Mr. ———, not wanting his wife to divorce him, asked me to intercede on his behalf because his wife and I were such good friends! Obviously, had I been the "other woman," as some "informant" allegedly told the FBI, Mr. ——— certainly wouldn't have come to me for help in saving his marriage, and Mrs. ——— certainly wouldn't be counted among my close friends.

As for the entertainer for whom I was an affiant in support of a passport application, the report neglected to say that he was black. The man was as much a Communist as was Thomas Jefferson or Abraham Lincoln. Let's not forget that this "intelligence" was gathered during the McCarthy Era. Apparently that era still lives within the cloisters of our nation's intelligence agencies. The only entertainers I know who performed for Communists are those who, in recent years, have traveled to Russia or China during our cultural exchange program.

With the exception of the NSA, the agencies seem abnormally preoccupied with sex. I could write a chapter disclaiming the nymphomaniacal image cast upon me by an unnamed informant or informants. But it's easy to prove that you *are* something, almost impossible to prove that you're not. I could cite dozens of informants who think me puritanical. But to what point? Gossips will believe what they *want* to believe, the facts notwithstanding.

What is equally appalling is the fact that my dossier is one of thousands. There were no less than fifteen special agents named in my dossier, and who knows how many unnamed agents, secretaries, filing clerks, typists, and others were involved in the gathering of this "subversive" file? Multiply this by thousands (representing other dossiers). Can you imagine the cost to taxpayers? And that money could have been put to good use—back in the taxpayers' pockets, for example.

The first thirty-two chapters of this book show how inaccurate these reports are. There may have been a William Kitt, or there may have been a man named William who was Pearl's father. But I never heard of him. Besides, my aunt's name was Kitt too. Obviously, then, my mother kept her maiden name. But that's in keeping with the rest of my dossier's "facts." I wonder if a reliable informant came up with William Kitt, too?

34

Cotton and Caviar

The author Gene Fowler once said that one never finishes a book, one abandons it, meaning of course that an author is never truly satisfied with the final product of his labor and could keep rewriting and revising forever. I think this doubly true of autobiography, and more literally true in that, unlike fiction, an autobiography has no end. Life goes on.

I began working on this book in the spring of 1974, and while working on it have appeared professionally in Hong Kong, Tasmania, Australia, Sweden, Denmark, England, and other countries. And I am happy to report that, since beginning work on this second autobiography, I have been getting work in America and am even now getting more and more offers.

It would be delightful if I could wrap this chapter up with a 1940s vintage Hollywood ending by saying that all the loose threads of my personal life have been neatly tied. But that's not the case. I finally found my two half-sisters, Pearl and Almita. Both are happily married and living in the Northeast, and both have families. I had never known Almita; she was the child born shortly before our mother's death, while Pearl and I were living with the Stern woman. And I hadn't seen Pearl since she was five or six. The reunion wasn't as I—and probably they—had imagined it would be. We were like strangers, despite not wanting to be. We had lived divergent lives and had nothing in common except our mother. We went our separate ways, strangers when we met and nearly strangers now.

Today I live alone with my daughter, and I like it. I love my home, with its garden and chickens and pets and friends and books. And I still love show business, I loved being married too, and I don't rule it out for the future, but the idea both attracts and scares me. Love is still synonymous with rejection in my mind. I have a constant fight within myself about this, and I've had to learn to live with the fact. And I only hope I have enough strength to endure and even overcome the inner battle.

Having the opportunity to tell my life story has been a healthy experience. Too often we're so wrapped up in the present and hopes for the future that we don't take time to reflect. I have had to discipline myself to look back—there was a lot I didn't want to look at—and in doing so I've relived the painful moments and rediscovered some of the wonderful ones as well. Overall, I've had a very good life, a life of cotton and caviar. And the cotton years have made the caviar years far more savory than they would have been had my early life been an easy one.

I've been blessed in a number of ways: blessed with talent that has given me a good living and an outlet for self-expression; blessed with good friends—and even a stranger or two—who helped me at crucial times.

Blessed with my daughter; blessed with my mother-in-law, who, until her death, proved to me that love doesn't have to be transitory; and blessed with the realization that, unlike the popular song goes, I did *not* do it my way—I did not do it alone.

My first autobiography, *Thursday's Child*, ended while I was starring on Broadway in *Mrs. Patterson*, with critical notices beyond belief. And I ended the book with Eartha Mae commenting, "But it seemed really true that Eartha Kitt had become a star." Now, twenty years later, I've lived the adage that stardom can be fleeting. The title of the book was taken from the poem that goes in part, "Monday's child is fair of face / Tuesday's child is full of grace...Thursday's child has far to go." In essence, I'm a sophisticated cotton picker. And I'm still Thursday's child.

Index

271